GENOCIDE NEVER SLEEPS

Accounts of international criminal courts have tended to consist of reflections on abstract legal texts, on judgements and trial transcripts. *Genocide Never Sleeps*, based on ethnographic research at the International Criminal Tribunal for Rwanda, provides an alternative account, describing a messy, flawed human process in which legal practitioners faced with novel challenges sought to reconfigure long-standing habits and opinions while maintaining a commitment to 'justice'. From the challenges of simultaneous translation to collaborating with colleagues from different legal traditions, legal practitioners were forced to scrutinise that which normally remains assumed in domestic law. By providing an account of this process, *Genocide Never Sleeps* not only provides a unique insight into the exceptional nature of the *ad hoc*, improvised ICTR and the day-to-day practice of international criminal justice, but also holds up for fresh inspection much that is naturalised and assumed in unexceptional, domestic legal processes.

NIGEL ELTRINGHAM is a Reader in Social Anthropology at the University of Sussex. He has written extensively on the aftermath of the 1994 Rwandan genocide. He is the author of *Accounting for Horror: Post-Genocide Debates in Rwanda* (2004); contributing editor of *Identity, Justice and "Reconciliation" in Contemporary Rwanda* (2009) and *Framing Africa: Portrayals of a Continent in Contemporary Mainstream Cinema* (2013); and contributing co-editor of *Remembering Genocide* (2014). He served as Executive Secretary and then Vice-President of the International Network of Genocide Scholars, and has held visiting lectureships at the universities of Gothenburg and Cornell.

CAMBRIDGE STUDIES IN LAW AND SOCIETY

Founded in 1997, Cambridge Studies in Law and Society is a hub for leading scholarship in socio-legal studies. Located at the intersection of law, the humanities, and the social sciences, it publishes empirically innovative and theoretically sophisticated work on law's manifestations in everyday life: from discourses to practices, and from institutions to cultures. The series editors have longstanding expertise in the interdisciplinary study of law, and welcome contributions that place legal phenomena in national, comparative, or international perspective. Series authors come from a range of disciplines, including anthropology, history, law, literature, political science, and sociology.

Series Editors

Mark Fathi Massoud, *University of California, Santa Cruz*

Jens Meierhenrich, *London School of Economics and Political Science*

Rachel E. Stern, *University of California, Berkeley*

A list of books in the series can be found at the back of this book.

GENOCIDE NEVER SLEEPS
Living Law at the International Criminal Tribunal for Rwanda

Nigel Eltringham
University of Sussex

CAMBRIDGE
UNIVERSITY PRESS

CAMBRIDGE
UNIVERSITY PRESS

University Printing House, Cambridge CB2 8BS, United Kingdom

One Liberty Plaza, 20th Floor, New York, NY 10006, USA

477 Williamstown Road, Port Melbourne, VIC 3207, Australia

314-321, 3rd Floor, Plot 3, Splendor Forum, Jasola District Centre, New Delhi - 110025, India

79 Anson Road, #06-04/06, Singapore 079906

Cambridge University Press is part of the University of Cambridge.

It furthers the University's mission by disseminating knowledge in the pursuit of
education, learning and research at the highest international levels of excellence.

www.cambridge.org
Information on this title: www.cambridge.org/9781108707398
DOI: 10.1017/9781108757195

First published 2019
First paperback edition 2021

A catalogue record for this publication is available from the British Library

Library of Congress Cataloging in Publication data
Names: Eltringham, Nigel, author.
Title: Genocide never sleeps : living law at the international criminal tribunal for Rwanda /
Nigel Eltringham.
Description: Cambridge, United Kingdom ; New York, NY : Cambridge University Press,
2019. | Series: Cambridge studies in law and society | Includes bibliographical references
and index.
Identifiers: LCCN 2019019493 | ISBN 9781108485593 (hardback)
Subjects: LCSH: Genocide – Rwanda. | Rwanda – History – Civil War, 1994 – Atrocities. |
Tutsi (African people) – Crimes against – Rwanda – History – 20th century. | International
Criminal Court. | BISAC: POLITICAL SCIENCE / Political Freedom&Security / Human
Rights.
Classification: LCC KTD454 .E47 2019 | DDC 345/.0251–dc23
LC record available at https://lccn.loc.gov/2019019493

ISBN 978-1-108-48559-3 Hardback
ISBN 978-1-108-70739-8 Paperback

Cambridge University Press has no responsibility for the persistence or
accuracy of URLs for external or third-party internet websites referred to in
this publication, and does not guarantee that any content on such websites is,
or will remain, accurate or appropriate.

CONTENTS

List of Figures   *page* vi
Acknowledgements   vii

Introduction: Judging the Crime of Crimes   1

1 'When We Walk Out; What Was It All About?'   26

2 'Watching the Fish in the Goldfish Bowl'   56

3 'Who the Hell Cares How Things Are Done
   in the Old Country'   84

4 'They Don't Say What They Mean or Mean
   What They Say'   118

5 'We Are Not a Truth Commission'   152

   Conclusion   181

Bibliography   189
Index   216

FIGURES

1.1 Wanted for genocide (Courtesy of the ICTR) *page* 30
2.1 The Public Gallery (Courtesy of the ICTR) 62
2.2 The Arusha International Conference Centre (Courtesy of the ICTR) 67
2.3 Inside a courtroom at the Tribunal (adapted from ICTR 2005a:16) 73
2.4 Judges' Bench from the defence end showing ICTR Emblem (Courtesy of the ICTR) 74
2.5 The UN Emblem and Seal of the ICTR 75
2.6 The Courtroom from the prosecution end (Courtesy of the ICTR) 78

ACKNOWLEDGEMENTS

I am grateful to the Nuffield Foundation (SGS/32034) and British Academy (SG-47168) for the generous support of the research for this book conducted under COSTECH (Tanzania Commission for Science and Technology) Research Permit No. 2006–304-CC-2006–122.

I am indebted to colleagues for invitations to present early versions of chapters at various seminars, including Johan Pottier (School of Oriental and African Studies), Lars Waldorf (School of Advanced Study), David Pratten (University of Oxford), Jens Meierhenrich (London School of Economics), Dan Rosengren (University of Gothenburg), Fredrik Söderbaum (University of Gothenburg), Gerhard Anders (University of Edinburgh), Barrie Sander and Jakob v. H. Holtermann (University of Copenhagen) and Maja Gudim Burheim (University of Oslo). Likewise, for invitations to present at conference panels, including Suzanne Chenault (ICTR Legacy Conference), Alexander Hinton (American Anthropological Association), and Gerhard Anders and Olaf Zenker (European Conference on African Studies). Thanks to all those who participated in the seminars for their questions, observations and suggestions. Thanks also to those who have invited me to contribute to publications, including Barrie Sander and Jakob v. H. Holtermann (*Humanity*), Cody Henson (*New England Journal of International and Comparative Law*), Alexander Hinton (*Transitional Justice: Global Mechanisms and Local Realities after Genocide and Mass Violence*) Julie Billaud and Luigi Achilli (*Allegra*), Alasdair Mckay (*E-International Relations*) and Gerhard Anders and Olaf Zenker (*Development and Change*).

I am particularly grateful to colleagues who read drafts of various articles that have contributed to this book, including Simon Coleman, Jane Cowan, Jon Mitchell, Filippo Osella, Zdenek Kavan, Anthony Good and Richard Wilson.

Special thanks go to Marita Eastmond and Joakim Öjendal for the invitation to be a visiting researcher at the School of Global Studies, University of Gothenburg. The period of time spent in Gothenburg was immensely productive and a wonderful experience for myself and my family. Final edits of the book were completed whilst I was a visiting lecturer at Cornell University and I am thankful to Lori Leonard and Fouad Makki for the invitation and support.

Those who deserve my thanks at the ICTR are too numerous to mention. The research in Arusha would not, however, have been possible without the initial and on-going support and guidance of Moustapha Hassouna and Straton Musonera to whom I am very grateful. Special thanks also to Aatsa Atogho, a former interpreter at the ICTR, for clarifying details of the simultaneous interpretation system.

Finally, and most of all, I thank my wife, Anna, and our daughters for their unswerving support.

Parts of this book were previously published, in a different form, in the following places: (2010) 'Judging the "Crime of Crimes": Continuity and Improvisation at the International Criminal Tribunal for Rwanda' in Hinton, A. (ed.) *Transitional Justice: Global Mechanisms and Local Meanings in the Aftermath of Genocide and Mass Atrocity* (New Brunswick, NJ: Rutgers University Press), 206–26; (2008) '"A War Crimes Community": The Legacy of the International Criminal Tribunal for Rwanda Beyond Jurisprudence', in *New England Journal of International and Comparative Law*, Vol. 14, No. 2, 309–18; (2009) '"We are not a Truth Commission": Fragmented Narratives and the Historical Record at the International Criminal Tribunal for Rwanda', in *Identity, Justice and "Reconciliation" in Contemporary Rwanda, Special Issue of Journal of Genocide Research*, Vol. 11, No. 1, 55–79; (2012) 'Spectators to the Spectacle of Law: The Formation of a "Validating Public" at the International Criminal Tribunal for Rwanda', in *Ethnos: Journal of Anthropology*, Vol. 77, No. 3, 425–45; (2014) '"When we walk out; what was it all about?": Views on "new beginnings" from within The International Criminal Tribunal for Rwanda', in *Development and Change*, Vol. 45, No. 3, 543–64; (2014) 'A legacy deferred?: The international criminal tribunal for Rwanda at 20 years', in *E-International Relations*; (2015) 'Rescuing (cosmopolitan) locals at the International Criminal Tribunal for Rwanda', in *Allegra: A Virtual Lab of Legal Anthropology*; (2017) '"The judgement is not made now; the judgement will be made in the future": "politically motivated" defence lawyers and the International Criminal Tribunal for Rwanda's "historical record"', in *Humanity: An International Journal of Human Rights, Humanitarianism and Development.*

INTRODUCTION: JUDGING THE CRIME OF CRIMES

Between 7 April and mid-July 1994 an estimated 937,000 Rwandans (according to a 2001 census the vast majority of whom were Tutsi), were murdered in massacres committed by militia, the gendarmerie and elements of the army, often with the participation of the local population (see Des Forges, 1999; Eltringham, 2004; IRIN, 2001). On 13 April 1994, Claude Dusaidi, the representative at the United Nations (UN) of the Rwandan Patriotic Front (the predominantly Tutsi rebel group that had entered into a power-sharing agreement with the government in August 1993), wrote to the President of the UN Security Council stating that a 'crime of genocide' had been committed against Rwandans in the presence of UN peacekeepers (UNAMIR[1]) and that the Security Council should establish a war crimes tribunal (Carlsson *et al.*, 1999: 68). As de facto custodian of the term genocide, the UN was, however, slow to designate the events as such (see Melvern, 2000). Only in his report of 31 May 1994, did the UN Secretary-General declare genocide had been committed (United Nations, 1994b, UN Doc. S/1994/1125: para 36). In a letter to the President of the UN Security Council on 28 September 1994, the post-genocide Rwandan government requested that an international tribunal be established (United Nations, 1994c, UN Doc. S/1994/1115) a suggestion supported by a UN Commission of Experts on 4 October 1994 (United Nations, 1994b: paras 133–42)[2]; the

---

[1] United Nations Assistance Mission for Rwanda, established 5 October 1993 by Security Council Resolution 872 (1993), UN Doc. S/RES/872.
[2] The Commission of Experts initially suggested that the ICTR be subsumed into the ICTY.

President of Rwanda on 6 October (United Nations, 1994a, UN Doc. A/49/PV.2: 5) and, on 13 October 1994, by the Special Rapporteur of the Commission on Human Rights on the situation of human rights in Rwanda (Degni-Ségui, 1994: 19). This resulted in a UN Security Council Resolution on 8 November 1994 (United Nations, 1994e, UN Doc. S/RES/955 (1994)), initially sponsored by the United States and New Zealand creating the 'International Criminal Tribunal for the Prosecution of Persons Responsible for Genocide and Other Serious Violations of International Humanitarian Law Committed in the Territory of Rwanda and Rwandan Citizens Responsible for Genocide and Other Such Violations Committed in the Territory of Neighbouring States, between 1 January 1994 and 31 December 1994' (see Chapter 1).

From 1996 to 2014, the ICTR's offices and four courtrooms were located in two rented wings of the Arusha International Conference Centre in Tanzania. The ICTR consisted of three principal organs: the Office of the Prosecutor (which investigated allegations; issued indictments and prosecuted the case in court); the Registry (administration); and three 'Trial Chambers' composed of 16 permanent and nine *ad litem* ('for the case') judges. There was no jury; the three judges who sat in each trial assessed the evidence and issued a judgment. The ICTR had jurisdiction over any person accused of committing the following in Rwanda in 1994 (and if Rwandan in neighbouring territories): genocide (as defined by the 1948 UN Convention on the Prevention and Punishment of the Crime of Genocide)[3]; crimes against humanity (a widespread or systematic attack on a civilian population)[4] and 'war crimes' (Article 3 common to the 1949 Geneva Conventions)[5]. Trials

---

[3] Genocide means any of the following acts committed with intent to destroy, in whole or in part, a national, ethnical, racial or religious group, as such: (a) Killing members of the group; (b) Causing serious bodily or mental harm to members of the group; (c) Deliberately inflicting on the group conditions of life calculated to bring about its physical destruction in whole or in part; (d) Imposing measures intended to prevent births within the group; (e) Forcibly transferring children of the group to another group. 3. The following acts shall be punishable: (a) Genocide; (b) Conspiracy to commit genocide; (c) Direct and public incitement to commit genocide; (d) Attempt to commit genocide; (e) Complicity in genocide (United Nations, 1994e: Art. 2).

[4] The International Tribunal for Rwanda shall have the power to prosecute persons responsible for the following crimes when committed as part of a widespread or systematic attack against any civilian population on national, political, ethnic, racial or religious grounds: (a) Murder; (b) Extermination; (c) Enslavement; (d) Deportation; (e) Imprisonment; (f) Torture; (g) Rape; (h) Persecutions on political, racial and religious grounds; (i) Other inhumane acts (United Nations, 1994e: Art. 3).

[5] These violations shall include, but shall not be limited to: (a) Violence to life, health and physical or mental well-being of persons, in particular murder as well as cruel treatment such as torture, mutilation or any form of corporal punishment; (b) Collective punishments; (c) Taking

began in 1996 and lasted an average of four years (one lasted nine years) (GADH, 2009a: 76).

The Office of the Prosecutor indicted 93 persons, of whom 62 were convicted and 14 acquitted. A further ten indictees were referred to national jurisdictions, two died prior to or during trial, two indictments were withdrawn before trial and three remain fugitives. The ICTR was the subject of sustained criticism during its operation regarding the selection of the accused; cost ($1.5 billion); and length of trials (see International Crisis Group, 2003; Peskin, 2008: 151–234).

In 2009 the UN Security Council (United Nations, 2009b, UN Doc. S/RES/1901 (2009)) called on the ICTR to complete its work by the end of 2012. On 20 December 2012, the judges passed the final sentence (apart from appeals) on Augustin Ngirabatware (Minister of Planning during the genocide) to 35 years' imprisonment for genocide and crimes against humanity. Two years earlier, the UN Security Council had created the Mechanism for International Criminal Tribunals (MICT) tasked with continuing the 'jurisdiction, rights and obligations and essential functions' of the ICTR and the International Criminal Tribunal for the Former Yugoslavia (ICTY, established in 1993) including the tracking and prosecution of remaining fugitives, appeals proceedings, retrials, trials for contempt of court and false testimony, judgment review, protection of witnesses and victims, the enforcement of sentences and assistance to national jurisdictions (United Nations, 2010, UN Doc. S/RES/1966 (2010)). The MICT is also responsible for the preservation and management of the ICTR archives which contain the transcripts of witness testimony, audio-visual recordings and documents entered as evidence. The UN Security Council (United Nations, 2010) chose Arusha as the site for storing the physical archive, in spite of the Rwandan government's insistence it should be transferred to Rwanda (Hirondelle News, 2009).

THE 'INNER WORKINGS' OF LAW

With the future of the ICTR's archives secure under the MICT, much of which is available online (http://jrad.unmict.org/), the story of the

of hostages; (d) Acts of terrorism; (e) Outrages upon personal dignity, in particular humiliating and degrading treatment, rape, enforced prostitution and any form of indecent assault; (f) Pillage; (g) The passing of sentences and the carrying out of executions without previous judgement pronounced by a regularly constituted court, affording all the judicial guarantees which are recognized as indispensable by civilized peoples; (h) Threats to commit any of the foregoing acts (United Nations, 1994e: Art. 4).

ICTR's creation and operation would appear to be secure and publicly available. And yet, what the archives contain is only part of the story:

> documents that have been produced in such profusion are there for all men to read. What alone is missing is the emotion, the colour, the movement that characterizes these days. . . . how shall that be captured, and when captured, how shall it be recorded?
>
> (Hyde, 1964: 504).

This diary entry, written by Norman Birkett, the British Alternate Judge, during the Trial of the Major War Criminals before the International Military Tribunal (the Nuremberg Trials 1945–6) suggests that trial archives, including those of the ICTR, fail to capture and preserve an account of the environment experienced by participants; an account, it can be argued, that is necessary if one is to assess such trials in relation to the claims made by advocates of criminal prosecution in the aftermath of mass atrocity crimes. While firsthand accounts of the Nuremberg Trials (see Gaskin, 1990; Neave, 1978; Stave *et al.*, 1998; Taylor, 1992) go some way to capturing what Birkett considered to be lacking from archives, few studies have 'sought to get inside the inner workings' of contemporary international tribunals, as John Hagan (2003: 3) notes in his path-breaking study of the Office of the Prosecutor at the ICTY.

The need to consider the 'inner workings' of law has been a longstanding concern of anthropologists in the context of domestic courts. John Conley and William O'Barr (2005: 2) have argued for a need to see law's power not as a distant abstraction confined to textual rules, but as something that manifests itself in the 'thousands of mini-dramas enacted every day in lawyer's offices, police stations and court-houses'. Rather than attending to 'inner workings', scholarly literature on contemporary international tribunals (the ICTR, the ICTY) has been dominated by the analysis of the expanding case law and precedents that have emerged from these institutions in relation to a variety of issues including command responsibility, judicial notice of genocide, rape and sexual violence and the 'right to counsel'.[6] The same trend has

---

[6] Command responsibility (Williamson, 2002); concurrent jurisdiction (Morris, 1997); crimes against humanity (Cerone, 2008; Mettraux, 2002); disclosure of evidence (Nahamya and Diarra, 2002); hate speech (Davidson, 2004; Gordon, 2004; Obote-Odora, 2004); international humanitarian law (Boed, 2002); judicial notice of genocide (Mamiya, 2007; Shannon, 2006); prosecutorial strategy (Obote-Odora, 2001; van den Herik, 2005); provisional release (Rearick, 2003); rape and sexual violence (Askin, 1999; Chenault, 2008; Green, 2002; Haffajee, 2006; Haddad, 2011; Obote-Odora, 2005; MacKinnon, 2006; McDougall, 2006; Nelaeva, 2010;

been apparent in literature on other transitional justice institutions. Writing on the South African Truth and Reconciliation Commission (SATRC), Lars Buur (2003b: 67, note 68) notes that much of the academic commentary on the commission contained 'no information about its everyday aspects ... as if the everyday work is just a neutral medium for information gathering and processing, a means to an end'.

This omission of 'everyday aspects' has been rectified to some extent as regards the ICTY in the aforementioned work by John Hagan (2003), by Pierre Hazan (2004) and in a series of articles by an ICTY judge, Patricia Wald, (2000; 2001a; 2001b; 2002; 2004a; 2004b; 2006). Regarding the ICTR, Rosemary Byrne (2010: 247–8) drew on trial observation to move beyond 'traditional legal analysis focused on the formal rules, decisions and judgments' to explore the 'hidden art of international criminal trial practice' (see Chapter 3). These works correspond to what Kieran McEvoy (2007: 414) describes as 'thick' writings on transitional justice that 'reflect critically on the actions, motivations, consequences, philosophical assumptions or power relations which inform legal actors and shape legal institutions' in contrast to 'thin' writings that 'tend to emphasize the formal or instrumental aspects of a legal system'. McEvoy (2007: 412–13) argues that the predominance of 'thin' writings means that the literature on transitional justice has become 'over dominated by a narrow legalistic lens which impedes both scholarship and praxis' (see also Lundy and McGovern, 2008: 275). Combined with a lack of 'on the ground' research, this has resulted in a 'very simplistic sense of what makes international law hang together' (Meierhenrich 2013: 9; see also Wilson 2007: 366).

Other authors have made similar observations regarding the need for 'thicker' accounts. In her discussion of the mobile personnel who moved from one international criminal tribunal to another, Elena Baylis (2008: 364) notes that although scholars have concerned themselves with the 'analysis of processes, norms, and institutions', there has been 'little examination of the people involved and the roles they play'. Likewise, Jenia Iontcheva Turner (2008: 543, note 555) notes that writing which has considered defence lawyers practising in

Oosterveld, 2005; Van Schaak, 2009; Wood, 2004); rules of evidence (Dixon, 1997); sentencing (Hola et al., 2011; Keller, 2001; Sloane, 2007; Szoke-Burke, 2012); the crime of genocide (Akhavan, 2005; Aptel, 2002; Eboe-Osuji, 2005; Greenfield, 2008; Gunawaradana, 2000; Zorzi Giustiniani, 2008; Obote-Odora, 2002; Schabas, 2000); the protection of witnesses (Pozen, 2005; Sluiter, 2005); transfer and extradition (Bohlander, 2006; Jalloh et al., 2007; Mujuzi, 2010; Melman, 2011); and 'right to counsel' (Niang, 2002; Wladimiroff, 1999).

international tribunals has focused 'on the rules governing the conduct of attorneys and not on the perspectives of attorneys themselves'. Regarding the importance of understanding such perspectives, Richard Wilson (2011: 14) documents, in his study of whether international trials can generate valid historical narratives, 'why prosecutors, defence counsel, and their respective expert witnesses argue about the past; what their motivations are; and what they hope to achieve' (see Chapter 5). In a similar vein, Jonneke Koomen (2013: 255–6 262) has noted that there has been lack of exploration of the 'social lives of these institutions' and argues that there is a need to direct attention to an institution's 'everyday tasks, routines, and cultural practices', and to the fact that while international justice 'masquerades in the language of the universal', it is 'always made possible through local encounters'. It is the local, 'social encounter' that has gone 'largely unaddressed' in literature on international criminal trials as Tim Kelsall (2009: 18) observes in his study of trials at the Special Court for Sierra Leone (SCSL, established 2002). In this way, while international criminal justice is fuelled by 'aspirations to fulfil universal dreams and schemes', there is a need to appreciate that it can only be enacted in the 'sticky materiality of practical encounters' (Tsing, 2005: 1).

Commenting on the aforementioned 'thin' legal literature on international tribunals, Jens Meierhenrich (2013) observes that such accounts are 'so preoccupied with the technical minutiae of prosecution and adjudication ... that the structured action of individual agency is not noticed, let alone studied'. Meierhenrich promotes 'practice theory' as one way of rectifying such omissions. In place of a unified 'practice theory', Meierhenrich (2013: 13) quotes Davide Nicolini's (2013: 3) summary of features common to different 'practice' theorists:

> [it] foregrounds the importance of activity, performance, and work in the creation and perpetuation of all aspects of social life. Practice approaches are fundamentally processual and tend to see the world as an ongoing routinized and recurrent accomplishment. .... institutions, and organizations are all kept in existence through the recurrent performance of material activities, and to a large extent they only exist as long as those activities are performed.

While the book does not apply 'practice theory' systematically throughout, it seeks to fulfil Meierhenrich's requirement 'to get readers to understand, first and foremost, the particularity of practices' in 'a specific time, place, and concrete historical context' by paying close attention to the 'doings and sayings of practitioners' (Meierhenrich 2013: 56–7). In this way, this book builds on the call by Hagan, McEvoy, Meierhenrich, Baylis, Byrne, Turner, Koomen, Kelsall and Wilson to explore the 'actions, motivations, consequences, philosophical assumptions [and] power relations' (McEvoy, 2007: 414) at play within institutions such as the ICTR through the 'people involved and the roles they play' (Baylis, 2008: 364).

Such an approach resonates with the 'legal realism' movement prominent in the United States in the 1930s and 1940s. Although an eclectic movement with a contested legacy (see Schauer, 2013: 749, note 742), it is best summarized by Karl Llewellyn's (1930: 447–8) distinction between 'paper rules' and 'real rules' where the former is 'what the books say "the law" is' and the latter being what actually happens in court (see Pound, 1910). Such a distinction challenged 'legal formalism', the assumption that law (statute and precedent) can be mechanically applied to 'fact' and also challenged the claim that the practice of law is a 'closed' system insulated from social and political bias. In contrast to 'legal formalism', Llewellyn detected a gap between rules and practice and demonstrated that 'legal doctrine ordinarily does not determine legal outcomes without the substantial influence of nonlegal supplements' (Schauer, 2013: 754). A central 'nonlegal supplement' identified by the legal realists was judicial discretion in which judges apply an 'unwritten real rule' (Schauer, 2013: 769).

Not only does this book resonate with elements of 'classic' Legal Realism it also reflects the New Legal Realism (NLR) that has emerged in the last ten years (see Nourse and Shaffer, 2010) with its focus on the transnational flow of legal ideas and personnel and exploration of 'international law, human rights law, and transitional justice' (Merry, 2006a). The gap between 'paper' and 'unwritten rules' is explored in Chapter 3, where I consider a whole set of 'unwritten' habitual assumptions that inform the operation of the courtroom drawing on Pierre Bourdieu's (1987: 831, 820) discussion of the 'written and unwritten laws' of the judicial field and Peter Zoettl's (2016) ethnography of Portuguese and German criminal trials. Zoettl (2016: 5–7) demonstrates that although every moment of the trial is scripted, not all of that script is codified as written, public rules. Standing and sitting and the bodily postures required of defendants by judges are, for example, part of a 'hidden' script, one that only becomes apparent 'when something goes wrong' (Zoettl, 2016: 4). There is, therefore, both a codified, public script (such as the ICTR's Rules of Procedure and Evidence - the

RPE or RPEs) and a hidden script which only becomes apparent when it is infringed. Given that the legal practitioners at the ICTR were drawn from a variety of legal jurisdictions there was frequent infringement of the 'hidden script' increasing the visibility of habitual, 'unwritten rules'.

The importance of 'unwritten rules' in the courtroom challenges the privileging of the 'written word' in the practice of law. In their ethnography of UK barristers, John Morison and Philip Leith (1992: 3) note that those who teach law seem to consider it as only having life in 'the gradations of the printed word: case notes, legislation, law reports'. Such a tendency is apparent in Bruno Latour's (2004: 101, 196) study of the French *Conseil d'État* which demonstrates how the law subordinates the 'real world' to a 'close-edited diagram' (Geertz, 1983: 173) by reducing 'the world to paper' so that texts 'replace the external world, which is in itself unintelligible'. While, as Richard Wilson (2007: 363–4) warns, Latour was concerned with the very particular practices of French administrative law, it can still be argued that legal practitioners tend to privilege texts because they are considered to represent 'stability, dispassionate fairness, fidelity to truth without prejudice, the blindness of the law' in contrast to the theatricality of the courtroom with its 'artifice, emotion, deception, seductive appearances, the instability of truth' (Stone Peters 2008: 199) (see Chapter 2).

The tendency to textualize the world was apparent at the ICTR where the transcript of witness testimony provided by stenographers was immediately available on lawyer's and judges' laptops via 'LiveNote', a transcript management software (see Chapter 2). This transcript was then used by judges' Assistant Legal Officers (ALOs) to produce 'witness summaries' for each witness which were used by judges in the drafting of the judgement. By applying the law (a text) to evidence (rendered as a text in two stages) another text was produced (the judgement). Like Latour's (2004: 102) *conseillers*, ICTR judges were not so much triers of 'fact' (in an external world), but triers of distilled texts. Given the privileging of text in ICTR trials (speech instantaneously turned into text via LiveNote), it is not surprising that scholarship on the ICTR has tended to concentrate on analysing residual texts (judgments and transcripts) rather than the working lives of the lawyers and judges who produced those texts or the environment in which they operated.

This is an unfortunate tendency for, as Morison and Leith (1992: vii) argue, the domination of this 'text based view of the law' obscures the reality of the practice of law and that if 'only one percent of the time spent in textual analysis [was] spent on analysing law in practice, we would have a completely different view of the nature of the law'. They suggest, for example, that it is a mistake to envisage the UK barrister's daily routine as one of 'scholarship and oratory', where, in reality, it is 'extra-legal' knowledge that is paramount (whether that be knowledge of the judge's temperament, the reputation of the opposition, the barrister's relationship with the solicitor etc.) (Morison and Leith, 1992: 17). They suggest that a more accurate portrayal of the barrister is as a 'fully social individual who must satisfy all sorts of competing demands' (Morison and Leith, 1992: 19). Elena Baylis (2008: 377), writing specifically on international criminal tribunals, concurs, suggesting that while relevant knowledge for international lawyers and judges is assumed to be restricted to 'a limited set of authoritative legal documents and texts' (a position exemplified by the legal scholarship on the ICTR), other forms of knowledge, including forms of bureaucratic organization and personal networks of practitioners are, in reality, more pertinent. This includes 'relational skills: a sense of cosmopolitan flexibility and cultural flexibility ... to work successfully with a diverse set of international co-workers from numerous legal backgrounds' (Baylis, 2015: 273) (see Chapter 3). Such skills are, however, rarely discussed in accounts of international criminal justice (see Mégret, 2016: para 45).

The domination of the 'text based view of the law' also obscures much that happens in the courtroom despite the profuse production of documents therein (see Hyde, 1964: 504). Transcripts, for example, are only a residue of a process and omit not only important elements of talk, including 'emphasis, intonation, volume, and pauses' (Eades, 1996: 217), but also 'gestures, hesitations, clothing, tone of voice, laughter, irony' (Clifford 1988: 290). The importance of such 'extratextual and subtextual language' (Martin 2006: 10–11) is apparent in anthropologist Alexander Hinton's (2016) account of the trial (2009–10) of 'Duch' (Kaing Guek Eav) by the Extraordinary Chambers in the Courts of Cambodia (ECCC) for war crimes and crimes against humanity committed at the S-21 ('Tuol Sleng') detention centre between 1975 and 1979. Having observed much of Duch's trial, Hinton takes care to record the mannerisms of the defendant, lawyers, judges and observers, the way they spoke and moved. Such details are not cosmetic, but central to Hinton's (2016: 67) main concern, asking whether the simplistic question of whether Duch was a 'man or monster' was at odds with the different *personae* Duch displayed in the course of the trial 'the man, teacher, lawyer, judge, defendant, victim, perpetrator, repentant, monster and so forth'. Hinton (2016: 56–8), for example, describes Duch delivering a prepared statement at the start of the trial:

> Duch the teacher rose from his seat, ready with a reprimand. Gazing toward the prosecutors, as if lecturing students who had gotten the facts wrong ... Putting on his glasses, Duch began reading from a prepared statement. ... His voice quivered slightly as he said [the number of those killed under Khmer Rouge rule]. Then he paused and glanced over at the civil parties [representing victims] before expressing 'my regret and my deepest sorrow' ... After taking a deep breath, Duch acknowledged his 'legal responsibility' for the crimes committed at S-21 ... his voice became increasingly soft, his arms barely moving. Having completed his statement, Duch set down his glasses and clasped his hands. Glancing alternatively between the judges and civil parties, he said that he wanted to express 'the remorse I have felt all my life' ... His voice sounding more confident, like the teacher who had first chided the prosecution.

Hinton (2016: 58) notes that having watched this performance, many observers wondered which Duch was authentic: the confident, former maths teacher reprimanding the prosecution, or the contrite defendant on the verge of tears? Such wonder in the minds of observers, was not simply a response to the words used by Duch (recorded in the transcript), but in the manner in which he had spoken those words. Relying on the transcript would not, therefore, communicate a key aspect of that moment in Duch's trial (see Chapter 2).

For Morison and Leith (1992: vii), an account of the 'non-textual nature of law' which would take such issues into account (both inside and outside the courtroom) would not only be more accurate, but, they argue, lawyers, academics and the public would benefit if we 'move from accepting ideologically based pictures of law, to seeing law as a necessarily flawed human process'. The legal scholar Bernard J. Hibbitts (1995: 52) gives an indication of what such an alternative account of law would consider:

> We must not overlook unwritten forms of expression and experience that shape our understanding and appreciation of law in practice ... Even in a society saturated by the written word, law lives in the speech of lawyers and clients, in the gestures of attorneys and witnesses, and in the multi-sensory 'performances' of persons party to wills, marriages and

trials. It resides in the setting and structure of courthouses, in the design and decoration of courtrooms, and the costume and accoutrements of judges. Notwithstanding our traditional inclination to ignore them, these and other 'alternative' legal texts have always had presence and power.

A primary purpose of this book is to give an account of Hibbitts' (1995: 52) different '"alternative" legal texts' at the ICTR. Hence, gesture and performance is considered in Chapter 2 and the setting and structure of courthouses is considered in Chapter 3.

COSMOPOLITAN LOCALS

While the literature on international criminal tribunals has adopted a narrow legalistic lens reliant on texts (transcripts and judgements), another body of scholarship has attended to the degree to which 'transitional justice' (in the form of international criminal tribunals and truth commissions) has been 'localised' (see McEvoy and McGregor, 2008). Scholars have argued that transitional justice institutions, including international tribunals, should be more attuned to the specificities of the contexts in which they operate (see Betts, 2005; Shaw and Waldorf, 2010). Although an essential adjustment to 'top down' interventions, the emphasis on how 'transitional justice' is received in 'local communities' may have inadvertently detracted attention from 'local communities' of lawyers and judges. Just as scholarship on international development has tended to be interested in the complexity of 'developees' and ignored the similar complexity of 'developers' (Hindman and Fechter, 2011: 12), so in emphasizing the complexity and diversity of the 'locals' and their response to transitional justice institutions, there has been a tendency in the transitional justice literature to homogenize 'internationals'. Tshepo Madlingozi (2010: 225), for example, speaks of 'transitional justice entrepreneurs' whom he describes as 'A well-travelled international cadre of actors [who] theorize the field; set the agenda; legitimize what constitute appropriate transitional justice norms and mechanisms'. Kieran McEvoy (2007: 424–6) similarly observes of transitional justice institutions that 'actors within such institutions develop a self-image of serving higher goals' and notes 'the tendency of international lawyers to eulogize the glory and majesty of international law'. This, however, obscures the diversity of those who inhabit(ed) such institutions, including the ICTR, both in terms of career trajectory and their assessment of international criminal justice (see Mégret 2011: 1013). Regarding career trajectories, Elena Baylis (2015: 252–6), describes diversity in terms of time spent at institutions, distinguishing between 'justice junkies' who change jobs rapidly; 'long-timers' who spend a decade or more working in a particular institution; and 'litigators' who, having established domestic careers, shift between domestic and international work as cases start and come to an end. Kamari Clarke (2009: 64) also notes that the 'cosmopolitan elite' that inhabits international criminal tribunals is diverse and that the:

> interests that tie these individuals to their elite enterprise are varied – shaped by professional ambitions, corporate economic interests, a personal desire for travel, idealistic aspirations for world peace, a commitment to the moral project of human rights through rule of law mechanisms, or a combination of these.

This diversity in both why judges and lawyers found themselves at the ICTR and their assessment of international criminal justice is discussed in Chapter 1.

By concentrating on the encounter of powerless 'locals' with externally imposed 'transitional justice', scholars may have inadvertently contributed to obscuring the activities of the powerful. Just as scholarship on international development tends to ignore development workers because there is a 'need to emphasise the suffering of aid recipients rather than aid workers' (Hindman and Fechter, 2011: 3), so a concentration on how local communities respond to international criminal tribunals may obstruct attention being directed towards legal practitioners. Privileging 'the powerless' may not only obscure the 'internal workings' of institutions like the ICTR, but can also strengthen the voices of those who speak on behalf of such institutions to mask internal discord and cultivate a 'public image of cohesion and shared belief' (Scott, 1990: 55) (see Chapter 1).

There is, therefore, a paradox that the literature concerned with 'localising' transitional justice which suggests that 'the values and ideas informing justice may need to be articulated within and by each community, based on its specific realities and needs' (Lundy and McGovern, 2008: 274), tends to assume that the 'specific realities and needs' of a community of judges and lawyers are homogeneous and unproblematic. This is contrary to 'New Legal Realism' which insists that empirical research should be both 'bottom up' (measuring the impact of law on ordinary people's lives) and 'top down' (under-standing the institutions which enact law) (Erlanger *et al.*, 2005: 339–40).

What Rwandan 'locals' thought about the ICTR appears to have been of marginal concern to ICTR officials. While the Prosecutor's spokesperson speculated that 'Testifying often has a cathartic effect that allows victims to let go of their hurt and to more easily embrace forgiveness and reconciliation with those who have harmed them' (Gallimore, 2008: 240, 243),[7] he admitted that there had been no comprehensive study to assess whether or not the victims of the Rwandan genocide 'feel vindicated or that their injuries and grievances have been redressed by the outcome of the trials'. As a Registry official told me in 2005 (nine years after the ICTR was established):

> We're planning to conduct a survey among the Rwandan population. To me it seems like putting the cart before the horse. Such a survey should have been done in 1996 to see what the expectations of the population were so that we could be informed about what they think and respond to that.

While not consulting Rwandan 'locals' about a court designed to serve them (see Chapter 1) can be seen as a failure, I would argue that the ICTR itself should also be considered as a locale, populated by a diverse groups of 'locals', judges, lawyers and other practitioners with varied interests, motivations and needs. As I have argued elsewhere (Eltringham, 2010: 208) international tribunals are sites of local 'ver-nacularisation' (Merry, 2006b; see Tsing, 2005: 8–9), where assump-tions and claims regarding 'transitional justice' are mediated, appropriated, translated, modified, misunderstood or ignored by 'cos-mopolitan locals' just as they are by 'locals' in Sierra Leone (Shaw, 2007); East Timor (Kent, 2011) or Bosnia (Selimovic, 2010). Given that international criminal justice can only be enacted in the 'sticky materiality of practical encounters' in specific localities (Tsing, 2005: 1), the courtrooms and offices of an international criminal tribunal are just as amenable to a 'place-based' approach as are these other localities (Shaw and Waldorf, 2010: 5).

It is possible that a preference for studying the responses of local communities to transitional justice, rather than 'cosmopolitan locals'

---

[7] The claim that participation in transitional justice is therapeutic for victims has been ques-tioned (see Brounéus, 2008; O'Connell, 2005). For a discussion of the ICTR impact on 'reconciliation' in Rwanda, see (Nsanzuwera, 2005).

(judges, lawyers etc.) in the institutions themselves, may be influenced by notions of 'authentic' research (Wilson, 2003: 383). Akhil Gupta and James Ferguson (1997: 13) describe a 'hierarchy of purity' in anthropological field sites, where those at the top of the hierarchy are 'distant, exotic and strange'. Despite a longstanding tradition of research among elites (see Abbink and Salverda, 2012; Cohen, 1981; Marcus, 1983), the 'hierarchy of purity' perpetuates 'dominant-subordinate' relationships with pliable 'locals' which leads to a preference for studying the culture of powerlessness rather than the culture of power (Nader, 1969: 289; see Hannerz, 1998: 109) so that the 'rich and the powerful' remain 'culturally invisible' (Gusterson, 1997: 115). The reasons for this are not clear. On one hand it may be that institutions inhabited by the 'rich and powerful' obstruct access (see Rogers, 2012; Thomas, 1995: 5–6). Alternatively, Annelise Riles (2006: 53) suggests that the fault lies with the researcher who may be intimidated by research subjects who match him or her 'in terms of levels of expertise, authority or status', while Peter Redfield (2012: 358), in the context of his ethnography of *Médecins Sans Frontières*, suggests that the fault lies with a readership for whom only the per-spectives of the marginalized will 'count' as ethnography (see Autesserre, 2014: 45). Whatever the reasons, this book argues that there is a need to examine the powerful as much as the powerless, so that the former do not remain 'culturally invisible' (Gusterson, 1997: 115).

THE ICTR AS 'SUPER-PERSON'

So far, I have suggested that the primacy of the text and privileging the response of 'local communities' to 'transitional justice' institutions distracts from examining the 'inner workings' of an institution like the ICTR. A further obstacle is the tendency, as noted by Elena Baylis (2008: 368), to speak of institutions like the ICTR as if they 'were singular entities that could act independent of human volition'. On one hand, Meierhenrich (2013: 9, 78) has noted the tendency of scholars (especially legal scholars and those from international rela-tions) to speak of such institutions as an 'undifferentiated whole' or 'virtually indistinguishable unitary actors'. On the other hand, lawyers and judges themselves perpetuate this tendency by employing figures of speech that displace agency away from individuals to the institution or 'the law'. This includes practices that efface the individual identity of those who participate in a trial. In his discussion of the theatrical qualities of the courtroom, Milner Ball (1975: 109) notes how the artificial persons of the *personae juris* correspond to the artificial persons of the *dramatis personae* (see Chapter 2). The 'defendant', for example, appears not as herself, but as a *persona*, a 'face' or mask' that acts as a 'dignifying, public identity' that ensures that they are protected and taken seriously. The same applies to judges and lawyers. Like the theatre, the courtroom drama is performed 'by those specially trained to shed their own identities and "represent" others' (Peters, 2008: 180). At the ICTR, for example, the presiding judge would be referred to in court as 'Mr President' although she or he was not the President of the Tribunal (the 'chief' judge); the Examining Prosecution lawyer would become 'Mr Prosecutor' although she or he was not the Prosecutor; the court usher would become 'The Registrar' although she or he was not the Registrar.

The shedding of individual identity, and the implications of that for the location of individual agency, went further. Observing trials at the ICTR, I was struck by the constant displacement of the sovereign centre of the court. Lawyers and judges alternated between three, seemingly interchangeable, terms: 'the Chamber', 'the Court', 'the Tribunal'. A lawyer, for example, over a period of 30 minutes, referred to documents 'in front of the court', 'in front of the Tribunal' and asked a witness 'Could you give the trial chamber some insight into … ?'. Despite the use of these diverse terms, the judges were, obviously, the centre of authority. Although often left unsaid, it was occasionally made explicit, as when an exasperated defence lawyer said to a witness 'Don't tell me, tell the judges, it's the judges who need to know your evidence.' This would also, occasionally, be made explicit by a presiding judge:

> The Trial Chamber must see and appreciate what is being confirmed. There are no shortcuts to that. The witness will have to observe, and then be asked the questions so that the dialogue between counsel and the witness is seen and appreciated by the Trial Chamber. Everything is done by way of questioning the witness, but it is being done for and on behalf of the Trial Chamber for it to see.

Although this statement explicitly places authority with 'the Trial Chamber', the three judges who constituted that chamber would also disassociate themselves from individual authority. When a contentious issue was raised, the three judges would form a huddle and, having conferred, the presiding judge would announce 'this will be the ruling of the Trial Chamber' rather than 'this will be our ruling' (see Steinitz, 2007: 15). Likewise, a presiding judge would ask a defence lawyer 'Is there some action you would like the court to take?' rather than 'Is there some action you would like us/me to take?'

These choices were not innocent figures of speech. In the seemingly insignificant act of conflating three persons into a depersonalized one ('the Chamber'), the judges colluded in creating an image of 'transcendent justice', the notion that 'justice itself is somewhere else: it cannot be ... confined totally to persons' (Garapon, 2001: 28). Shifting the focus away from themselves conveyed a sense of an authority that transcended individuals. The insinuated location of that authority was always elsewhere, always beyond an individual speaker, passed in relays from lawyers to judges and from judges to 'somewhere else, always out of reach' (Feldman, 2004: 193). The constant displacement of responsibility away from individuals allowed judges to take 'refuge behind the appearance of a simple application of the law' which expressed neither the will nor 'the world-view of the judge but the will of the law' (Bourdieu, 1987: 823, 828). Just as Stone Peters (2008: 199) suggests that legal texts are privileged because they represent 'stability, dispassionate fairness, fidelity to truth without prejudice, the blindness of the law' (see above), so judges employed figures of speech that disassociated the operation of law from themselves, contributing further to obscuring the fact that law is 'a necessarily flawed human process' (Morison and Leith 1992: vii).

This displacement of agency in the courtroom was replicated by those who spoke on behalf of the ICTR who tended to assign agency not to the individuals whose work propelled the trials, or even the ICTR's constituent organs (Registry, Prosecution, Defence, Judiciary) but to an aggregated 'Tribunal'. This can be seen in statements by the Registrar who, following Rule 33 of the ICTR's RPE was its 'channel of communication'. Discussing the choice of those who had been indicted, the Registrar wrote:

> The Tribunal has followed a thematic and geographical approach to its work based on the patterns of involvement of leading individuals in several sectors of society – politicians, military, civil administrators, media, and clergy – and the locations of the crimes alleged (Dieng, 2001).

It was not, however, 'the Tribunal' that had chosen who to prosecute, but the Prosecutor, for it was neither the Registrar, the judges nor, obviously, defence lawyers who chose who was to be indicted. On one hand, the Registrar's statement reflects the ICTR's poorly worded 1994 Statute, which states that it 'shall have the power to prosecute persons' and does not distinguish between the Prosecutor who prosecutes persons and judges who assess the prosecution's case (United Nations, 1994e: Art. 1). Despite this ambiguous sentence, the more detailed sections of the Statute (United Nations, 1994e: Art. 10, 20) do designate and circumscribe the power of the ICTR's 'independent' organs: 'The Chambers' (judges); 'The Prosecutor'; 'Registry' (administration); and defence lawyers. Indictments had to be approved by the judges (United Nations, 1994e: Art. 18), but it was the Prosecutor who chose whom to indict (United Nations, 1994e: Art. 17).

Like the judges' conflation of three persons into a depersonalized one ('the Trial Chamber'), the Registrar's reference to 'the Tribunal' is not innocent. In his discussion of the way in which spokespersons, like the ICTR Registrar, represent an institution, Pierre Bourdieu (1991: 204) notes that 'in appearance the group creates the man who speaks in its place ... whereas in reality ... it is the spokesperson who creates the group' and the group 'would not exist ... if he were not there to incarnate it'. Put another way, the ICTR Registrar 'speaks in the name of something which he brings into existence by his discourse' (Bourdieu 1991: 204). An institution did, of course, exist in Arusha, Tanzania; but to represent it as 'the Tribunal' was a particular choice made by the Registrar and others tasked to speak on the ICTR's behalf. Speaking of the ICTR in this way transformed a collection of diverse individuals with varied roles into a 'moral person', a 'social agent' which enabled:

> what was merely a collection of several persons, a series of juxtaposed individuals, to exist in the form of a fictitious person, a *corporation*, a body, a mystical body incarnated in a social body, which itself transcends the biological bodies which compose it (Bourdieu 1991: 207).

This corresponds with Michael Taussig's (1992: 112) discussion of the 'fiction of the state'. Like the state, 'the Tribunal' was presented as 'a being unto itself, animated with a will and mind of its own' when it was, in reality 'a collection of individual human beings connected by a complex system of relations' (Radcliffe-Brown, 1955[1940]: xxiii).

As already indicated, to speak of the ICTR as if it were a 'social agent' that 'could act independent of human volition' (Baylis, 2008: 368), was not to engage in an innocent figure of speech. Rather, the 'insubstantiability' of 'the Tribunal' was important for its political legitimation (Taussig, 1992: 112–13; see Trouillot, 2003: 81–2) as it strengthened the sense of transcendent justice which could not be 'confined totally to persons' (Garapon, 2001: 28).

Speaking of the ICTR as if it acted independently of human volition was also a means of obstructing scrutiny. In her exploration of public administration in Sweden, Barbara Czarniawska (1997: 1–2) suggests that knowledge about the internal functioning of organizations like the ICTR is often 'blackboxed', that those speaking on behalf of such organizations employ the idea of the institution as 'super-person' because they are unwilling to 'reveal the everyday muddle' (see also Meierhenrich 2013: 9). This corresponds with David Mosse's (2006: 938) observation that institutions of international development engage in impression management in order to 'constantly organize attention away from the contradictions and contingencies of practice and the plurality of perspectives' (see Chapter 1).

Central to this blackboxing is the anthropomorphization of institutions, in other words attributing human characteristics to the non-human ICTR and portraying it as a 'super-person' (Czarniawska, 1997: 40–1). Czarniawska (1997: 46) suggests that this persists because 'the rules for constructing personal and organizational identities are very much alike', in that both are dependent on a 'continuous process of narration where both the narrator and the audience are involved in [re] formulating, editing, applauding, and refusing various elements of the ever-produced narrative'. In other words, organizations like the ICTR are spoken of as if they were 'super-persons' with an autobiography (Czarniawska, 1997: 40, 46, 50). This can be seen, for example, in the production of a list of 'The Achievements of the ICTR' (see Chapter 1).

Speaking of the ICTR as a 'super-person' in this way suppresses attention to the 'contingencies of practice and the plurality of perspectives' (Mosse, 2006: 938) and 'the everyday muddle' (Czarniawska, 1997: 2). The diverse opinions of judges and lawyers, and the 'everyday muddle' in which they operated can, however, be accessed because each person who encountered the ICTR's (autobiographical) narrative was also a narrator. Each judge and lawyer at the ICTR was constantly 'involved in [re]formulating, editing, applauding, and refusing' (Czarniawska, 1997: 46) the narrative disseminated by those tasked with speaking for the ICTR as 'super-person'. And it is there, in that constant narration, that one can find a commentary that can enrich our assessment of the ICTR. That commentary runs throughout this book.

Just as the judgment of the ICTR's precursor, the Trial of the Major War Criminals before the International Military Tribunal (the Nuremberg Trials 1945–6), stated that 'Crimes against international law are committed by men, not by abstract entities' (International Military Tribunal, 1947: 233) so, in turn, I would argue that we should distinguish between attempts to portray the ICTR as a disembodied, abstract 'super-person' and the ICTR as what it actually was, a collection of situated persons. There is a need, as Meierhenrich (2013: 8) notes, to recognize that the ICTR was 'produced, reproduced, and reconfigured as a result of the particular and contingent beliefs, preferences, and strategies of the individuals (as well as collectivities)' acting within it. The same can be said of all courts, as Antoine Garapon (2001: 45) notes:

> [The court] only exists by the life that we give it. Without judges and lawyers, without skills, without its density of emotion, without that concentration of anguish and at times joy, without that race for notoriety, advancement or successful outcome, without hurried, worried or idle people, the court does not exist.

A PROCESS ENDURED

The discussion above has suggested that the primacy of texts, the privileging of 'local' communities and displacing agency from individuals to the ICTR as 'super-person' combined to distract attention from the 'everyday muddle' of the ICTR. This resonates with research on the day-to-day experience of aid workers. Heather Hindman and Anne-Meike Fechter (2011: 2–4), for example, note that the role played by aid workers has been neglected because the concern with development outcomes directs attention to retrospective analysis of what is 'achieved' rather than with the process in which the aid workers were engaged. The legal literature on the ICTR reflects a similar concern with outcome rather than process. Among those I met at the ICTR, however, it was process that was emphasized. Lawyers and judges criticized academic commentary that they considered disconnected from day-to-day, routine process, for example, 'Academic papers are very abstract. Not only abstract, but detached. When you listen to a traumatized witness, not just once, but over a number of days, then the reality of the work here is much clearer' (prosecution lawyer). Such comments suggest a need to explore the 'how' of international criminal justice, not just the 'what' (see Autesserre, 2014: 54).

Lawyers explained that this detached abstraction was because academics did not attend trials, that 'Academics don't have a clue. They've never set foot in a courtroom – an amazing, toxic place. They only write treatises on things' (prosecution lawyer).[8] Many of the lawyers and judges I encountered at the ICTR impressed upon me that trials were an endurance test, both in terms of the emotional impact of the trials and tedium. The emotional impact of 'toxic' trials was a constant topic of conversation, that 'Nothing prepares you for the work here. The sheer scale of the atrocities takes its toll emotionally. Very few people in a national jurisdiction are exposed to this' (prosecution lawyer) (see Koomen 2014a: 588–9). A story recounted by an ALO concerning a prosecution colleague illustrates the impact:

> Last week I got a phone call from my friend asking 'can we meet at lunchtime; it's been a terrible morning'. She had been interviewing a witness who, in a matter of fact way, had been describing how he killed, 'butchered' twenty children. My friend had heard such things before, but because it was children it had affected her very badly. Also, the translator, was a Tutsi woman. She left the room in tears, she'd had to translate this talking about the killing in a matter of fact way.

The visceral response felt by ICTR practitioners was further illustrated by a European registry official who described the first time he saw a high-profile defendant in the courtroom:

> I wanted to kill him, if I'd had a stone I would have thrown it. I went back to my office and cried, I was crying uncontrollably, I was frightened that my colleagues would hear me, I couldn't control myself, I was frightened that someone would come in.

Despite such impact, practitioners complained that the ICTR provided no psychological support. Lawyers contrasted this with support 'back home', where 'there's psychological support from the Bar Association if you're the lawyer in an armed robbery case'. While I was told that a lot of 'Tribunal people' had visited a private psychologist in Arusha,

---

[8] This is perhaps curious given that, as Leslie Vinjamuri and Jack Snyder (2004: 359) note, individuals operating in international criminal justice 'move between roles as scholars, advocates and practitioners'. And yet, 'The writings of the barrister turned academic gave no hint of the complexity of life in the courtroom' (Morison and Leith, 1992: 4).

a request from a registry official for the human resources department to provide an in-house psychologist had been rejected.

While extremes of emotion had to be endured, so did boredom.[9] For example, at a morning coffee break, sitting with the defence and prosecution lawyers from a trial I had been watching the previous day, I asked how a witness (who had been giving testimony for a number of days) was doing. The defence lawyer responded 'It's fucking boring, minutia, it's just fucking minutia'. 'How long do you think he'll be on the stand?', I asked. 'At this rate, for fucking ever' the lawyer replied. On another occasion, a defence lawyer explained to me that 'The judges in our case are good. I like them. They're very attentive. When we're doing things that bore me to tears I can see that they're attentive, at least they're still paying attention.' In private, however, judges conveyed to me the same despondency, that 'Our proceedings can be very boring with arid, dry evidence. Very often I'm actually totally bored, but we judges cannot switch off' and:

> It's a boring, boring exercise. We hear the same information many, many times. Lawyers make reference to the same documents – internal legislation, UN telegrams – it's not very interesting from a human position. In fact, ordinary people would die from these proceedings. The first two or three months are OK, but then . . .

Even the ICTR's former spokesperson acknowledged that 'As in all criminal trials . . . the daily courtroom tedium that follows some interesting moments is absorbing only to true believers in justice, or victims' (Moghalu, 2005: 179). On one hand, this reminds us that the documents on which 'thin' legal scholarship tends to rely are only a spectral residue of a tedious, laborious process that has been endured (see Chapter 2). Residual documents which are 'there for all men to read' in the ICTR Archives (transcripts, judicial decisions and judgments;

---

[9] The fact that trials are boring is found in commentary on the ICTR's precursors, the Trial of the Major War Criminals before the International Military Tribunal (the Nuremberg Trials 1945–6). The journalist Rebecca West (1984[1955]: 3, 8) describes the Nuremberg courtroom as a 'citadel of boredom', a place of 'extreme tedium', a 'water-torture, boredom falling drop by drop on the same spot on the soul'. This is, perhaps, not an unsurprising response from a layperson, unaccustomed to the monotony of any trial. And yet, the barrister Airey Neave (1978: 260) (Assistant Secretary to the International Military Tribunal) talks of the 'relentless hours of boredom' while Norman Birkett (1964: 506) (British Alternate Judge) recalled a particularly 'awful cross-examination' and writes that 'with complete murder in my heart I am compelled to sit in suffering silence, whilst the maddening, toneless, insipid, flat, depressing voice drones on in endless words which have lost all meaning'.

see Chapter 5) do not convey the sense of how trials were endured, that 'The process is much more challenging than the end result' (judge).

The daily tedium of trials also offers an explanation of why residual documents (transcripts and judgments) are treated as if they are a sufficient record. When I asked an ICTR defence lawyer whether he attended trials other than his own, he replied:

> I read a lot of transcripts. I sometimes attend a trial if a witness is going to appear in my trial, but, it's easier to read a transcript in one and a half hours than spending a whole day in a court which can be very boring.

If this was the case for a defence lawyer *in situ* in Arusha, all the more so for scholars at a distance who use transcripts to 'cut to the chase'. And yet, the sense among lawyers and judges at the ICTR of trials as something endured further strengthens the need to understand that trials are the outcome of 'everyday tasks, routines, and cultural practices' (Koomen, 2013: 255) and it is those which are the subject of this book.

'DEEP HANGING OUT' IN THE 'GENEVA OF AFRICA'

Given that this book aspires to speak to readers beyond my own academic discipline of social anthropology, there is a need for me to briefly explain the methodology used to collect the material on which the discussion draws. To collect that material, I employed ethnographic data collection methods. Galit Sarfaty (2009: 651) notes in her analogous study of the internal dynamics of the World Bank that ethnographic research seeks to answer a question(s) rather than test a hypothesis. As Sarfaty points out, however, what those question(s) might be emerges only in the course of the fieldwork, as the researcher continually oscillates between collecting and analysing data. That was certainly my experience at the ICTR, the key questions gradually coalescing over the course of the fieldwork into the themes around which the chapters are organized. As regards the methods used to collect the data, ethnographic research:

> involves the researcher participating, overtly or covertly, in people's daily lives for an extended period of time, watching what happens, listening to what is said, and/or asking questions through informal and formal interviews, collecting documents and artefacts – in fact gathering whatever data are available to throw light on the issues that are (the) emerging focus of inquiry (Hammersley and Atkinson 2007, 3).

This reflects my approach during the primary period of fieldwork from 2005–7, during which I spent a total of eight months at the ICTR in Arusha, Tanzania (described in 2000 by Bill Clinton as the 'Geneva of Africa'). During this period, I conducted semi-structured interviews with 12 of the 25 judges. I conducted a further 55 semi-structured interviews with defence and prosecution lawyers, Registry officials, interpreters, witness protection officers and other staff members. Additional semi-structured interviews were conducted in Europe and the USA. Of equal, if not more, value to the research than semi-structured interviews was my 'deep hanging out' (see Clifford 1997: 56), the informal conversations held during the day at coffee, tea and lunch breaks and in the evenings and weekends in bars, at dinner parties and on day trips. While these conversations and interviews play an important part in the discussion that follows, sustained trial observation over eight months was essential for me to begin to explore the relationship between what lawyers and judges told me they were doing and what they actually did. By combining trial observation, interviews and conversations, the 'doings and sayings of practitioners' (Meierhenrich 2013: 56–57) could be given equal attention. My attendance at a conferences organized by the ICTR (in 2007; see Chapter 1) and by ADAD (*Association des Avocats de la Défense* in 2009, see Chapter 5) were additional opportunities to conduct interviews and collect relevant documents. Finally, the (temperamental) online ICTR archive gave me access to trial transcripts, judgements and exhibits.

CONCLUSION

One o'clock in the morning. The crowd packing Via Via bar, in Arusha, Tanzania is made up of Tanzanians, backpackers and staff from the ICTR. I stand at the bar with two lawyers. One bemoans another late night, 'What we need is a decent cinema or a bowling alley, something other than drinking, then I can get some sleep.' "No", his colleague jokes, "genocide never sleeps and neither should we", and raises his glass in a mock toast, "genocide".

Such irreverence may shock and seem irrelevant to the obscene crime of genocide and the aspiration that the ICTR would 'contribute to the process of national reconciliation and to the restoration and maintenance of peace' (United Nations 1994f, UN Doc. S/PV.3453). This episode, however, speaks to a central theme of this book, that despite efforts by those who spoke on behalf of the ICTR to 'organize attention away from the contradictions and contingencies of practice' (Mosse 2006: 938), international criminal justice is a 'flawed human process'

(Morison and Leith 1992: vii). It is a relentless, demanding process to be endured (it never sleeps) and it is enacted not by an institution, but by flawed (occasionally irreverent) humans.

I started this Introduction by suggesting that the ICTR archives do not capture these characteristics. I have argued that this should be rectified, that there is a need for 'thick' accounts of international tribunals (McEvoy 2007) that pay attention to 'everyday tasks, routines, and cultural practices' (Koomen 2013: 255). The question may be asked, however, of why such a 'thick' account, however interesting, is relevant to the project of international criminal justice? Hinton (2018: 5) asks the simple question 'What is the point of holding international tribunals?' Those tasked with speaking on behalf of institutions provide answers, ranging from discovering and publicizing the 'truth'; punishing perpetrators; responding to the needs of victims; promoting the rule of law; and promoting reconciliation (Fletcher and Weinstein 2002: 586–601; see Chapter 1). Hinton (2018: 21, 9) describes such answers as a 'justice façade', the 'face' of institutions masking the 'lived experience and practice' that lies within. Problems arise, I would argue, when both detractors and advocates of international criminal justice take this façade at face value and praise or condemn according to its narrow list of objectives. In contrast, a 'thick' account of international criminal justice requires both detractors and advocates to be diligent, irrespective of their final judgment, in recognizing that the success/failure of grandiose claims is undergirded by a 'muddled' and 'flawed human process' (Morison and Leith 1992: vii) which resists a simple success/failure assessment.

This book is not, however, concerned with international criminal justice in isolation. Seeking a fuller understanding of the practice of international criminal justice within the context of the improvised, ad hoc ICTR is also an opportunity to scrutinize the practice of law in domestic contexts. As an exceptional context, the ICTR was an opportunity to re-assess what passes as unexceptional in domestic trials. Chapter 2, for example, explores whether the observations on the role domestic court buildings play in constructing the courtroom as a site of power (see Hanson, 1996; Mulcahy, 2007) are also applicable to the ICTR, located in a converted conference centre. Similarly, while the role of demeanour has been researched in the context of domestic trials (see Levenson, 2007), the use of simultaneous interpretation at the ICTR provided an opportunity to further assess the relationship between the oral and the visual in domestic as much as international trials (see Chapter 2). While the importance of 'unwritten rules' oper-ating in the courtroom has been explored extensively in domestic trials (see Zoettl, 2016), the ICTR was an invaluable opportunity to further scrutinize these rules given that the diverse provenance of legal practi-tioners required that much of what would ordinarily be taken for granted had to be explicitly articulated and (re)negotiated (see Chapter 3). Chapter 4 interrogates assertions that 'Rwandan culture' impeded witness testimony at the ICTR (see Combs, 2009), by employ-ing research from domestic contexts that highlights the distinction between everyday storytelling and the expectations of testimony in a criminal trial (Conley and O'Barr, 2005; Eades, 2008: 210). Finally, the consideration in Chapter 5 of the value placed on the 'historical record' by judges and lawyers at the ICTR is an opportunity to revisit a debate as applicable to domestic trials as it is to international criminal justice on whether a trial should stick to the 'main business' of deter-mining the guilt or innocence of defendants (Arendt, 1994[1963]: 253), or whether a trial should have salutary repercussions beyond the individual case. In this way, while a full(er) understanding of the ICTR as a 'flawed human process' allows for a more nuanced assessment of 'exceptional' international criminal justice, the ICTR was also an opportunity to scrutinize 'unexceptional' practices that underpin the operation of domestic law.

1

'WHEN WE WALK OUT; WHAT WAS IT ALL ABOUT?'

On my first day at the ICTR in 2005 I met with an external relations officer. 'I haven't sold my soul to the devil yet' he told me, 'but there are plenty of people willing to raise the flag and let it flutter in the wind'. He handed me a pamphlet entitled 'ICTR: Challenging Impunity'. 'Here's the propaganda' he said, and told me to go and speak to a particular prosecutor, who would, he predicted, give me the 'official line' that 'He claims that a purpose of the ICTR is deterrence. But, just look what's happening in Darfur' waving his hand northwards. 'This place is a salve for the conscience of an organization that could have done something in 1994.'

A few days later, I met with two defence lawyers in a hotel bar. 'It's a victor's court, a persecution of Hutus' one began, 'a way of concealing the responsibility of the International Community'. 'Will it contribute to reconciliation?' I asked. One of the lawyers replied, 'The claim for reconciliation is puzzling. The Tribunal is actually a persecution of Hutus. No Tutsi have been brought here. This is a victor's court. That is how the Hutu in Rwanda and in the diaspora see it, as persecution.' 'But' the other defence lawyer interjected, 'The accused persons say, and keep saying, we shouldn't give up. We are putting everything on record for history. The truth will come out one way or another. "Put everything on the record", they say, "and then later our children will decide on the truth".'

With that conversation fresh in my mind, I met with a judge in his office. Our conversation began with a discussion of how the accused were selected. Picking up a ring-bound document on his coffee table he proceeded to quote from the ICTR's 1994 Statute and read "'Upon a determination that a *prima facie* case exists, the Prosecutor shall prepare an indictment", that's in Article 17.' I then asked about the Preamble to the Resolution which states that one of the purposes of the ICTR was to 'contribute to the process of national reconciliation'. The judge replied,

> If the Tribunal does its work properly it will contribute to reconciliation. But, we judges simply evaluate the credibility of evidence and relate it to the crimes alleged. The introduction of political objectives like reconciliation would undermine the quality of justice. My thoughts are governed by my judicial function. If I go into the court thinking about "purposes", then I would not be a judge.

That afternoon, I finally met the prosecutor recommended to me on my first day. I explained that I was interested in knowing what those who work at the ICTR thought its purpose was. 'Let's take a look at the resolution', he said as he went across to his desk and picked up the same bound set of documents consulted by the judge. He read from the Preamble, "'will contribute to ensuring that such violations are halted and effectively redressed" – will end the cycle of impunity – and make a "contribution to peace and reconciliation". Therefore, we are making peace. This is a fundamental part of what we do.' So ended my first two weeks in Arusha.

During a conversation with me, a prosecution lawyer once mused, 'When we walk out; what was it all about?' The comments above demonstrate that those who worked at the ICTR answered that question in diverse ways. In contrast to this diversity, the Registrar of the ICTR wrote in the first edition of the 'ICTR Newsletter' in June 2003:

> As you all know, the Tribunal is striving to effectively discharge its mandate of trying persons accused of being responsible for genocide and other serious violations of humanitarian law committed in Rwanda in 1994. By so doing, the Tribunal is playing an effective role in promoting international peace and security and putting to an end such crimes. The Tribunal is also sending a strong message, regionally and internationally, that the international community is determined to put to an end the culture of impunity, which is a hallmark of such crimes. Also, by discharging its mandate, the Tribunal is contributing to the national reconciliation and unity in Rwanda. Unfortunately, little is known about how the daily activities of the ICTR are conducted

> (Dieng, 2003: 1).

Employing 'Tribunal' as if the ICTR were a singular entity that 'could act independent of human volition' (Baylis, 2008: 368) (see Introduction), the statement contains rhetorical claims for international criminal justice, including promoting international peace and security, deterrence and contributing to reconciliation (see Fletcher and Weinstein, 2002; Turner, 2008: 537–42). And yet, in light of the diverse opinions contained in the opening section, the phrase 'As you all know' reads more like an instruction, intended to cultivate a 'public image of cohesion and shared belief' (Scott, 1990: 55). The Registrar's reference to hidden 'daily activities', however, raises questions about how those immersed in the activities of the ICTR related to its purported purposes?

The legal scholar Frédéric Mégret (2016: para 30) suggests that there is a tendency to see international criminal justice as a 'movement speaking with one voice ... in ways that minimise the element of internal struggle'. As discussed in the Introduction, such a perspective is cultivated by those who speak on behalf of such institutions who tend to refer to international tribunals as social agents that can 'act independent of human volition' (Baylis, 2008: 368). As Mégret (2011: 1013) notes, however, the role of an international criminal tribunal will mean 'very different things for different people', so that in the aftermath what is left is a 'collection of complex individual narratives' shaped by 'the nature of the work one did for it, how one was personally affected by it, or what one hoped it would achieve in the first place'. The assessment of international criminal justice that lawyers and judges now hold, while not pre-determined by the institutional location an individual occupied, will have been forged by the specific power(lessness) that accompanied their institutional location, whether judiciary, prosecution or defence. The chapter will gain entry to these diverse assessments by focusing on the lack of indictments against members of the Rwandan Patriotic Front/Army (RPF/A) for alleged massacres in Rwanda in 1994. First, however, the chapter will consider the claims made for the ICTR on its creation and how these were modified over time.

THE CREATION OF THE TRIBUNAL

As is apparent from my conversations in those first two weeks, a key source for the ICTR's 'purposes' was the UN Security Council Resolution (drafted by the USA representative, see Moghalu, 2005:

30) that brought the ICTR into existence in November 1994 (United Nations, 1994e, UN Doc. S/RES/955 (1994)). Four purposes of the ICTR are given in the Resolution's Preamble (which precedes the Statute): to bring to justice those responsible for violations of international humanitarian law (referring to genocide, crimes against humanity and war crimes); to 'contribute to the process of national reconciliation and to the restoration and maintenance of peace'; and to halt violations of international humanitarian law (deterrence). The reference to 'reconciliation' was innovative, given that such an objective did not appear in the Statute of the International Criminal Tribunal for the Former Yugoslavia (ICTY) established a year earlier (United Nations, 1993, UN Doc. S/RES/827 (1993)).

Despite this apparent clarity of mission, it was clear even during the Security Council debate immediately following the Resolution's adoption that the relative weight given to these four purposes, and their relationship with one another, was a matter of perspective. Although some members reiterated that the ICTR would be an 'instrument of national reconciliation' (United Nations, 1994f, UN Doc. S/PV.3453: 6) others were less certain, commenting that 'The Tribunal might become a vehicle of justice, but it is hardly designed as a vehicle of reconciliation' (United Nations, 1994f: 7). There were also more subtle divergences. While for some members of the Security Council the ICTR would ensure that 'normality is restored to the country' (United Nations, 1994f: 12), for others the status quo was the problem, and the intention was that the ICTR would end Rwanda's normal 'cycle of violence' (United Nations, 1994f: 5), characterized as a 'culture of impunity' (United Nations, 1994f: 7). Rather than restoring a pre-genocide dispensation ('the restoration and maintenance of peace'), the fight against 'impunity' would require, in the words of the representative of Rwanda on the Security Council, that Rwandans 'learn new values' and participate in the 'construction of a new society' (United Nations, 1994f: 14).

Alongside these 'local', Rwanda-specific objectives, hopes were expressed that the ICTR would contribute to the global project of international criminal justice and 'provide international penal experience which will be useful for the establishment of the future permanent court [the International Criminal Court]' (United Nations, 1994f: 4) and 'signify a breakthrough in creating mechanisms that would impose international criminal law' (United Nations, 1994f: 7). Rather than only serving Rwandans, the ICTR was perceived as a means to further

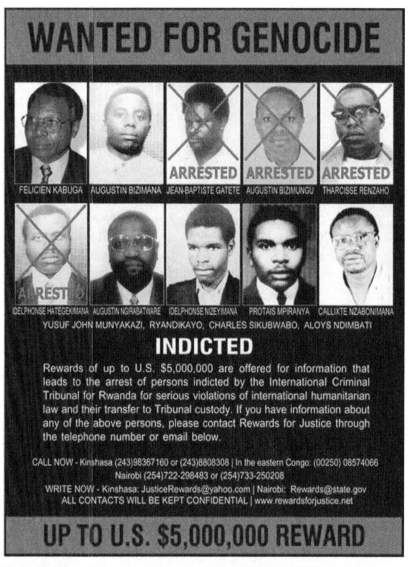

Figure 1.1 Wanted for genocide (Courtesy of the ICTR)

resuscitate the project of international criminal justice that had stalled after the International Military Tribunal at Nuremberg (1945–6) and The International Military Tribunal for the Far East (1946–8). Given that such diverse positions on the purposes of the ICTR were present in the first hours after its creation, it is no surprise that those who I met in my first two weeks in Arusha held equally diverse opinions. Given the diverse ways the mission of the ICTR could be articulated, those tasked with promoting the institution to an external audience had been required to make choices regarding the relative weight to assign these different 'purposes'.

THE ICTR 'AT A GLANCE'

When I first arrived at the ICTR, 'peace' and 'reconciliation', as found in the Preamble to the 1994 Statute, permeated its public presentation. The ICTR's website banner reproduced part of a speech made in September 1998 by the then UN Secretary-General, Kofi Annan: 'For there can be no healing without peace; there can be no peace without justice; and there can be no justice without respect for human rights and rule of law.' Over my first few days at the ICTR, I became aware of other allusions to the Preamble of the 1994 Statute. At the entrance, under the ICTR's emblem (the scales of justice superimposed on a 'dove of peace'), there was a plaque which read 'Dedicated to the memory of our beloved colleagues and friends who have lost their lives whilst in the service of the ICTR towards peace and justice.' Pinned to a noticeboard outside the library there was a list of 'New Acquisitions & Highlights', the header of which read 'Information for Justice and Reconciliation'. On my first day, I was handed a 26-minute video produced in 2005 entitled *Towards Reconciliation* and a leaflet entitled 'The ICTR at a Glance' (ICTR, n.d.) which stated that the ICTR was created 'to contribute to the process of national reconciliation in Rwanda and to the maintenance of peace in the region, replacing an existing culture of impunity with one of accountability'.

Writing on the ICTY, Mégret (2011: 1035) distinguishes between an '"internal" or "forensic"' vision of international criminal justice that is focused on the trial and an '"external" or "strategic"' vision concerned with the repercussions of trials beyond the courtroom. Mégret (2016: para 50) notes that while there is a 'constant effort [by the ICTY] to sell its goals and achievements', these oscillate between 'grandiose statements about its supposed benefits ("peace", "transition", "truth", "reconciliation"), and sober reassessments of its goals (to prosecute and nothing else)'. I encountered the same oscillation at the ICTR (see Chapter 5). The oscillation between the grandiose and the sober resonates with Sally Falk Moore's (2000: 2) observation that while 'ordinary experience' suggests law and legal institutions can only 'effect a degree of intentional control of society', this 'limited degree of control and predictability is daily inflated in the folk models of lawyers and politicians all over the world . . . as if there were no possible uncertainties in the results'. This inflation of what trials can achieve also relates to John Conley and William O'Barr's (1990: 163–5) distinction between law as being considered 'enabling' (a 'force for the righting of wrongs' that will 'punish wrongdoers and compensate victims') when the 'official ideology' of legal systems is that 'the law is limited to dealing with violations of specific rules of narrow applicability'. This tension was clear at the ICTR where 'The ICTR at a Glance' leaflet or the Preamble to the 1994 Statute ('will contribute to the process of national reconciliation and to the restoration of peace') reflected 'strategic', 'enabling' claims made for law, while the judge's comments in the opening section ('we judges simply evaluate the credibility of evidence and relate it to the crimes alleged') reflect an 'internal', 'limiting' and 'sober' assessment of law.

I became aware at the ICTR that rather than discuss whether the ICTR had achieved objectives associated with an 'enabling' view of law (reconciliation; peace) or the effect on victims; officials tended to foreground the strictly quantifiable (number of arrests; number of convictions) and the tangible contributions to the global project of international criminal justice (jurisprudence). Under the heading 'The Achievements of the ICTR', the leaflet 'The ICTR at a Glance' (ICTR, n.d.) provided the following list:

- Obtained the cooperation of the international community in the arrest of suspects, the travel of witnesses to Arusha, and the detention of convicted persons and, in general, support for its aims and activities.
- Secured the arrest of about 70 individuals accused of involvement in the 1994 genocide in Rwanda. Completed trials of several of those arrested . . .
- Laid down principles of international law, which will serve as precedents for other International Criminal Tribunals and for courts all over the world . . . [1]

---

[1] This included being the first international tribunal to interpret the definition of the UN Convention for the Prevention and Punishment of Genocide and enter a judgment for genocide (Jean-Paul Akayesu in 1998); to define rape in international criminal law and to recognize it as a means to commit genocide; and to issue a judgment against a former head of government (Jean Kambanda in 1998) (see Møse, 2005).

- Established a complex international institution based in Arusha and Kigali. The institution includes four modern fully equipped court-rooms and the first ever Detention Facility to be set up and run by a United Nations body.

In other words, that which was quantifiable and tangible was cele-brated as an 'Achievement' rather than more intangible contributions to 'peace' and 'reconciliation'. This public emphasis on the global ('Laid down principles of international law') was replicated in internal documents. Of the nine 'accomplishments' outlined in an internal discussion paper on the 'legacy' of the ICTR and ICTY (ICTR, 2005b), only two were concerned with Rwanda ('improved the chances of reconciliation between Rwanda's ethnic groups'; 'impact of the rule of law' in Rwanda) the remaining seven concerned 'unique and inno-vative' legal decisions and judgments which contributed to interna-tional criminal justice (ICTR, 2005b: 14). The emphasis was on the tangible (number of arrests/completed trials; jurisprudence) rather than the intangible (national reconciliation, peace, deterrence).

On one hand, as a UN institution, the emphasis on transferable contributions to international criminal justice corresponds to Sally Merry's (2011: 84) account of UN indicator culture that constantly converts 'complicated contextually variable phenomena into unambig-uous, clear and impersonal measures' (for a critique of assessing inter-national tribunals in this way see Stahn, 2012: 264–6). This desire for 'unambiguous, clear and impersonal measures' suggests that the primary audience was not Rwandans. Rather, 'decision makers' at the ICTR saw, as at the ICTY, 'New York, Washington, Berlin, London, Paris, Moscow as their constituents. That is where they looked for approval or support.' (Mégret, 2011: 1030–5). On the other hand, Merry's 'indica-tor culture' also dovetails with the status of the ICTR as a legal institu-tion, for as Kieran McEvoy (2008: 22) suggests, the confusion and 'messiness' that characterizes daily reality are 'thinned out' by human rights discourses into a 'legalese of international standards, legal cer-tainties, and political objectivity'. This process corresponds to what happens in criminal trials, in which the 'messiness' of events is replaced by a 'skeletonisation of fact' (Geertz, 1983: 170) (see Chapter 4). It is possible, therefore, that those who spoke on behalf of the ICTR (pre-dominantly legal practitioners) employed the same 'thinning out' to organize the way in which they spoke of the ICTR's tangible 'achieve-ments'. In both its guises (as UN body and as legal institution) those who spoke on behalf of the ICTR felt propelled to foreground the tangible (number of arrests/completed trials; jurisprudence) and ignore the unquantifiable, context-specific questions of reconciliation, peace and deterrence.

A LOCAL OR GLOBAL PURPOSE?

Having considered the nature of the 'strategic' vision of the ICTR's work disseminated by those tasked with promoting the institution, what of the 'internal' views I encountered among judges and lawyers (see Mégret, 2011: 1035)? Before answering that question, there is a need to understand who populated the ICTR. Officially, the 1994 ICTR Statute only provided criteria for judges ('persons of high moral character, impartiality and integrity who possess the qualifications required in their respective countries for appointment to the highest judicial offices' (United Nations, 1994e: Art. 12 (11)). A 1996 Directive laid out requirements for defence lawyers ('admitted to practice law in a State, or is a professor of law at a university or similar academic institution and has at least 10 years relevant experience') (ICTR, 1996: Art. 13).[2] Such criteria do not, however, explain why legal practitioners found themselves at the ICTR in a context in which there was no established cadre of international criminal lawyers and judges, given that the project of international criminal justice had only been resuscitated in 1993 with the creation of the ICTY (see Eltringham, 2008).

One explanation would be an a priori commitment to (or opposition to) the project of international criminal justice. While a defence lawyer mocked the 'large number of the defence and prosecution lawyers who are here to "make a difference" and "improve the world"' an ALO explained to me that:

> There are zealots on both sides and zealotry is never attractive. There are people in the OTP [Office of the Prosecutor] who think that they're doing the work of God and they talk about it in that way and it's inappropriate. But there are also defence counsel who are deniers. So, there are zealots on both sides.

While such 'zealotry' may have developed in the course of working at the ICTR, none of the lawyers or judges with whom I spoke recalled

---

[2] Jenia Iontcheva Turner (2008: 547) found that among defence lawyers (ICTY, ICTR, SCSL) the majority had practised for at least 15 years and predominantly in criminal law.

a prior, burning commitment to (or aversion to) the project of international criminal justice. On one hand, judges and lawyers indicated to
me a degree of causal happenstance. A judge told me how he was
nominated by his home country 'without prior consultation'; that 'It
was not something I wanted to do. Before I had a chance to make up my
mind, I received a letter of confirmation.' The lack of preceding commitment to international criminal justice also expressed itself as doubt
about suitability, one judge confiding in me, 'I'm always asking myself
"Am I the right man to do this?" I try to prepare, read books, read
articles, but . . . ' A prosecution lawyer (who prosecutes and defends in
his home country) explained that, 'through a friend', he had been
a defence lawyer at another international criminal tribunal, had 'got
a taste for this' and did not feel he could go back to 'burglary or bank
robbery' because, 'In this field, one has a sense of importance, a sense of
history' and 'It's also a good career option.' A defence lawyer (who
prosecutes and defends in his home country) recalled how he ended up
in Arusha having received an email from a friend who 'wanted someone
with a bit of French and I thought it sounded interesting'. While ties of
friendship were one route, a defence lawyer spoke of the attractions of
a cosmopolitan lifestyle, that 'I wanted my children to be citizens of the
world; to live somewhere internationally.' Another defence lawyer was
more explicit, that it was 'An interesting case and overseas travel. But,
I don't have any burning interest in International Criminal Law.'
Others spoke of a simple desire for a change. A prosecution lawyer,
for example, having been a banking lawyer for 17 years simply 'wanted
to do something different'. Only two defence lawyers among those with
whom I spoke suggested a degree of prior interest, one that 'I got
involved in the case because I wanted to know about how international
tribunals worked' while another told me 'I was always interested in
international law.' Taken together, my discussion with lawyers corresponds to Jenia Iontcheva Turner's (2008: 548) findings from research
among defence lawyers (at the ICTY, ICTR and the Special Court for
Sierra Leone), that the principal initial reason was 'professional curiosity' and 'taking on a new professional challenge' rather than commitment to the 'grandiose' claims made for international criminal justice
('peace' and 'reconciliation').

When asked for their evaluation of the work of the ICTR,
judges and lawyers could choose to refer to a range of ICTR
objectives, some of which were tangible (number of arrests/com-
pleted trials; jurisprudence), some more speculative (national

reconciliation, peace, deterrence). Some objectives fulfilled aspirations found in the Preamble to the 1994 Resolution (number of arrests/completed trials; national reconciliation, peace, deterrence) and some did not (ending the 'culture of impunity'; jurisprudence). Some objectives focused on Rwanda ('ending the "culture of impunity"'; national reconciliation, peace, deterrence) others were more concerned with the global project of international criminal justice (jurisprudence).

The way that lawyers and judges drew upon these possible objectives in their evaluations of the ICTR can be illustrated by considering two prosecution lawyers. The prosecutor quoted at the start of this chapter appears invested in the Rwanda-specific promises of the Preamble ('[W]e are making peace. This is a fundamental part of what we do.'). Within minutes of having said this, however, he told me, that the ICTR's 'legacy' was not its 'local' contribution, but its contribution to the global project of international criminal law:

> We think of it as stitching together a fabric. The Tribunal, its law, its definitions of crimes, these are now all available to other institutions. This Tribunal has made an enormous contribution to the international legal regime. The Tribunal was not explicitly created for the purpose of knitting the fabric together, but these definitional achievements are consistent with that defining Statute. We see our legacy as our jurisprudence.

For this prosecution lawyer, the legacy was straightforward; an 'enormous contribution to the international legal regime'. But, his use of the plural pronoun ('We see our legacy as our jurisprudence.') was deceptive because not everyone at the ICTR, or even in his own office, shared his views. For example, five days later I met with one of his colleagues in the prosecution. I began by asking him whether he thought that lawyers, on first arriving at the ICTR, believed it could achieve the promises of the Statute's Preamble ('peace' and 'reconciliation')? He responded with a far less celebratory tone than that of his colleague, 'We operatives of international justice assumed it would be simple, we would come and dispense justice, end the culture of impunity, establish peace and then go away. But, it didn't happen that way.' He then employed tangible, quantifiable criteria, 'At Nuremberg only twenty two tried, even at the Special Court for Sierra Leone, with all the gruesome acts there, only thirteen persons on trial.

But, in Rwanda, on the contrary, we have tried fifty people. So, what are we doing wrong? But, nobody makes a good comparison between the ICTR and Sierra Leone or Nuremberg.'

Having indicated his feeling that the ICTR's quantifiable achievements were insufficiently recognized, I asked the prosecution lawyer whether he considered jurisprudence to be an 'achievement' of the ICTR? 'Jurisprudence is not an excuse', he replied, 'It's one of the complexities that we argue with; it's part of our legacy.' I asked him to expand on the statement that 'jurisprudence is "not an excuse"'. Talking first about the failure of the ICTR Statute to provide compensation to victims he then spoke of his worries about how the ICTR was perceived in Rwanda:

> To a Rwandese who know that the Akayesu trial [1997–1998] cost the International Community US$600,000 and victims are dying by their hundreds every day, can we say that we are delivering justice as a legacy? Victims continue to die while those detainees who would have died of AIDS have been kept alive. Therefore, when we go we will say that we have 'delivered justice', but will that resonate with the victims? Our legacy will be measured by how we improve the lives of Rwandese and stopped impunity.

Compared to his colleague, he articulated a very different idea of what constituted the ICTR's purpose and, by extension, how he understood the work he was doing. He did not contradict his colleague's assessment ('We see our legacy as our jurisprudence.'), but bequeathing globally useful jurisprudence did not, for him, excuse local failure. The two lawyers (located in the same organ of the ICTR) proposed different ways in which the ICTR could be evaluated; simply as a court of law ('we have tried 50 people'); as benefiting Rwanda ('improve the lives of Rwandese and stopped impunity'); or as benefiting the project of international criminal justice ('We see our legacy as our jurisprudence.') These two colleagues represent, in microcosm, the diversity I encountered among lawyers and judges. I will now broaden the exploration of different perspectives by considering how judges and lawyers relate to the accusation that the ICTR was a 'victor's court' because no one from the Rwandan Patriotic Front/Army (RPF/A, the party which took power following the 1994 genocide) was indicted for alleged massacres committed in 1994.

VICTOR'S JUSTICE: THE ELEPHANT IN THE COURTROOM?

It was jurisprudence as legacy that the ICTR Registry chose as the theme of a three-day Symposium in November 2007 entitled 'The Legacy of International Criminal Courts and Tribunals for Africa with a Focus on the Jurisprudence of the International Criminal Tribunal for Rwanda'. Panel themes included 'Genocide, Crimes Against Humanity and War Crimes: Case Studies in Criminal Responsibility'; 'Freedom of Speech and Incitement to Criminal Activity: A Delicate Balance' and 'Sexual Violence Under International Law'. At that time, the ICTR completion strategy (following UNSC Resolution 1503 (2003)) required all trials (excluding appeals) to be completed by the end of 2008. With 13 months left, it was the globally relevant and tangible jurisprudence, rather than the local and intangible ('reconciliation' and 'peace') that would be considered by more than 200 participants congregating at the New Arusha Hotel (see Eltringham, 2008). While the intention was to celebrate the ICTR's jurisprudential achievements, the lack of indictments for members of the RPF/A would be raised by defence lawyers almost as soon as the Symposium began, thereby implying that rather than advancing international criminal law, the ICTR had simply resurrected the 'Nuremberg paradigm of international criminal justice', the paradigm of 'victor's justice' (Reydams, 2005: 981).

Before considering the 2007 Symposium in detail, it is necessary to outline the accusations against members of the RPF/A. References below to documents that were presented in evidence in ICTR trials demonstrate that this was a prominent subject in the courtroom, despite the lack of indictments of members of the RPF. As discussed in the Introduction, the ICTR was created in response to the interim report of a UN Commission of Experts (4 October 1994) which concluded that Tutsi had been victims of genocide between 6 April and 15 July 1994 (United Nations, 1994b, UN Doc. S/1994/1125: paras 44, 124, 133, 148). The report, however, also stated that there were 'substantial grounds' to conclude that 'Tutsi elements' had committed 'mass assassinations, summary executions, breaches of international humanitarian law [i.e. war crimes] and crimes against humanity' (United Nations, 1994b: para 82). The Commission stated that it had received from UNHCR 'extensive evidence of systematic killings and persecution ... of Hutu individuals by the [Rwandan Patriotic Front] army' (United Nations, 1994b: 30). This would appear to be a reference to a report sent to the High Commissioner for Refugees by Robert Gersony who, having led a UNHCR mission in Rwanda (1 August to 5 September 1994) to investigate the repatriation of refugees, had, on 19 September 1994, presented evidence to UN officials in Kigali of 'calculated, preplanned, systematic atrocities and genocide against Hutus by the RPA'; claiming that 30,000 had been massacred; that the 'methodology and scale' suggested a 'plan implemented as a policy from the highest echelons of the government'; and that 'these were not individual cases of revenge and summary trials but a pre-planned, systematic genocide against the Hutus' (ICTR, 2006a: para 5; see also Khan, 2000: 51–4). Although the UNHCR subsequently denied the existence of Gersony's report (see Des Forges, 1999: 726), it appears that Gersony also briefed US diplomats in Kigali on 17 September 1994 (ICTR, 2006c) and that based on this briefing and other reports (ICTR, 2006d) a US State Department memo (dated 21 September 1994) anticipated that the UN Secretary-General would announce that there is 'evidence that the RPA is involved in ethnic cleansing, acts of genocide, or war crimes' (ICTR, 2006b). On 10 October 1994 the UN Commission of Experts met with UNHCR officials including Gersony (United Nations, 1994d, UN Doc. S/1994/1405: para 20) and in its final report (9 December 1994) recommended that 'an investigation of violations of international humanitarian law and of human rights law attributed to the Rwandese Patriotic Front [RPF] be continued by the Prosecutor for the International Tribunal for Rwanda' and that it would hand over 'all relevant files' to the UN Secretary-General (United Nations, 1994d: para 100; see Sunga, 1995: 124).

That the ICTR would prosecute 'both sides' (those responsible for the genocide and the RPF/A for war crimes and crimes against humanity), remained a publicly stated intention in the early years of the ICTR's operation. In February 1995, the UN Secretary-General justified the choice of Arusha (Tanzania) as the seat of the ICTR by saying that it would ensure 'complete impartiality and objectivity in the prosecution of persons responsible for crimes committed by both sides to the conflict' (United Nations, 1995 UN Doc. S/1995/13: para 42) while Judge Laity Kama (President of the ICTR 1995–9) stated, in September 1998 that 'All parties, including the RPF, who have committed crimes against humanity must be prosecuted. It is a simple question of equality. The credibility of international justice demands it' (Hazan, 1998). Despite the information transferred to the ICTR by the Commission of Experts, Richard Goldstone (ICTR/ICTY Prosecutor 1994–6) argued that he 'didn't have evidence of mass crimes committed by the RPF' (Peskin, 2008: 189). According to Bernard Muna (Deputy Prosecutor 1997–2002), he and Goldstone's successor Louise Abour (ICTR/ICTY Prosecutor 1996–9) initiated discussions with the Rwandan government on the subject of RPF/A indictments in 1997 and that the Rwandan Vice-President Paul Kagame was positive (Moghalu, 2005: 138). What were to be called 'Special Investigations' were finally opened by the ICTR Prosecutor in February 1999 (Cruvellier, 2010: 240–1) and made public by Carla Del Ponte (the ICTR's third Prosecutor) on 13 December 2000 (ICTR, 2000).

In mid-2002, obstruction by the Rwandan government (dominated by the RPF) prevented prosecution witnesses from travelling to Arusha. This was interpreted at the time as a response to the threat of indictments for members of the RPF/A (see ICTY, 2002; Peskin, 2008: 207–25; United Nations Wire, 2002). Although both the ICTR President (ICTR, 2002) and Prosecutor (ICTY, 2002) registered formal complaints to the UN Security Council (in July and October 2002 respectively) it was only in August 2003 that the UN Security Council issued a resolution calling on Rwanda to 'render all necessary assistance to the ICTR, including on investigations of the Rwandan Patriotic Army' (United Nations, 2003b, UN Doc. S/RES/1503 (2003): para 3).

On 28 July 2003, Kofi Annan sent a letter to the UN Security Council recommending that the, until then, joint position of ICTY/ICTR Prosecutor be split. According to Pierre Richard Prosper (ICTR prosecution lawyer 1994–6 and US Ambassador-at-Large for War Crimes Issues 2001–5) it was the UK government that suggested splitting the role of prosecutor (Moghalu, 2005: 135) because it, together with the USA, did not want RPF indictments (Peskin, 2008: 221). Carla Del Ponte, the ICTR Prosecutor, indicated at the time that she believed 'pressure from Rwanda contributed to the non-renewal of my mandate' (Hirondelle News, 2003). In 2007, Florence Hartmann, Del Ponte's former spokesperson (2000–6) published a book in which she alleged that US diplomats had pressured Del Ponte not to indict the RPF and had, ultimately, been instrumental in removing her as ICTR Prosecutor (Hartmann, 2007: 261–79). Del Ponte confirmed these allegations in her autobiography published in 2009 (Del Ponte and Sudetic, 2009: 234–9; see Moghalu, 2005: 125–51). Kingsley Moghalu (2005: 148), former Special Counsel and Spokesman of the ICTR, believes that it was virtually impossible for Del Ponte to survive such a 'determined and carefully orchestrated political onslaught by Rwanda and the great powers'. Although the succeeding ICTR Prosecutor, Hassan Bubacar Jallow, revived the 'Special Investigations' in 2004 (GADH, 2009b: 45), the prosecutorial strategy outlined in the ICTR President's 'Completion Strategy' in May 2004 indicated that only genocide cases would be prosecuted (ICTR, 2004). No indictments against members of the RPF/A were forthcoming before the ICTR ceased operations.

Part of the reason why indictments were not forthcoming was that the Rwandan government, dominated by the RPF/A, was in a position to obstruct the operation of the ICTR given that around 80 per cent of witnesses travelled from Rwanda and the Office of the Prosecutor was located in Kigali. When it appeared that RPF/A soldiers would be indicted in late January 2002, the two main genocide survivor organisations in Rwanda, *Ibuka* and *Avega,* boycotted the ICTR 'with pivotal backing from the Rwandan government' thereby diverting 'attention away from the government's continuing refusal to abide by its obligations to cooperate with Del Ponte's investigations of RPF atrocities' (Peskin, 2008: 200). In June 2002, Rwandan authorities blocked travel of genocide survivors who were to give testimony and two trials had to be repeatedly postponed (Peskin, 2008: 212). When 'Special Investigations' into RPF/A alleged crimes were put on hold soon after, the Rwandan government allowed witnesses to travel (Peskin, 2008: 219).

DEBATING 'LEGACY'

Returning to the 2007 Symposium. Although commentators persistently accused the ICTR of 'victor's justice' (see Reydams, 2005; Human Rights Watch, 2002; Human Rights Watch & FIDH, 2002; 2006) and allegations against the RPF/A were part of the judicial record (as indicated by the references to trial exhibits above), the issue was not present in the programme for the 2007 Symposium. This was the fourth major symposium organized by the ICTR Registry, following symposiums on reconciliation (2002),[3] the work of prosecutors (2004)[4] and

---

[3] 'Promoting Justice and Reconciliation in Africa: Challenges for Human Rights and Development' together with the Office of the High Commissioner for Human Rights (Arusha, 24–6 May 2002).

[4] 'Colloquium of Prosecutors of International Criminal Tribunals (Arusha, 25–7 November 2004).

challenging 'impunity' (2006).[5] The 2007 Symposium was designed to be a final reflection on the ICTR's achievements given that, at the time, the ICTR's completion strategy (following UNSC Resolution 1503 (2003)) required the ICTR to complete all trial activities of first instance by the end of 2008, and to complete all work, including appeals, by the end of 2010.

The Symposium resulted in a special issue of the New England Journal of International and Comparative Law[6] and a report produced by the International Center for Ethics, Justice and Public Life at Brandeis University[7] which had co-sponsored the Symposium. If one were to read these two accounts, one would be left with the impression of a confident ICTR that had bequeathed a legacy of jurisprudence to international and domestic criminal justice. Exchanges in the first couple of hours of the Symposium, however, suggest an alternative reading.

Opening the Symposium, a judge declared that the ultimate goal over the next three days was to 'achieve the greatest diversity of voices and opinion as possible. Everyone is encouraged to ask questions.' The first hour was occupied by five presentations: three by academic 'outsiders'; one by a former prosecution lawyer (an 'outsider/insider'); and one current 'insider' from the Office of the Prosecutor. When the floor was opened to questions, a defence lawyer asked the judge why, given the commitment to a 'divergence of voices', only one defence lawyer was due to speak among 30 presenters? The judge explained that the panels were composed of people not involved in cases currently before the ICTR and that she was 'acting as a moderator and not as a panellist'. Immediately, the same defence lawyer who posed that question asked 'Will the Tribunal follow the example of South Africa and uphold the rule of law for all parties who were accused of committing crimes during the temporal jurisdiction? Will Kagame [President of Rwanda and leader of the RPF in 1994] be indicted?' Ignoring an interjection by the Rwandan government's observer at the ICTR that it was not appropriate 'to raise an issue which has never been an issue' another defence lawyer directed a question to the prosecution lawyer on the panel:

[5] 'Conference on Challenging Impunity' (Kigali, 7–8 November 2006).
[6] Available at www.nesl.edu/students/ne_journal_icl_vol14.cfm
[7] Available at www.brandeis.edu/ethics/pdfs/internationaljustice/Legacy_of_ICTR_in_Africa_ICEJPL.pdf

> How can you talk about combating impunity if the Chief Prosecutor [Carla del Ponte] was removed for threatening to indict members of the RPF? I'm citing Florence Hartmann's book. The ICTR was established to prosecute both sides. If it fails, will it not discredit the hard work of the judges, other prosecution and defence lawyers? This must change because it discredits all the work of the Tribunal and serves only to perpetuate the notion of 'victor's justice'?

During these exchanges, I noticed two defence lawyers walking round handing binders to delegates. When I received my copy, I discovered it was a 109-page dossier prepared by ADAD (*Association des Avocats de la Défense*) entitled 'Avoiding a "Legacy" of Victor's Justice and Institutional Impunity: Challenges for the ICTR and the United Nations Security Council'. The preface explained that ADAD had 'prepared this small dossier to assist Symposium participants in under-standing some of the issues which may not be raised or discussed at the Symposium, at least according to the published programme'. The dos-sier's preface referred to the allegations in Florence Hartmann's book which claimed that the UK and US governments had interfered to protect their ally, the post-genocide government of Rwanda,[8] and the dossier contained an English translation of the relevant passage from Hartmann's book. The preface also highlighted inclusion in the dossier of an affidavit by Michael Hourigan, a former investigator for the OTP, who, in 1997, recommended the prosecution of Paul Kagame and was told to 'destroy his notes' by Del Ponte's predecessor Louise Arbour. Just before the panel session came to an end, the prosecution lawyer on the panel responded to the defence lawyer's earlier question about 'victor's justice':

> Regarding Mr [name of defence lawyer's] question about my Prosecutor, my 'Chief Prosecutor'. I have no 'Chief Prosecutor', I just work for a Prosecutor and we all work for the ICTR, Prosecutors and Defence and we all, Prosecutors and Defence, collect a pay cheque at the end of the month from the ICTR.

At first sight the exchanges during this first panel suggest a contest between defence lawyers on one side and judges and prosecution lawyers on the other. But the interaction is more nuanced. By asking whether our hard work will be discredited ('If it fails, will it not discredit the hard work of the judges, other prosecution and defence lawyers?'),

---

[8] Regarding US and UK support for the post-genocide government, see (Commonwealth Human Rights Initiative, 2009) and (Pottier, 2002).

the defence lawyer seeks to establish collegiality with the prosecution lawyer and he cites the book by Florence Hartmann (a former spokesperson for the Prosecutor). If Hartmann is to be believed, the defence lawyer implies, then the Prosecution have been victims of extra-judicial interference. And how does the representative of the Prosecution respond? Rather than dismiss the defence lawyer's accusations of 'victor's justice' as being without foundation, he also asserts collegiality, affirming their common location as legal practitioners ('we all . . . collect a pay cheque at the end of the month from the ICTR'). As for the judge chairing the session, she replicates the inscrutable role she plays in the courtroom and refuses to offer an opinion.

The fact that defence lawyers would raise 'victor's justice' at the earliest opportunity indicates the importance they placed on this issue. But more telling is the fact that neither the judge nor the prosecution lawyer took the opportunity in this public forum, one designed to project the image of the ICTR in the most positive light, to dismiss the accusation as being without basis or as irrelevant. Rather, they avoided the question; the prosecution lawyer deftly dissembling, the judge pleading neutrality. Observing these exchanges, I interpreted them in a particular way because, through preceding conversations, I knew that judges and prosecution lawyers held views that, although not entirely concordant with those of the defence lawyers who spoke at the symposium, were not diametrically opposed to them either. To me, the responses of the prosecution representative and of the judge further indicated that legal practitioners, enmeshed in an institutional order, must self-censure on certain issues while struggling with the fact that, given their prescribed spheres of action, they were unable to alter situations they may privately consider objectionable. It is to these hidden views that I now turn.

HIDDEN VIEWS ON 'VICTOR'S JUSTICE'

Compared to the reticence of the judge and prosecution lawyer at the 2007 Symposium, I found in conversation that the accusation of 'victor's justice' was a ubiquitous concern among legal practitioners. Among the prosecution lawyers with whom I spoke, none dismissed allegations against the RPF/A. A number were adamant that there should be RPF/A indictments, while others did not dismiss allegations against members of the RPF/A, but argued that the genocide, as the 'major crime base', had to remain the priority to ensure the rights of defendants to as speedy a trial as possible.[9] When, for example, I asked a prosecution lawyer whether he was concerned about the accusations of 'victor's justice', he replied:

> We are required to investigate RPF crimes because they are under our jurisdiction. But, it needs to be approached diplomatically. We are accused of 'victor's justice', but, our major crime base is the genocide. We still have people in detention awaiting trial. This must be the priority. How can we take on new cases when people have been in detention for 4–5 years and we are accused of violating their rights to a fair trial? There is a potential for the Rwandan government to disrupt trials. We are never sure that if we take up the issue what will happen.

When I asked another prosecution lawyer (in 2006) about the ability of the Rwandan government to disrupt trials if the issue of RPF/A indictments was raised again, he replied, 'It would be possible for us [the prosecution] to do our cases without anyone from Rwanda, but the defence would cry blue murder because all of their best witnesses are there.' Whether propelled by a sincere commitment to the rights of the accused or because infractions of the accused's rights would disrupt the prosecution's case, this prosecution lawyer was keenly aware that the power of the OTP to indict members of the RPF/A was curtailed by the Rwandan government. Rather than a principled opposition to RPF/A indictments, this gave rise to a sense of pragmatism among prosecution lawyers. As another prosecution lawyer explained to me:

> Like Nuremberg, we are accused of enacting 'victor's justice'. Given that the RPF committed atrocities, although not genocide, the fact that the Prosecutor is unable to provide justice for those from the other side of the conflict continues to haunt us. The dilemma we face is that the Rwandan government can disrupt our trials. When we close, that is one of the criticisms we will face. We cannot complete trials without the help of the RPF. We want international justice, but we cannot avoid dilemmas.

At the start of the chapter, I recounted a judge's response to my question on how the accused had been selected and he responded by reading from the 1994 Statute 'Upon a determination that a *prima facie* case exists, the Prosecutor shall prepare an indictment.' The judge circumscribed (and thus defined) his own power (he cannot indict) by indicating where that power lay (with the OTP). And yet, as the

---

[9] As required by the 1994 Statute, 'The Trial Chambers shall ensure that a trial is fair and expeditious' (United Nations 1994c, UN Doc. S/1994/1115: Art. 19 (1)); 'To be tried without undue delay' (United Nations 1994c: Art. 20 (4c)).

comment above indicates, prosecution lawyers were all too aware that this was not a power the OTP could exercise in relation to the RPF/A. What I found surprising was defence lawyers' sympathy for the prosecution's powerlessness in this regard. A defence lawyer, for example, told me that 'The prosecution are tying themselves to the Rwandan government in order to get access to witnesses. It's not that the prosecutors are bad, but they're concerned with institutional survival.' Another defence lawyer observed that 'You can't charge the RPF, because Kagame would close down the Tribunal.' Even when a defence lawyer began by criticizing the prosecution he still acknowledged this dilemma, 'The Prosecution has an attitude that taints all things because they are only prosecuting one side. But, the witnesses all come from Rwanda. Therefore, the Prosecutor is stuck in this and cannot manoeuvre. The Rwandan government can close the doors and the Tribunal at a functional level will not operate.'

The revelations by Hartmann and Del Ponte regarding US pressure not to indict members of the RPF/A further enhanced defence 'sympathy' for the dilemmas faced by the prosecution. While in 2005 a defence lawyer told me that 'When Del Ponte said on 13 December 2000 she would indict the RPF, she had the powers and the evidence, but no intention', by the 2007 Symposium defence lawyers were distributing copies, translated from French, of the relevant sections of Hartmann's 2007 book, sections that effectively exonerated Del Ponte from obstructing RPF/A indictments. And yet, such 'sympathy' often had a strategic edge, with some defence lawyers using an appreciation for the prosecutor's 'dilemma' to imply that all the convictions were in doubt, as indicated by one of the defence lawyers at the 2007 Symposium quoted above, who stated that if 'The Tribunal was created to combat impunity' then one-sided convictions questioned 'the legitimacy of all judgments'.

Strategically deploying the term 'victor's justice' to question the work of the ICTR as a whole was not, however, a uniform position held by defence lawyers. One defence lawyer mocked attempts to use alleged RPF/A crimes as a defence against indictments for genocide, suggesting it was like saying 'OK I killed my wife because he did' (the *tu quoque* defence (see Wilson, 2011: 155–67)) adding that because lawyers 'have been here for a long time, they build up personal relations with the defendants which can lead them to a loss of objectivity'.

In the discussion above I warned that it would be a mistake to interpret the exchanges at the 2007 Symposium as reflecting a division between defence lawyers and judges and prosecution lawyers regarding RPF/A alleged crimes. It would, however, be equally wrong to assume homogeneity among defence lawyers. While representatives of ADAD challenged prosecution lawyers at the 2007 Symposium (see above), another defence lawyer described ADAD as being 'full of politically-motivated and self-promoting nitwits'. The same defence lawyer who mocked the use of the *tu quoque* defence described himself in the following terms:

> [M]y job is no different from a plumber. There's a legal leak, you need a technician to fix it. We'd rather do interesting work and if the client isn't a sleaze ball, all the better. But, it's a technical exercise and we're fitted to do it by our abilities and our training.

Emphasizing his 'technical skills' he distinguished himself from 'politically motivated people'. A prosecution lawyer echoed this position, that 'At the English Bar you never get involved in your own case. You need detachment, you learn this.' Another defence lawyer contrasted this with how a fellow defence lawyer 'is so political. The clients all love it because he says what they want to hear, but his fellow defence lawyers hate him for it because it doesn't help their case.' In other words, some defence lawyers denounced those who employed accusations of 'victor's justice' against the ICTR as being 'political' and neglecting the core responsibility of defending their clients.

The use of such language ('politically motivated') resonates with the notion of 'cause lawyering' – a form of 'moral activism' where lawyers do more 'than simply deploy their technical services on behalf of their client' (McEvoy, 2011: 354; see Sarat and Scheingold, 1998). In her study of cause-lawyering among defence lawyers in the USA, Margareth Etienne (2005: 1197) notes the concern that the pursuit of the lawyer's cause may at times conflict with the client's interests as they relate to the outcome of the trial. Such 'causes' include defence lawyers using individual cases to reform the criminal justice system (potentially 'sacrificing' the interests of one client to help future clients) or giving a defendant inappropriate ownership of the process. One lawyer interviewed by Etienne (2005: 1214) spoke in terms similar to that employed by ICTR defence lawyers, that clients 'appreciated their story being put forth even though they knew the chances of winning were very, very low'. Overall, however, Etienne (2005: 1198, 1201, 1208) questions the utility of the category of 'cause lawyer' given that all the defence lawyers she interviewed were 'motivated by a range of moral and political beliefs', that these motives are 'as mixed and varied as the lawyers themselves' and that such motivations are not only 'notoriously difficult to discern', but change over time. This implies that all lawyers have their 'causes', it is just a question of whether they make them explicit (see discussion of Legal Realism in Introduction). This implies that one should be suspicious of a lawyer who claims that he is simply a 'technician' devoid of ulterior motivation.

As noted above, Turner (2008: 548) found that most defence lawyers (at the ICTY, ICTR and the Special Court for Sierra Leone) were driven not by 'political or ideological motivations' (other than a commitment to a fair trial), but 'professional curiosity'. Furthermore, Turner (2008: 531, 561) found that the majority of the defence lawyers she interviewed believed that international trials in which they defended did serve an adjudicative purpose (determining guilt or innocence through fair procedures) rather than a political purpose; that acquittals were possible; providing a fair trial was the priority; and that, as a consequence, defence lawyers were not inclined to politicize proceedings in a way that may hurt clients. I too encountered predominantly positive assessments of the ICTR from the defence lawyers with whom I spoke:

> [What do you think the legacy of the Tribunal will be?] It's very hard to say. Ultimately, I'm very positive. The international community is prosecuting atrocities on a grand scale. It's the only way it could be done. It will, however, be remembered for being extremely slow and for the failure to prosecute the RPF because of political expediency.

The defence lawyers described by their colleagues as 'politically motivated', however, voiced complex evaluations of the ICTR. One defence lawyer (among those described as 'politically motivated' by colleagues) described the ICTR in the following terms:

> This is a political institution. The idea that it has anything to do with criminal justice is a façade. It was established to demonize one side, protect those who came to power, cover up what the great powers had done in Central Africa and propagate a certain thesis. They're revisionists – even though they call us revisionists – it does not have a criminal justice purpose. It's just a bunch of white people condemning Africans to show what will happen if they do not toe the line.

And yet, even with this vehement denunciation, the same defence lawyer also conceded that 'because the trials are adversarial it means that we can present to the public some reality in some small way, more and more stuff has come out'.

This position, that although the ICTR was a 'victor's court' there were elements of the trials that were redeemable, was something I encountered among other defence lawyers. To return to the conversation with the two defence lawyers that I described at the start of the chapter. Although they described the ICTR as a 'victor's court' and 'a persecution of Hutus' they tempered their assessment by describing the trials as a mechanism to preserve history:

> The accused persons say, and keep saying, we shouldn't give up. We are putting everything on record for history. The truth will come out one way or another. Put everything on the record and then later our children will decide on the truth. People will be able to read and make their own decisions in the future. We have all the records. The judgement is not made now; the judgement will be made in the future.

Like their colleague ('more and more stuff has come out') these defence lawyers saw trials as a mechanism to establish the 'true' history of the 1994 genocide. Although condemning the ICTR as a 'victor's court' these defence lawyers also spoke of their clients' commitment to the trial; that the trial provided an opportunity for creating a 'record for history'; and that failures at the ICTR did not mean that the project of international criminal justice was universally suspect.

The idea that ICTR trials, whatever their shortcomings, were redeemable as a mechanism to record 'history' was conveyed by other defence lawyers. A defence lawyer told me that his client had told him 'We appreciate what you have done, that our children's children will know the truth, that truth was spoken and that truth cannot be hidden forever.' In their writings, defence lawyers have also indicated that, for all its weaknesses, the ICTR trials have been an opportunity to preserve history and to tell 'the untold story of the Rwanda War' (Erlinder, 2009: 20). While denouncing alleged influence of UN member states in the prosecutorial strategy, the defence lawyer Peter Erlinder (2009: 20), states that 'disclosure requirements may be creatively used by the defence to reveal a more accurate and balanced recreation of history than would have been possible in the absence of the tribunal disclosure system'.

Erlinder cites the disclosure and admission into evidence of various documents, including the 'Gersony Report' (see above) and other UNHCR documents alleging RPF/A killings and ICTR testimony by

Joshua Ruzibiza and Jean Marie Vianney Ndagijimana claiming inter-national knowledge of these reports, including the US Secretary of State, Kofi Annan and Brian Attwood (Chief of USAID). Arguing that such documents, especially UN and US government files, would not have come into the public domain so quickly had it not been for the ICTR's disclosure requirements, Erlinder is effectively saying that with-out the ICTR trials, the 'truth' would not be known. Rather than an unequivocal rejection of the ICTR as a 'victor's court', Erlinder (2009: 20) states:

> despite [the] limitations that are built into the system of international tribunals, the . . . use of disclosure principles to tell 'the untold story of the Rwanda War' demonstrates that legal rules, when taken seriously and aggressively pursued, make it possible for the 'vanquished' to prevent the wholesale 'falsification of history' by victors . . .. perhaps, for the first time in history.

A defence lawyer described as 'politically motivated' by defence col-leagues, Erlinder combines criticism of the ICTR (for perceived prose-cutorial partiality) with praise for the way in which the trials, especially disclosure requirements, had enabled the preservation of a 'historical record' awaiting future analysis irrespective of the final, legal judgment (see Chapter 5). The fact that Erlinder has established a website with access to the documents accessed via disclosure further demonstrates this position[10].

Such views were not, however, universally held by defence lawyers. Another defence lawyer described as 'politically motivated' by collea-gues commented that although 'We contribute nuggets, they [the judges] will create a bullshit narrative.' Such ambivalent assessments of the ICTR by defence lawyers were also seen in the way in which some used the example of other international criminal justice institutions to denounce the partiality of the ICTR but, at the same time, demonstrate their belief that the project of international criminal justice was not intrinsically flawed. The two defence lawyers quoted at the start of the chapter observed that 'In Sierra Leone, all the parties in the conflict were indicted [by the Special Court for Sierra Leone]' and another defence lawyer told me that 'At the ICTY the prosecutor brings cases from both sides' and that 'The ICTY and the International Criminal Court treat all suspects equally' (on 'distributive justice' see Mégret,

---

[10] www.rwandadocumentsproject.net/gsdl/cgi-bin/library.

2011: 1041–44). In other words, defence lawyers denounced the ICTR, but not the whole project of international criminal justice.

So far I have suggested that in relation to accusations of 'victor's justice', prosecution lawyers tended to argue that the prosecution's hands were tied, while defence lawyers were split between those who considered the accusation of 'victor's justice' against the ICTR to be a distraction from defending a client and those who thought it condemned the ICTR, although for the latter this did not necessarily mean that the trials were useless as they preserved 'truth'. So what of the publicly inscrutable judges?

When I first met the judge quoted at the start of the chapter, I asked not about allegations against the RPF/A, but simply how 'the Tribunal' chose who was indicted. The judge responded 'I don't have a direct answer, but I can say two things. First, the Prosecutor is an independent organ of the Tribunal. The decision to prosecute is made by the Prosecutor without any influence. Therefore, it is not "the Tribunal" which selects the accused.' I have already discussed above how those who spoke on behalf of the ICTR assigned such agency to 'the Tribunal' rather than the Prosecutor (see also Introduction). Here, however, the judge explicitly disaggregated 'the Tribunal', delineating the power of the Prosecutor in order to demarcate his own relative power(lessness). To further emphasize this, the judge reached for a binder of the ICTR's key legal documents resting on his coffee table and read to me the article of the 1994 Statute which declares the Prosecutor's independence (United Nations, 1994e: Art. 17). By exhibiting the 'cult of the text' (Bourdieu, 1987: 851; see Introduction), by deferring to an immutable text that assigns roles and power, the judge was making clear to me that while judges must approve an indictment prepared by the prosecution (United Nations, 1994e: Art. 18 (11)), they cannot order the indictment of anyone or review the Prosecutor's decision not to indict someone who has been investigated. Unprompted by me, the judge continued:

> Selective prosecution has been a judicial question, that we only prosecute Hutu people when Tutsi people also committed crimes against humanity ... you know, this idea of 'victor's justice' that has been around since Nuremberg and that it is no different here. I, from a judicial point of view, would not describe it as this, but judiciary are not involved in the selection of who to prosecute.

I found it significant that it was the judge who introduced the issue of 'victor's justice'. In this light, his reiteration of his earlier emphasis on the independence of the judiciary ('judiciary are not involved in the selection of who to prosecute') suggests 'victor's justice' was an accusation from which the judge was seeking to pre-emptively insulate himself before I raised it.

While abdicating responsibility was one response I encountered among judges, I also encountered other positions. One judge, for example, told me (in 2007) that 'It's essential that the RPF is put on trial. UN Security Council Resolutions 1503 [(United Nations, 2003b)] and 1504 [(United Nations, 2003c, UN Doc. S/RES/1504 (2003)] include the RPF.' When, later in the conversation, I asked him whether he thought one of the objectives of the ICTR was to create an 'historical record' (see Chapter 5), the judge replied that if it 'established facts in an unemotional, detached way', it would 'contribute to reconciliation'. He continued, however, in a more cryptic fashion:

> There are small contributions here and there. The acquittals, for example, or those who have been convicted, but acquitted on some counts, demonstrate that reality is not black and white, but a mixture. Asking questions such as who shot the plane down etc.? The important thing is that it's perceived as being fair and not short-sighted. At the same time we've included references to books, the testimony of experts etc. But, they cannot take over, it's a court. There are negatives, but also blaming it for what it didn't do.

The phrase 'There are small contributions here and there' resonates in a surprising way with the ('politically motivated') defence lawyers quoted above who suggested that during the course of the ICTR trials 'more and more stuff has come out' and 'We contribute nuggets'. In addition, the judge chooses to mention the attack on 6 April 1994 on the plane carrying the Presidents of Rwanda and Burundi which signalled the start of the genocide, an attack blamed by some on the RPF/A (see Oosterlinck et al., 2012; Thalmann, 2008). His reference to acquittals and part-acquittals suggests balance while his comment that 'reality is not black and white' suggests the weakness of the binary of Hutu perpetrators vs. Tutsi victims. Perhaps it is 'books, testimony of experts' that refer to alleged crimes of the RPF/A that he has in mind, such as the book by ICTR witness Joshua Ruzibiza (2005) in which he maintains that he was part of an RPF/A team that had shot the plane down on 6 April 1994. And by 'negatives' does the judge mean the failure to indict members of the RPF/A? Again, the judge responded to a question I had not posed. Having indicated that he believed the RPF/A should be indicted, he appeared to be arguing that RPF/A culpability had been acknowledged as far as possible within the trials the Prosecutor had given him and his judicial colleagues to adjudicate.

The judge's phrase, 'blaming it for what it didn't do' suggests a concern that the failure to indict members of the RPF/A would eclipse what the ICTR had accomplished. Conversations with the judges' ALOs also gave some insight into judges' fear that they would be blamed in the future. An ALO told me (in 2006) that the Prosecutor was just waiting to finish presenting evidence in two prominent cases, for which he needed 'the cooperation of the Rwandan authorities', but that 'I bet my bottom dollar that when these are over there will be RPF indictments'. A year later, however, the Prosecutor had made public the last 'sealed indictments' which, it transpired, were not for members of the RPF/A. Commenting on this, another ALO told me (in 2007) that 'everyone had thought that the three sealed indictments were RPF and everyone, including judges, were shocked when they discovered they weren't'. In a similar vein another ALO (also in 2007) told me that 'Up until four months ago everyone thought they were the RPF, that at the eleventh hour they were finally going to put things right. I think some of the judges were convinced they were and were disappointed.'

While judges impressed on me that that they were not responsible for who was indicted ('the Prosecutor exercises independent judgement') and that the allegations against members of the RPF/A had been acknowledged as far as was possible ('There are small contributions here and there') reports from ALOs that judges hoped the Prosecutor would 'put things right' and that judges were 'shocked' and disappointed' when this did not happen suggests that judges feared such considerations would not insulate them from criticism in the long term. Such a fear was no secret, as seen in the comments of the 'politically motivated' defence lawyer at the 2007 Symposium, 'If it fails [to indict the RPF/A], will it not discredit the hard work of the judges, other prosecution and defence lawyers?' The fear that 'the Tribunal' would be held to account for this failure (rather than just the Prosecutor) was increased, of course, by the tendency of those who spoke on behalf of the ICTR to speak of 'the Tribunal' and not carefully distinguish (as the judge did) between those who had the power to indict and the other organs of the ICTR (see Introduction).

CONCLUSION

> Although great efforts have been made to show that this is to be a fair trial, by the provision of counsel and full facilities for calling witnesses and producing documents, and in many other matters, I yet greatly fear that ... all these efforts will be in vain. ... there has been much weakness and vacillation, and, above all, a failure to appreciate that the trial is only in form a judicial process and its main importance is political (Hyde, 1964: 514–15).

> Human affairs are always rather confused, with positive and negative elements mixed together (Röling and Cassese, 1993: 89).

These two quotes do not refer to the ICTR, but to the genesis of the project of international criminal justice, the International Military Tribunal (the trial of the Major War Criminals) at Nuremberg (1945–6) and The International Military Tribunal for the Far East (1946–8). The first quote is an extract from the diary of Norman Birkett, the British Alternate Judge at Nuremberg; the second by Bert Röling, Dutch Judge at Tokyo. Given the discussion above, there is no doubt that Norman Birkett's comment could be mistaken for a statement about the ICTR in relation to 'victor's justice'. But, it is perhaps Röling's comment that is most apt given my survey of how judges and lawyers reflect on the ICTR's 'achievements' from their specific institutional locations. Such a survey suggests that 'Human affairs are always rather confused'.

In the Introduction to this book the argument was made that there is a need to examine the powerful (at the ICTR) as much as the powerless (the 'locals' in Rwanda). The discussion in this chapter has, inevitably, suggested that the powerful are by no means homogenous and their power always relative. There is a need to recognize that the appearance of having effective power is always in a relationship with powerlessness that circumscribes it and that practitioners are acutely aware of this. Judges appear to be the ultimate power, but they cannot choose who will be prosecuted, and, fearing association with a tarnished legacy, oscillate between arguing for recognition of what has been achieved ('There are negatives, but also blaming it for what it didn't do') and insulating themselves from responsibility ('the Prosecutor is an independent organ of the Tribunal'). In turn, however, prosecution lawyers are all too aware that their institutional location is not 'independent', their power constrained by a reliance on 'national interest' in Rwanda and the machinations of the 'great powers'. Celebrating the contribution to the global project of international criminal justice ('We see our legacy as our jurisprudence') cannot wish that powerlessness away or the feeling that principles are compromised by 'dilemmas' and that having 'assumed it would be simple' found that it was not. And then there is the defence. Ostensibly the least powerful, even those (self) ascribed as 'politically motivated' speak of the ICTR as an opportunity that empowered them to tell 'the untold story of the Rwanda War'.

What this reminds us is that, just as the judgment of the precursor institution of which Birkett speaks (the Nuremberg Tribunal) stated that 'Crimes against international law are committed by men, not by abstract entities' (International Military Tribunal, 1947: 233) so, in turn, any attempt to assess an institution like the ICTR, by either proponents or detractors, must distinguish between the ICTR as a disembodied 'abstract entity' and the ICTR as what it actually was: a collection of situated persons negotiating their simultaneous empowerment and disempowerment, 'involved in [re]formulating, editing, applauding, and refusing' (Czarniawska, 1997: 46) the narrative disseminated by those tasked with speaking for the ICTR as 'super-person'.

2

'WATCHING THE FISH IN THE GOLDFISH BOWL'

It is around 3pm, and a defence lawyer had just completed the examination-in-chief of a protected Rwandan witness:

Defence Lawyer: Mr President, I don't know what the situation is for you, but here it's intolerable. It's very, very humid here. There's something wrong in this courtroom and it's very, very difficult for us to work under these conditions.

Presiding Judge: Yes. Madam Registrar, could you give us a report on what happened today.

Registrar: Thank you, Mr President. They told us that they had resolved the situation. And after the morning coffee break, I believe the place was cool enough. I don't know what has happened now after the lunch break. We will call them to come back again during the tea break.

Presiding Judge: Mr [name of prosecution lawyer], is it any better on your side?

Prosecution Lawyer: Not at all, Mr President. Certainly less than the situation on Mr [name of defence lawyer's] side because he's talking. But when I start talking, I too will be sweating and I will be spending a lot of energy, and I will probably feel the same way as him. So I totally agree with him that something should be done about the problem.

Presiding Judge [to the Prosecution Lawyer]: May the uncomfortable conditions cause you to speak a bit less? [generalized laughter in the courtroom].

As discussed in the Introduction, scholarship on international criminal justice has tended to concentrate on texts (judgments and transcripts). These texts are, however, a residue of dynamic, situated encounters (see Buur, 2003b: 67; Robben, 2010). As the episode above illustrates, the courtroom is a place in which people occupy specific positions, sweat and expend energy. Such details have been largely absent from scholarly literature on the ICTR (on the Extraordinary Chambers of the Courts of Cambodia, see Hinton 2016: 47–8, 229–32, 254–5). In contrast, those who observed precursors at Nuremberg and Jerusalem took pains to record such details (see Arendt, 1994[1963]: 3; Gouri, 2004: 144, 171, 297; Neave, 1978: 47, 253, 263; West, 1984[1955]: 7). For example, Telford Taylor (1992: 224–31), who was assistant to Chief Counsel (Prosecutor) Robert H. Jackson at the Trial of the Major War Criminals before the International Military Tribunal at Nuremberg, goes to some length in his memoir to describe the layout of the courtroom, including the location and seating order of the judges, the position of the 'Tribunal Secretariat' (who 'ran errands for the judges'); the simultaneous translators; the defendants (who 'remained the magnet for the eyes of all those visiting the trial for the first few times'); the court reporters (whose area 'was in nearly constant motion'); the cameras ('High along the walls ... just below the ceiling ... making a visual record of the trial'); movement within the room; what participants wore ('defence counsel [most of whom] wore simple black robes, but a few were silk-lined and more colourful') and mundane issues, such as the initial provision of smaller chairs for the 'alternates' (deputies) of the four voting judges.

The concern of participants like Telford Taylor with the physical features of the courtroom at Nuremberg contrasts with the contemporary legal literature on international criminal justice that tends to concentrate on the texts produced in the courtroom (see Introduction). This reflects a broader trend in the ethnography of contemporary courtrooms which has been dominated by a concern with speech and the 'ethnography of discourse' (Conley and O'Barr, 1990: 35; see Atkinson and Drew, 1979; Philips, 1998) which analyses transcripts of what has been said (Conley and O'Barr, 2005: 20). This emphasis on speech rendered as text replicates 'lawyers' obsession with the word' (Mulcahy, 2007: 384) and the domination of the 'text based view of the law' (Morison and Leith, 1992: vii).

Transcripts, however, are only a residue of a process (Mosse, 2011: 2). The trial transcript, 'turns aural objects into visual ones, which inevitably implies reduction' (Portelli, 1981: 97; see Portelli, 1985: 13–14; Walker, 1986) and fails to capture important elements of talk including 'emphasis, intonation, volume, and pauses' (Eades, 1996: 217). In her research on UK asylum hearings of gay and lesbian claimants, Toni Johnson (2011: 59) recalls her need to record not only what was said, but 'atmospheric details about the hearings', including the physical layout, the mannerisms of the participants, nervousness etc. because the 'sterility of the notes [of what was said] would have done a disservice to the atmosphere and context of the court'. Describing the courtroom as a 'theater of dramatic gestures', James Clifford (1988: 290) also notes how a trial transcript 'omits gestures, hesitations, clothing, tone of voice, laughter, irony ... the sometimes devastating silences'. Such gestures are part of what Carol Martin (2006: 10–11) describes as the 'extratextual and subtextual language' of the courtroom. Discussing examples of documentary/verbatim theatre (in which transcripts from trials are restaged), Martin (2006: 11) notes that in order to give documentary/verbatim theatre the quality of 'real life and believability', actors and directors are required to create what is 'outside the archive', in other words they need to re-introduce the 'glances, gestures, body language, the felt experience of space and the proximity of bodies'. This suggests that the very thing that brings the courtroom 'to life' is not recorded in the transcript.

This was all too apparent in the trials I observed at the ICTR. On one occasion a five-minute extract from a BBC report about the genocide showing children with machete wounds was shown on the courtroom monitors (without sound) as part of the examination-in-chief of a European defence witness. When the video finished, the CCTV camera focused on the witness who was clearly very distressed, tears running down his face. After a moment the Presiding Judge asked 'Witness, would you like to have some time off?' All that was recorded in the transcript prior to the judge's question was '(Video played)'. Other unrecorded silences were less 'devastating', but frequent. For example, a defence lawyer passed a document to a witness. The transcript reads: 'Witness: kindly give me a few moments to peruse the document', followed by 'Lawyer: Very well. Thank you'. But, between the lawyer's 'Very well' and 'Thank you', five and a half minutes passed. During this time, 20 legal practitioners sat in complete silence, the only sound coming through the headphones that of the witness whispering to himself in Kinyarwanda as he read the document.

These episodes indicate the importance of the visual as much as the spoken in the courtroom. This was all the more apparent at the ICTR given the reliance on simultaneous interpretation in English, French and Kinyarwanda (see Chapter 3). In his discussion of language interpretation in international criminal tribunals, Joshua Karton (2008: 24, note 138) notes that 'interpreters generally insist on sitting where they can clearly see the witness'. This enables interpreters to draw upon 'paralinguistic (non-verbal) communication' which he describes as 'the emotional content and background of utterances, as expressed through the speaker's body language, linguistic style and nuance, pauses, hedges, self-corrections, hesitations and displays of emotion' (Karton 2008: 17, 24). Reflecting this, the Code of Professional Ethics of the International Association of Conference Interpreters (2015), of whom the majority of interpreters at the ICTR were members, states that members 'require a direct view of the speaker and the room and therefore will not agree to working from screens except in exceptional circumstances where a direct view is not possible'. Such requirements make explicit what is necessary for all trial participants in all trials, international or domestic. As Julienne Hanson (1996: 55) notes, 'the practicalities of the trial make it imperative that everyone who is in any way involved must have perfect knowledge of one another, both visually and audibly'. And yet, only the audible is recorded in the transcript.

The preceding discussion has drawn attention to the 'extratextual and subtextual language' of the courtroom (Martin 2006:10–11). Rather than simply being concerned with the extratextual activities of those who participate in trials, the chapter will go further and also explore the way in which the configuration of the space in which those activities take place also (silently) affected those activities. First, the chapter will reflect on the spatial organization of the court complex and courtroom (drawing on a longstanding comparison of courtrooms and theatres) to explore the ways in which the organization of space con-stitutes the courtroom as a 'play-ground' in which an 'absolute and peculiar order reigns' (Huizinga, 1949: 10). Second, having noted the specific spatial organization of the courtroom, the chapter will return to the theme of the necessity to 'see and be seen' in the courtroom and the importance of space in relation to demeanour. The argument here is that the extraordinary, ad hoc nature of the ICTR court complex reveals aspects of the creation of judicial space that are otherwise naturalized and hidden in domestic court complexes.

THE COURT AS THEATRE

In her discussion of demeanour in US jury trials, Laurie Levenson (2007: 574, 579), dismisses the conventional analogy of the courtroom as a 'controlled laboratory' in which lawyers present evidence, the judge ensures quality control and a jury provides a result for the experiment. In its place, Levenson suggests the analogy of the courtroom as a theatre in which 'jurors use all of their senses' and where 'nonverbal communication subtly effects the entire proceedings of a trial'.

The analogy of trials as theatre is longstanding (see Bentham, 1978[1827]: 353). Hannah Arendt (1994[1963]: 4), for example, compared the usher's shout at the beginning of each session at the 1961 trial of Adolf Eichmann with the 'effect of the rising curtain' while Haim Gouri (2004: 192), having observed the same trial, noted that 'Every courtroom seems at times like a theatre, an arena. Along with the ultimate seriousness you can find an element of histrionics, of professional role-playing' (see Sontag, 1966: 126–7). Alexander Hinton (2016: 12) organizes his account of the trial of 'Duch' (Kaing Guek Eav) (2009–10) by the ECCC for war crimes and crimes against humanity committed at the S-21 ('Tuol Seng') detention centre as an 'ethnodrama', noting that:

> this book has a dramatic structure that includes a protagonist (Duch), an agonist (his victims), key roles and characters (defence, prosecution, judge), a stage (the courtroom where the trial took place), and dramatic action (events unfolding before an audience). Indeed, each morning the start of the proceedings was marked by the drawing of the curtains.

Exploring the theatre analogy further, Julie Stone Peters (2008: 185) suggests that law is the 'ultimate institution of twice-behaved behaviour'. Here she refers to Richard Shechner's (1985) 'twice-behaved behaviour' which refers to scripted behaviour that 'has been rehearsed or that consciously evokes formal templates that serve the same function as rehearsal' (Peters, 2008: 184; see Chapter 4 for a discussion of 'twice-behaved behaviour'). If performance is defined by the quality of being reiterative (that which can be repeated) then both theatre and trials display this quality in that both employ scripts (Peters, 2008: 184; see Huizinga, 1949: 10). In his ethnography of Portuguese and German criminal trials, Peter Zoettl (2016) notes how every moment of the trial is scripted, from the usher who calls for the defendant; to the order the judges enter; the form the defendant's plea must take; examination-in-chief, cross-examination, re-examination and so on. Zoettl (2016: 12) draws on Judith Butler's (1988) discussion of gender performativity to make a related point. Butler (1988: 526) compares the restrictions imposed on the gendered body to theatre scripts, in that 'gender is an act which has been rehearsed, much as a script survives the particular actors who make use of it, but which requires individual actors in order to be actualized and reproduced as reality once again'. Zoettl (2016: 12) suggests that the appearance of 'justice' being done corresponds with the performance of gender because justice 'has to be actualized and reproduced by individual acts . . . which are nevertheless bound to the corpus of scripts written by acts performed in the past'.

In addition to the reliance on scripts, there are also similarities in the way that space is organized in the theatre and the courtroom. As a defence lawyer said to me 'Courtrooms are created areas, they have to bring gravity to themselves. The courtroom is so abstracted from everyday life. That's why it's even more theatrical here. It's an empty shell up for grabs.' Milner Ball (1975: 83) states that the courtroom is 'a theatrical space, one which evokes expectations of the uncommon' and draws on Johan Huizinga's (1949: 8) classic reflection on the social function of 'play', defined as 'stepping out of "real" life into a temporary sphere of activity with a disposition all of its own'. Huizinga (1949: 10) emphasizes the special 'secluded' and temporal quality of play:

> The arena, the card-table, the magic circle, the temple, the stage, the screen, the tennis court, the *court of justice*, etc., are all in form and function playgrounds, i.e. forbidden spots, isolated, hedged round, hallowed, within which special rules obtain. All are temporary worlds within the ordinary world, dedicated to the performance of an act apart (emphasis added).

Huizinga (1949: 10 12 19) describes the 'play-ground' as a place in which the rules of ordinary life are suspended and an 'absolute and peculiar order reigns' (see Schechner, 1985: 114). For Huizinga (1949: 10) the demarcation of the 'play-ground' creates an 'absolute and supreme' order. In the context of a courtroom, this suggests that while it is rules explicitly enforced by a judge that appear to establish order, order is, in reality, a consequence of the demarcation of the space. Supporting this notion, Pat Carlen (1976: 31), in her study of magistrates' courts in the UK, found that while lawyers were deferential towards magistrates as embodying rules, the magistrates themselves argued that their own authority was invested in the place rather than their personal status. I will argue that this sense of place, of the courtroom as 'play-ground', relies, paradoxically, on those that appear to be most marginal: the spectating public.

THE NECESSARY PRESENCE OF THE PUBLIC

Rule 78 of the ICTR's RPE read 'All proceedings before a Trial Chamber, other than deliberations of the Chamber, shall be held in public, unless otherwise provided.' All four courtrooms at the ICTR had a public gallery with seats for around 25 visitors separated from the courtroom by a wall of bullet-proof glass. Lawrence Douglas (2006: 104) describes similar arrangements at the ICTY generating a feeling 'akin to watching an elaborate psychology experiment through one-way glass: the spectator cannot suppress the feeling that he or she is entirely invisible to the Tribunal'. Those in the ICTR courtroom told me that 'We are like fish, people looking at us' (judge) and 'It's a little disconcerting having someone watching the fish in the goldfish bowl. This is our water, this is our world' (defence lawyer) (see Steinitz, 2007: 10). While only the presence of those within the courtroom was formally recorded on trial transcripts, the presence of the public, and the fulfilment of Rule 78, was an issue of importance for many lawyers and judges with whom I spoke (see Byrne, 2010: 299).

This became most apparent when the public had to be excluded. According to Rule 79 of the ICTR's RPE (entitled

Figure 2.1 The Public Gallery (Courtesy of the ICTR)

'Closed Sessions'), a Trial Chamber could 'order that the press and the public be excluded from all or part of the proceedings' for reasons of 'Public order or morality', 'the interests of justice' or the 'Safety, security or non-disclosure of the identity of a victim or witness.' Furthermore, Rule 79 required that the Trial Chamber 'make public the reasons for its order'. All of the closed sessions I experienced were to ensure the non-disclosure of witness identity. Around 80 per cent of the approximately 3,200 witnesses who testified were protected (see Chapter 4). As a consequence, either the witness box was surrounded by a curtain or the public gallery was closed.

The frequency of 'closed sessions' resulted in lawyers re-affirming that the public ought to be present. After a morning of closed sessions, for example, a lawyer complained over coffee that 'After all, this is supposed to be a public trial. That's the whole point of this place, that it's heard in public.' Another lawyer, while acknowledging that the judges may have occasionally needed to exclude the public for a few minutes explained to me that 'People [in the public gallery] don't know that, they go away and don't come back. These trials should be open to the international public.' Lawyers also compared the ICTR with their domestic experience. A lawyer, commenting on whether judges gave decisions orally or in writing, told me 'For me, oral is preferable because it helps the publicity of the trial, because the public can follow the submissions. In my experience coming from [European country] a trial on criminal matters should be as public as possible.' The principle that the public is part of the trials was also made in the courtroom. For example, a defence lawyer argued that the report of a prosecution expert witness must be read in the courtroom 'to ensure that the public knows what his evidence is' adding that judges and the public are 'both vitals parts of this whole procedure', the defence lawyer finishing by saying that to not read the contents of the report would be 'contrary to the principle of open justice'.

Asked about the prevalence of closed sessions, judges also re-affirmed to me a commitment to the presence of the public that 'The principle is a public trial and we try to stick to this principle' and 'The public has a right to hear what he [the witness] says if not to know what he looks like. What they say about the accused must be known by the whole world.' A presiding judge told me that she did not allow closed sessions of longer than five minutes in her trial because they 'contradict the purpose of our existence' that 'our trials should be public'. I witnessed judges trying to restrict closed sessions, by instructing lawyers to 'organize your questions in such a manner that you collate all the sensitive matters pertaining to his identity, so that they could be asked in one closed session'.

Judges further demonstrated this principle in court. Some judges, for example, explicitly showed consideration for those seated in the public gallery when the court went into closed session, re-affirming the otherwise required presence of the public by stating, 'For the benefit of the public, I'm very sorry that we have to do this, but it's an essential action that we must take to protect the witness's identity at this stage. So we go into a closed session for a short time' or 'at this stage of the proceedings, members of the public may leave the public gallery. Sorry for that. We do hope it will be for a short duration.'

Following on from the analogy between the courtroom and theatre, Milner Ball (1975: 86) notes Jerzy Grotowski's (1991[1968]: 32) observation that theatre is 'what takes place between actor and spectator' is equally applicable to trials because 'Performance always intends an audience' (Kapferer, 1986: 192; see Steinitz, 2007: 16). But, this does not explain why law must be performed before an audience? On one hand, it can be argued that an audience is a safeguard of a fair trial as the presence of spectators ensures that the active participants perform their proper roles (Ball, 1975: 86). An alternative argument is that the coercive power claimed by judges must be acknowledged, that 'Legal rituals depend on the outside witness to confer on them not only recognition, but validity' (Baumann, 1992; see Hibbitts, 1995: 65, 69).

The argument that the public is necessary in order to acknowledge the coercive power claimed by judges finds support in Michel Foucault's (1991[1975]: 57) classic account of the judicial spectacle of execution, in which he states that in 'the ceremonies of public execution, the main character was the people, whose real and immediate presence was required for the performance'. When the spectacle of justice was transferred from execution to trial in post-Revolutionary France, Foucault refused to analyze courtroom trials, associating them with 'the uniform edifice of sovereignty' rather than with disciplinary power and normalization (Taylor, 1993: 5–6, 12; see Foucault, 1991[1975]: 183; 1980: 102, 104–6). And yet, given this transfer of the spectacle of justice from execution to trial, Foucault's key insight can be applied to contemporary trials: that 'the people' are still required to observe trials in order to re-assert that the power to try and punish does not belong to the 'multitude', but to the sovereign power whose authority has been affronted (Foucault, 1991[1975]: 36, 47). As with executions, without the 'real and immediate presence' of spectators, sovereign power as 'juridical monarchy' (Foucault, 1978: 89), cannot distinguish itself in this manner and cannot re-assert its monopolies of violence, censure and regulation. This is why the RPE required the presence of the public, a presence supported by judges and lawyers. However, I will go further and argue that the public also played an essential role (unbeknownst to them) in constructing the courtroom in the first place as a play-ground in which an 'absolute and peculiar order reigns' (Huizinga, 1949: 10).

ENTERING THE COURT COMPLEX

Catherine Bell (1992: 90) defines ritualization as 'a way of acting that specifically establishes a privileged contrast, differentiating itself as more important or powerful' through 'nuanced contrasts and the evocation of strategic, value-laden distinctions'. She also suggests that strategies of differentiation (ritualization) are 'rooted in a distinctive interplay of a socialized body and the environment it structures' (Bell, 1992: 7). If we accept that a space is constituted through prohibitions placed on the body, that 'Space commands bodies, prescribing or proscribing gestures, routes and distances to be covered' (Lefebvre, 1991: 143), then it can be argued that the privileged space of the courtroom 'reproduces itself within those who use the space in question' in the individual visitor's 'blind spontaneous and lived obedience' (Lefebvre, 1991: 137, 143) (see discussion of Pierre Bourdieu's 'corporeal hexis' in Chapter 3). We must, therefore, be attentive to both work done on the court visitor's body and the work the court visitor's body does to create the courtroom as privileged space, as a 'play-ground' in which the rules of ordinary life are suspended and an 'absolute and peculiar order reigns' (Huizinga, 1949: 10).

Antoine Garapon (2001: 46–7) suggests that courtrooms are always the culmination of a 'condensing passage', that, beginning at the court complex's entrance, 'complicated routes ... dramatize the spectacle of law' and direct 'mute injunctions directly to the body' (Bourdieu, 1999: 126) so that the visitor experiences a cumulative, emotional response (see Steinitz 2007: 10–11). Starting from the assumption that 'a space is not a thing but rather a set of relations between things' and that 'it is by means of the body that space [is] produced' (Lefebvre, 1991: 83, 162) it can be argued that the privileged space of the courtroom depends, therefore, both on its place in a wider complex and in the relation of active participants (lawyers, judges, interpreters, stenographers) to docile spectators, where the latter are formed in the passage through the complex as they make their way towards the courtroom. In this way, the ICTR courtroom was a privileged site not primarily because of what was said in the courtroom, but because of the measured obstruction and gradual incorporation of spectators as they approached the courtroom. In this way, the obstructed spectator-body following a pre-ordained route is 'at once result and cause, product and producer' (Lefebvre, 1991: 142, 195) of the privileged courtroom space. One must start, therefore, at the UN security check at the ICTR's entrance.

The ICTR occupied two of the three wings of the Arusha International Conference Centre (AICC). Built by the Chinese government in the 1970s, the AICC was established as a conference centre and as the headquarters of the East African Community (EAC) - the regional, intergovernmental organization of Kenya, Uganda, Tanzania, Burundi and Rwanda which was established in 1967, collapsed in 1977 and was re-established (again with the AICC as its headquarters) in 1999.

Diplomatic premises, such as the ICTR, are not, as is commonly assumed, extraterritorial or 'foreign territory'. The international conventions governing such premises do, however, construe them as distinct territories. The UN's 1996 agreement with the government of Tanzania (United Nations, 1996a, UN Doc. A/51/399: 20–35) which determined the status of the ICTR complex, was an amalgam of the Vienna Convention on Diplomatic Relations (United Nations, 1961) and the Convention on the Privileges and Immunities of the United Nations (United Nations, 1948). The agreement took from the Convention on Privileges and Immunities (Art. II. 3) and the Vienna Convention (Art. 22) the key principle that 'The premises of the Tribunal shall be inviolable ... The competent authorities shall not enter the premises of the Tribunal to perform an official duty, except with the express consent, or at the request of, the Registrar' (United Nations, 1996a : Art. V 1–2). In this way, while the laws and regulations of Tanzania did apply within the ICTR complex (United Nations, 1996a: Art. VI 2) and Tanzanian policemen were part of the detail that guarded the accused in the courtroom, the court complex was a distinct

Figure 2.2 The Arusha International Conference Centre (Courtesy of the ICTR)

sphere within which the Tanzanian state's authority to freely enforce national law was suspended.

This segregation between the Tanzanian nation-state and the ICTR complex was announced at the ICTR entrance by allusions to the imagery and practices of the nation-state. Given that ritual activity often 'plays off other forms and instances of ritual activity' (Bell, 1992: 116), so the ritual activity of crossing the frontier of a nation-state was used at the ICTR as a convenient means to establish 'privileged differentiation'. Having handed her passport to a UN guard and received a visitor ID badge, the visitor to the ICTR would pass through an x-ray arch then through a room-high revolving metal gate (opened by a UN guard pressing a button on the wall). The visitor would then continue to the courtrooms. What could be more natural for those who regularly pass through airports or enter public buildings (see Bajc, 2007: 1667)? And yet, ritualization (activity seeking 'privileged differentiation') always 'tends to see itself as the natural or appropriate thing to do in the circumstances' (Bell, 1992: 109) rather than an intentional distinguishing strategy.

That this is a distinguishing strategy and not just a matter of 'security' is illustrated by examining another entrance to the AICC. Running from the small building housing the UN security check to the base of the AICC was a waist-high steel fence in which there was a gate through which EAC officials entered. This gate was guarded by a single, khaki-clad Tanzanian policeman. Returning one day from lunch with a senior ICTR administrator (a UN careerist) we passed through the neighbouring UN security check. The ICTR employee disdainfully commented on how the 'EAC people' wanted to use 'their gate' and recalled that when the UN established the security check, the EAC had refused to participate and wanted to 'maintain their separate entrance'. He concluded: 'What hope is there for an international organization that does not have a security check?' His comments imply that, for him at least, the UN security check does not simply serve a practical purpose ('security'), but that it also strategically distinguishes what lies within.

A feature that distinguished the UN security check from the EAC entrance was the x-ray machines for possessions and bodies. Such machines are now ubiquitous at the entrances to court buildings in Europe and North America. Garapon (2001: 46–7) asks, 'Have the metal detector cabins that multiply at the entrances of courthouses for reasons of security not taken the place of the initiative passage?' Garapon is suggesting that the transformation once only achieved through the accumulative effect of a building's fabric (see Taylor, 1993) is now compressed into the x-ray arch (for a discussion of arches and 'frontier liminality', see van Gennep, 1960: 19–21). The x-ray machine takes on a particular significance if we accept that the distinguishing strategies of ritualization are rooted in the physical 'interaction of the social body within a symbolically constituted spatial and temporal environment' which is 'experienced as molding the bodies acting within it' (Bell, 1992: 101). In such an environment, the visitor's body is not simply a passive receptor, but is a vehicle for the strategies of differentiation which 'distinguish and privilege what is being done in comparison to other, usually more quotidian, activities' (Bell, 1992: 74). Visiting members of the public do not, however, perceive themselves as an essential, embodied element in this differentiation, but only as 'acting in a socially instinctive way to how things are' (Bell, 1992: 206) because x-ray machines at the entrance to public buildings in the name of 'security' are commonplace and unremarkable.

When I discussed the security check with those responsible for the management of visitors, they simply justified it as a matter of 'security'. As already noted, however, activity seeking 'privileged differentiation' always 'tends to see itself as the natural or appropriate thing to do in the circumstances' (Bell, 1992: 109). Furthermore, as Julian Pitt-Rivers (1986: 126) observes, such processes can fulfil both explicit, practical purposes ('security') and have other, implicit effects. There is, therefore, no tension between the explicit need for security and the implicit influence on visiting members of the public who, by having to pass through an x-ray arch, become embodied indicators of the privileged space within; a space supposedly privileged irrespective of their presence (see Butler, 1988; Zoettl, 2016). In this way, the trivial act of passing through an x-ray machine contributes to constructing the courtroom as privileged space precisely because 'it extorts the essential while seeming to demand the insignificant' (Bourdieu, 2003[1977]: 95).

SEPARATE CIRCULATION SYSTEMS

It would be tempting to assume that after the activity at the UN security check the passage of the visitor towards the ICTR courtroom played little role in constructing the courtroom as a 'play-ground' in which the rules of ordinary life are suspended and an 'absolute and peculiar order reigns' (Huizinga, 1949: 10). However, the role played by the public in distinguishing the courtroom continued inside the complex. Julienne Hanson (1996: 52–4, 55) suggests that while the contemporary design of court complexes has moved from the monumental and awe-inspiring, such as the Palais de Justice in Paris (see Taylor, 1993: 15–20) to the more practical, a fundamental continuity has remained in the 'spatial syntax' of 'physically discrete and segregated territories' within court buildings. Paul Rock (1993: 249, 254), for example, observes that although the public spaces in a new English Crown Court built in the 1990s were 'simple and comforting', the segregation of circulation systems and the surveillance of 'civilians' was even more emphatic than earlier buildings. These 'separate circulation systems' originally appeared in nineteenth century Europe and North America, so that judges, lawyers, court officials, witnesses and the public would each inhabit 'a little world with its own discrete entrances and exits, stairways, corridors and rooms ... insulated against the others by more or less visible barriers' (Rock, 1993: 204; see Hanson, 1996: 55; Mulcahy, 2007: 396–9; Taylor, 1993: 27–43).

The ICTR complex, like other court complexes, exhibited these 'separate circulation systems'. Accompanying lawyers in the secure area revealed a hidden warren of corridors, staircases and shortcuts. These played a part in differentiating the 'play-ground' of the courtroom, for, as Rock (1993: 234) notes, the courtroom was 'an extrusion of the building's surrounding sealed circulations systems' in that the wider court complex frames, and thus distinguishes, the courtroom as a privileged point (see Miller, 1987: 101). Garapon (2001: 38) goes further and suggests court complexes are structured around the 'well of the courtroom' (the space in front of the judges), an 'empty space [which] represents the place of the Law' and that it is around this 'directionless centre' (Geertz, 1980: 109) that the sealed circulatory systems are oriented. The consequence is that the ICTR courtroom was further differentiated as a space because it was the only place where the two circulation systems (for the public and for judges and lawyers) met. It is to the court-room that I will now turn.

THE COURTROOM

The discussion above has suggested that the efficacy of the 'absolute and peculiar order' (Huizinga, 1949: 10) in the courtroom depends on that space being defined as a privileged 'play-ground'; that entering the ICTR complex and the separate circulation systems generate this demarcation through 'the felt experience of space' (Martin, 2006: 11); that this 'spatial and temporal environment' is 'experienced as moulding the bodies acting within it' (Bell, 1992: 101) so that the body of the public spectator in this space is 'at once result and cause, product and producer' (Lefebvre, 1991: 142, 195) of the courtroom as privileged space. The effect of this process is further amplified by the way the courtroom only becomes a courtroom when the judges are present, as a defence lawyer explained to me:

> I cannot when the judges are present cross over the courtroom and talk to the prosecution. I cannot go and shake hands with the judge even if he is a good friend. I cannot pass documents to the judges or prosecution. If I want to speak to the prosecution I need to ask the judges' permission. When the judges are in the room it is a courtroom, when they leave, it is just a room.

Like Hurzinga, Erving Goffman (1959: 106, 159) noted that when a performance is given it is 'usually in a highly bounded region', and that as a 'front region' or 'setting' this space defines the situation for those who observe and participate in the performance. This 'front region' contrasts with the 'back region' where 'action occurs that is related to the performance but is inconsistent with the appearance fostered by the performance' (Goffman, 1959: 134; see Steinitz, 2007: 10). Goffman (1959: 127), however, also suggests that a single space can be transformed from one to the other, that 'a region that is thoroughly established as a front region for the regular performance of a particular routine often functions as a back region before and after each performance'.

This was certainly the case at the ICTR. Before a trial session, lawyers, Assistant Legal Officers (ALOs), registry officials etc. would mill around; wave at acquaintances in the public gallery; adjust their robes; struggle with the unwieldy curtains; untangle translation headsets; and fiddle with air-condition remote controls. Lawyers freely crossed to their counterparts' desks to hand over documents. Just before the judges entered, everyone would sit in silence in their appointed places. Through the headphones one would only hear a hiss; no one would speak into the microphones, required for simultaneous interpretation, while judges were not in the room.

This would all change when the judges entered. Carlen's (1976: 31) description of the entrance of magistrates in the UK corresponds with the ICTR:

> many of the organisational and ceremonial strategies of stage-management centre round the presentation of the magistrate. His entrance to the courtroom is both staged and heralded. The opening of the court is signalled by the usher calling 'All stand' and 'Silence in court'. When everybody in the courtroom is standing in silence the magistrate enters, his appearance being staged via the door of which he has the exclusive use and which appears to seal off those innermost areas of the court to which the public never has access.

At the ICTR a curtain would be drawn back at the entrance to the courtroom and the judges would enter (through a door leading to the judge's 'separate circulation system'). Lawyers, stenographers and the witness had to be in their places and seated, for only then could they acknowledge the transformation of the 'back region' in to 'front region' by standing when the judges, led in by an usher, entered the courtroom. Zoettl (2016: 2) suggests that such waiting before the start of the session and the 'highly scripted nature of the order of the appearance of the bench' is part of the 'dramaturgy of the trial', a 'public dramatization of hierarchy' (see Mulcahy, 2011: 397). The requirement of first sitting in order to then show deference by standing was strictly enforced at the ICTR. On one occasion, an expert witness stood in the witness box waiting for the judges to enter. The prosecution counsel, sitting, mouthed to the witness 'sit down'. A few minutes later, everyone noticed the movement of the curtain at the entrance and stood up. Before the judges could enter, the usher exclaimed, 'Le témoin? Le témoin?' The witness had gone to the toilet. The curtain remained open, the judges hovered at the entrance, everyone in the courtroom was standing, the witness ran back in past the judges to stand in the witness box, the usher shouted 'Le Tribunal' (the French equivalent of 'All rise'), the judges entered.

The entrance of the judges can be seen as an example of Bertrand Hibbitts' (1995: 60) 'ordinative' or order-giving legal gesture. As an embodied, personal, social, contextual, ephemeral act (all of which distinguish the legal gesture from the legal text) the entrance of the judges is a part of the process that signifies a change in condition, that 'divides legally-important words and behaviours from other words and behaviours' (Hibbitts, 1995: 54) and signals that an 'absolute and supreme' order operates in the courtroom now that the judges are present (see Huizinga, 1949: 10).

It became clear to me that judges were conscious of this transformative role. Whereas the 'separate circulation systems' in domestic court complexes are purpose-built, enabling judges to move around the building without having to engage with the public this was not the case for the whole of the ICTR given that it was located in a rented, retrofitted building. Judges did not, however, compensate for this by entering a courtroom when the court was not in session. An ALO explained to me that judges never used the courtrooms as thoroughfares, 'They will never use the court as just a space.' I witnessed an incident which demonstrated judge's aversion to being in the courtroom when it was not in session. To access Courtroom III, judges chose to walk along a corridor where the public waited for the session to begin when they could have avoided the public by walking through the courtroom. Seeing the judges resplendent in their scarlet robes returning from lunch, an Australian visitor (a lawyer) commented 'they have separate entrances at home. You never get to meet a judge or talk to one.' The judge's behaviour implies their awareness of the role they played in transforming the courtroom from 'back stage' to 'front stage'.

The discussion above regarding the UN security check and the 'separate circulation system' (Rock, 1993: 204) corresponds to Catherine Bell's (1992: 106) 'external strategy' of ritualization that demarcates activities as privileged in contrast to what surrounds them. Regarding the inside of these demarcated activities, Bell (1992: 106) notes an 'internal strategy' which involves 'schemes of opposition [and] hierarchization'. In the same way, Garapon (2001: 43) speaks of the judicial space as being 'divided and obligatory for its occupants; a space organised and hierarchised ... It embodies order, it creates order, it is order.' It is, therefore, through the organization of space within the courtroom (an 'internal strategy') as much as without (an 'external strategy') that an 'absolute and peculiar order reigns' (Huizinga, 1949: 10). How, therefore, was space 'organised and hierarchised' within the ICTR courtroom?

The three judges sat on a raised podium against the centre of the back wall. Below and to each side of the judges, at floor level, sat two stenographers (French and English). Immediately below them, at floor level, seated at a long desk, sat the judges' ALOs and Registry staff. Facing them was the witness box. The three desks of the defence were to the left and, facing them, were the two desks of the prosecution to the right.

On the wall behind the judges was the UN emblem, designed in 1945 by Donal McLaughlin, Chief of the Graphics Presentation Branch of the United States Office of Strategic Studies. It is a map of the world 'inscribed in a wreath consisting of crossed conventionalized branches of the olive tree' (United Nations, 1946, UN Doc. A/107 (1946)).

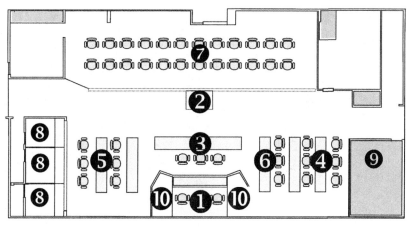

1 Judges	5 Prosecution Team	9 Technical Control Room
2 Witness Box	6 Defence Team(s)	10 Stenographers
3 Registry Officials	7 Public Gallery	
4 Accused	8 Interpreters	

Figure 2.3 Inside a courtroom at the Tribunal (adapted from ICTR 2005a:16)

When I commented on the emblem, a prosecution lawyer responded 'Oh that just makes good television.' He was referring to the CCTV systems installed in three of the four courtrooms (four to five cameras mounted in the ceiling), the images broadcast to screens on lawyers' and judges' desks; to monitors in the public gallery; and to offices throughout the building. The UN emblem framed the judges, but it also framed all that occurred in the courtroom, creating 'an axis of symmetry with the person of the judge[s]' (Garapon, 2001: 28) so that the 'distribution of space, of roles, of functions, the gestures of the judicial debate, take meaning in relation to that major axis' (Jacob, 1994; cited in Garapon, 2001: 28; see Hinton 2016: 230).

The positioning of the UN emblem maintained continuity with domestic courtrooms. Placed behind the judges, the emblem took the place of, for example, a county seal in the United States or the Royal Coat of Arms in the United Kingdom. The UN emblem inherited the role played by these objects, indicating a delegation/transference of authority from an exterior foundation of justice ('the people', 'the monarch') to the judges. At the ICTR, certain people bowed in the direction of the judges when entering

Figure 2.4 Judges' Bench from the defence end showing ICTR Emblem (Courtesy of the ICTR)

Figure 2.5 The UN Emblem and Seal of the ICTR

and leaving the courtroom, most notably Tanzanian Registry officials, but also guards, resident journalists and UN staff. In the trials that I observed, others, including French lawyers and the majority of stenographers did not bow. An American ALO and an American stenographer explained to me that there is no bowing in US courts and that this is a 'British Tanzanian thing'. In the United Kingdom, when one bows to a judge one is primarily showing deference to the 'presence' of the monarch in the form of the Royal Coat of Arms that is placed above/behind the judge. From 1919, the Royal Coat of Arms would have been behind or above judges with jurisdiction over Tanganyika. It appears, therefore, that a residual disposition has remained following independence in 1961. On one hand, people's relation to the emblem indicated a particular residue of local, Tanzanian courts and those from other Commonwealth jurisdictions, but it also indicated the preservation of a more general form found in many domestic jurisdictions, the presence of an emblem framing judges which indicates that they are delegates of a transcendent justice which is 'somewhere else [and which] cannot be contained in laws or confined totally to persons' (Garapon, 2001: 28) (see Introduction).

Echoing Garapon's (2001: 36) observation on the requirement for legal practitioners not to stray from the position 'allocated by the judicial liturgy' initiated by the entrance of the judges, Hanson (1996: 55) notes the contrast between the need for everyone to have 'perfect knowledge of one another, both visually and audibly' but that all concerned are confined to a specific location:

> Only the clerk normally moves about within the courtroom. For everyone else it is a frozen space in which the actors are separated from one another by the arrangement of barriers which breaks the courtroom into its separate territories. Despite co-presence in space, the participants in the trial occupy separate pavilions in the landscape which is the floor of the court. [This] is difficult to appreciate fully ... because the containment of the various territories within a single envelope gives them a semblance of spatial integration.

The ICTR courtroom was, likewise, composed of 'physically discrete and segregated territories' which meant that 'although the actors can see and hear each other ... they inhabit quite separate and mutually exclusive premises' (Hanson, 1996: 56–7). While defence and prosecution could move freely within their own enclosures, they were prohibited from moving beyond the front desk of their enclosure when the judges were present (see Hinton 2016: 230). Only the Registry usher was authorized to move about to collect and distribute documents (see Carlen, 1976: 31; Garapon, 2001: 4; Zoettl, 2016: 4). As the defence lawyer quoted above stated, 'I cannot when the judges are present cross over the courtroom and talk to the prosecution.' Such restrictions lead Hanson (1996: 56) to modify her analogy between trials and the theatre:

> a courtroom is like a theatre in that the negotiations must take place and be seen to take place in public, but unlike a theatre in that the 'stage' is compartmentalized into separate spatial domains, and the actors confront one another across an unbreachable physical divide.

While Hanson and Garapon's observations draw on the layout in English and French courtrooms, regarding 'physically discrete and segregated territories' (Hanson, 1996: 56–7) it is not universally applicable. As a US defence lawyer explained to me in the context of practising in her home jurisdiction, 'I love when it's a jury, you can control them, get up, walk around. But at the ICTR, I'm confined in 15 square inches. I'm used to controlling the courtroom by walking around.' The restrictions on movement required, for some lawyers, was an additional modification of habitual behaviour (see Chapter 3).

Hanson's observation that 'actors can see and hear each other', although applicable to all courtrooms, also requires a modification in the context of the ICTR. Goffman (1959: 106) defines 'regions' as places bounded by 'barriers to perception'. Coincidently, he uses the example of the 'thick glass panels' found in 'broadcasting control rooms' to illustrate this. This is applicable to the ICTR where the courtroom was acoustically compartmentalized by glass (separating the public gallery, interpreter booths and AV booth from the courtroom; see Parker, 2011). On one hand, these glass walls, especially those of the interpreter's booths, were not 'barriers to perception' as participants could still see and hear (via headphones) one another, but they did modify perception (how hearing was modified is discussed in Chapter 3 in relation to the influence of simultaneous interpretation on habitual practice). This brings us back to Hanson's (1996: 55) observation that 'the practicalities of the trial make it imperative that everyone who is in any way involved must have perfect knowledge of one another' not only aurally (which was recorded in the transcript), but also visually.

TO SEE AND BE SEEN

The chapter began by noting that transcripts fail to capture much that happens in the courtroom, a space imbued with a particular character by an 'external strategy' (the security check and 'separate circulation systems' that act upon a required public) and an 'internal strategy' (the entrance of the judges and the combination of visual freedom with constrained physical movement). Having considered the practices that create an arena for the visual (and not just the verbal as recorded in the transcript), I will now explore the 'glances, gestures, body language, the felt experience of space and the proximity of bodies' (Martin, 2006: 11) in the ICTR courtroom.

As in all courtrooms, non-verbal gestures were habitually employed by lawyers, judges and witnesses. Lawyers and judges would make wild hand gestures to indicate to a witness that he or she should stop speaking or slow down to enable interpretation and stenography (see Chapter 3). Stenographers, lawyers and judges would stab their fingers in the air to indicate to someone that they should turn a microphone on or off. Judges would bang their desk with the sides of their hands or throw headphones down when irritated by a lawyer. An interpreter would shake his head in exasperation because he was unable to keep up with the speed of a witness. A defence lawyer would hold up a document, the presiding judge would raise her copy of the same document and wave it up and down slightly to indicate they were 'on the same page'. A prosecution lawyer would turn to the interpretation booths (immediately behind him) hold up a document and point at the paragraph he was about to read, the interpreter nodding, the lawyer responding with a 'thumbs-up' sign. A defence lawyer who was cross-examining would sit down because he saw the judges were talking to one another. Non-verbal gestures were an essential component of the trials, but they were not recorded in the transcript.

It could be argued that that such visual communication was commonplace, but marginal to the outcome of the trial. On one hand, it is hard to envisage how the trial could have proceeded without these gestures. On the other hand, judge's assessment of witness demeanour appeared to be central to the outcome of the trial. On one occasion I observed a judge challenge a defence lawyer's questions with the following summary of the judge's role:

> At the bottom line, what we really are trying to do is get the testimony from this witness that we can assess in due course, and we look at the

Figure 2.6 The Courtroom from the prosecution end (Courtesy of the ICTR)

totality of the picture, his behaviour, his demeanour in the witness box; all these are part of the whole package that assists us in assessing his testimony.

In the Introduction, I quoted another presiding judge summarizing the judge's role in which he refers to sight three times:

> The Trial Chamber must see and appreciate what is being confirmed. There are no shortcuts to that. The witness will have to observe, and then be asked the questions so that the dialogue between counsel and the witness is seen and appreciated by the Trial Chamber. Everything is done by way of questioning the witness, but it is being done for and on behalf of the Trial Chamber for it to see.

The importance judges placed on looking and seeing was also attested to by their assistants. A key task of ALOs was the production of 'witness summaries', often using the transcript rather than being present in the courtroom when the witness gave testimony. One ALO implied the importance of demeanour, that 'When I'm preparing witness summaries I can detect contradictions etc., but I wasn't actually there, I didn't actually see them and assess their demeanour. All I can do is detect contradictions, I can't comment on demeanour.' Whether judges used their own assessment of demeanour to assess witness summaries was unclear, as the same ALO explained in relation to the three judges with which he worked:

> The judge's main job is to read the witness. It's a skill you develop, it's not taught at law school. One of the judges in my case takes notes on every witness. He's got notebooks of notes on every witness. The other two judges don't. But assessing demeanour is one of their main roles. I'm surprised that judge [name] does not take notes, while judge [name] doesn't remember the witness from last week! That's why judge [name's] notes will be so important, he'll be central to that judgment.

Lawyers also indicated that demeanour played a role in the judges' assessment of testimony. When I asked a prosecution lawyer whether simultaneous interpretation impeded assessment of demeanour (see Chapter 3), he replied 'I don't believe that the judges don't observe the demeanour of the witness. They're concerned with the record, yes, but they will notice that a fidgeting witness is probably lying, judges are far cannier than that.' This concern with demeanour emphasizes the need to 'see and be seen' and corresponds to comments by judges in a Jerusalem court who 'rather than embracing the criminal statute's focus on words', they highlighted the 'marginality of words' and the importance of the body; the 'body language' rather than 'word language' (Braverman, 2007 261–3; see Introduction).

A particular episode further emphasizes the imperative of visibility. In 2006, the prosecution in the case of Protais Zigiranyirazo (a Rwandan businessman and politician acquitted by the ICTR on appeal of genocide and crimes against humanity), requested that a detained witness, Michel Bagaragaza (Director General of the office controlling the Rwandan tea industry who pleaded guilty to complicity in genocide in 2009, having voluntarily surrendered to the ICTR in 2005) give testimony via video-link from The Hague due to concerns for his security. In response, the judges expressed concerns about their ability 'to effectively and accurately assess the testimony and demeanour' if the witness testified by video-link (ICTR, 2006e: 32), thereby highlighting the importance the judges placed on being able to observe the witness in the same room. The judges decided, therefore, to hear Bagaragaza's testimony in person in The Hague with Zigiranyirazo, the defendant, present. The Dutch authorities, however, said there would be a delay in allowing Zigiranyirazo to enter the country. In the end, Bagaragaza testified for two days in a courtroom in The Hague in the presence of the judges, while the defendant, Zigiranyirazo was in the courtroom in Arusha accompanied by one of his lawyers. To ensure some degree of fairness, the judges decided that both the prosecution's examination-in-chief and the defence's cross-examination would be conducted via video-link by lawyers in the Arusha courtroom.

Zigiranyirazo's defence lawyers, however, appealed, arguing that this arrangement violated the defendant's right, enshrined in the ICTR Statute (United Nations, 1994e, UN Doc. S/RES/955 (1994): Art. 20) ('To be tried in his or her presence'). The violation of this right was ultimately upheld by the Appeals Chamber and the testimony given by Bagaragaza in The Hague was excluded (ICTR, 2006f). Although ostensibly about the right of a defendant to be present at the examination of a witness, this episode reveals the extent to which visibility informs the practice of judges and lawyers. The judges made this clear in their original decision (the need 'to effectively and accurately assess the testimony and demeanour' (ICTR, 2006e: para 32)). On their part, the defence argued that they 'could not speak directly to the judges, gauge their reactions, and adjust the arguments and tenor of pleadings as if they were in open court with the members of the bench' (ICTR, 2006g: para 25) a complaint summarized by the Appeals Chamber as a denial of 'normal visual interaction with the proceedings' (ICTR, 2006f: 16). One of the lawyers involved, further elaborated in conversation with me:

> It's the case that the judges have to be able to see the witness and the accused. But, the camera was only on the witness, so we couldn't see the judges and the judges could only see my client when the camera was occasionally on him. All the time, it was just images of me looking down at my notes, because the judges weren't there. Now, if you and I are talking, I look at you. If the judges are there, I look at them. That's the real skill, that you can just take a little look at your notes, so that you're always looking at the witness or the judges. But, when they weren't there, I just looked down at my notes.

These comments correspond to the Appeals Chamber decision which highlights that 'normal visual interaction' must be reciprocal, that the judge's misgivings about being able to assess the demeanour of the witness via video-link 'must apply with equal force to the ability of the accused and his counsel to follow the evidence and proceedings' (ICTR, 2006f: para 19). There is a mutual need to 'see and be seen'.

The Zigiranyirazo Appeals Judgment's emphasis on 'normal visual interaction' corresponds with the opinions of judges, lawyers and ALOs considered above. The accepted notion that 'demeanour' is part of a witness's testimony obscures the fact that demeanour is something that all in the courtroom utilize. For example, while a transcript will record a defence lawyer's statement 'I will rephrase my question', it does not record the almost imperceptible movement made by a prosecution lawyer (noticed by the defence lawyer) which indicates that he will, if necessary, stand up and object. Likewise, the transcript records a defence lawyer rephrasing a question, but it does not record the judge, his arms wide open in a gesture of disbelief and puzzlement with an 'Oh come on!' look on his face.

The primacy of seeing was challenged by the introduction in 2004 of 'LiveNote' at the ICTR, a transcript management software program which allowed all in the courtroom (except the witness) to monitor the transcript instantaneously in 'real-time' on laptops. Sitting in the public gallery I could see, through the blue-tinted, bullet-proof glass, LiveNote on a lawyer's laptop. In the software, time was marked at the start of each line (hour: minute: second) and a yellow line ran along the bottom, within which pulsing words appeared as they were spoken. When a line was complete, the line of words moved up the screen and the yellow line moved down and continued to be filled with words. This allowed immediate revision of the transcript. For example, speaking at 11:05am, a judge said: 'There is one issue in the transcript on 1100:00 and 1100:36 ... The "yet" in both cases shouldn't be there.'

Watching LiveNote now competed with watching the demeanour of the witness. Judges, however, insisted to me that the witness's demeanour remained their priority and that LiveNote 'does not substitute for the witness. It's a way of coping with the witness because you can listen as well as watch.' Likewise, a prosecution lawyer told me:

> I don't want to be distracted, I focus so much on what the witness says. LiveNote takes something away from watching the demeanour of the witness. You need to do that for strategic reasons. I watch to see how he has answered, is he sure or unsure. I'll be nice when he's sure, but more aggressive when he's unsure. Sometimes you can tell from the voice, but you also need to watch them.

Whether or not all judges and lawyers operated in this way, LiveNote introduced a 'text based view of the law' (Morison and Leith, 1992: vii; see Introduction) into the very heart of the trial, reiterating the privileging of text because it represents 'stability, dispassionate fairness, fidelity to truth without prejudice, the blindness of the law' in contrast to the theatricality of the courtroom with its 'artifice, emotion, deception, seductive appearances, the instability of truth' (Peters 2008: 199). The desire for such 'fidelity to truth without prejudice' could not wait until a transcript could be consulted after a trial session, but had to be embedded in the very process itself.

CONCLUSION

Examining how the ICTR courtroom brought 'gravity' to itself, I have suggested that it is useful to see it as a 'play-ground' in which the rules of ordinary life are suspended and an 'absolute and peculiar order reigns'. This was achieved by an 'external strategy' (the security check and 'separate circulation systems' that acted upon a required public) and an 'internal strategy' (the entrance of the judges and the combination of visual freedom with constrained physical movement (see Bell, 1992: 106)). I am not the first person to discuss the 'external strategy' of the court complex (see Garapon, 2001; Hanson, 1996; Steinitz, 2007; Taylor, 1993) or the 'internal strategy' of the courtroom (Carlen, 1976; Mulcahy, 2007). I would argue, however, that the exceptional, improvised, ad hoc nature of the ICTR (located in rented, retrofitted building) brought these otherwise naturalized and hidden features of the operation of law into a clear and sharp focus. For example, Michel Bagaragaza's testimony in the case of Protais Zigiranyirazo was exceptional, and required judges to make explicit what is habitually taken for granted, the 'normal visual interaction with the proceedings' (ICTR, 2006f: 16).

While the chapter has gone some way to capturing activity in the ICTR courtrooms (which will be examined further in the remaining chapters), the chapter also contributes to broader questions about the nature of legal proceedings and responds to Bernard Hibbitts' (1995: 51) suggestion that a 'fully-accurate and nuanced understanding of how the law actually works requires an appreciation of other texts in law's semiotic field'. Hibbitts' suggestion corresponds with Morison and Leith's (1992: vii) call for an appreciation of the 'non-textual nature of law' and how this responds to the (New) Legal Realist's concern to identify the 'nonlegal [i.e. non-textual] supplements' (Schauer, 2013: 754) that enable law to operate (see Introduction).

3

'WHO THE HELL CARES HOW THINGS ARE DONE IN THE OLD COUNTRY'

A Rwandan prosecution witness is being cross-examined by an American defence lawyer. The witness has been giving testimony for eight days. The defence lawyer asks the witness whether he made notes when he gave his statement to the prosecution investigators and whether he has been consulting those notes in the evenings while he has been giving testimony. The presiding judge interjects and asks the defence lawyer to explain the relevance of this line of questioning:

Defence Lawyer: Mr President, if the witness has been reviewing documents concerning the events that he's testified about, that affects his credibility; his memory is being enhanced. And the defence is entitled to see those documents he has been reviewing.

Co-Judge: But he said these were his own notes.

Defence Lawyer: Yes, and if he's relying on notes to refresh his memory, the defence are entitled to see those notes.

Co-Judge: You're saying you're entitled to his own private notes?

Defence Lawyer: Yes. If he's used them to refresh his memory. Isn't that common practice in every jurisdiction, that a witness who's used material to refresh their memory has to produce that material?

Presiding Judge: I'm not aware of that rule. I'm not aware of any control over what he reads when he's not in the witness box.

Defence Lawyer: So if a witness has prepared some kind of document and uses that in the evenings, it's your understanding that it's only disclosable if he brings it to court with him? Maybe it's my national practice that I'm betraying knowledge of, but I'm not aware of that distinction.

Prosecution Lawyer: I think in that regard it must be a Californian practice because I practiced in New York and I've never heard an application quite like this one. In any case, I would suggest that there's nothing in our rules that require disclosure of a witness's own memoranda.

Presiding Judge: We rule that the witness's own notes are not disclosable.

The ICTR Statute (United Nations, 1994e, UN Doc. S/RES/955 (1994)) was a hybrid of civil and common law. In civil (or 'inquisitorial') procedure (France, Germany, Belgium etc.), judges determine the factual issues of a case on the basis of documentary evidence and written summaries of witness testimony. If live witnesses are called, it is the judge who poses questions, defence and prosecution lawyers playing a relatively passive role. In contrast, in the common law (or 'adversarial') system (United Kingdom, United States, Canada etc.) evidence tends to be heard orally, lawyers question witnesses and judges play a relatively passive role ensuring that procedure is followed. Reflecting on the hybridity of the ICTR Statute, scholars have suggested that lawyers and judges were able to accommodate these differences (see Ambos, 2003: 34, Ellis, 1997; Nice, 2001; Tochilovsky, 2004).

In the episode described above, the lawyers and judges all originated from common law jurisdictions. The fact that this antagonistic incident is between four practitioners from the same system raises alternative issues to the common law/civil law confrontation that has occupied scholars. The episode demonstrates, for example, that common law is varied ('I think in that regard it must be a Californian practice because I practiced in New York and I've never heard an application quite like this one') and that some lawyers were happy to abandon domestic habit ('I would suggest that there's nothing in our rules that require disclosure of a witness's own memoranda').

In the field of human rights, Sally Merry (2006b: 39) has described a process of 'vernacularisation' in which universal human rights are adapted to local conditions and in the process are 'mediated, appropriated, translated, modified, misunderstood [or] ignored' (Hinton, 2010: 12). At the ICTR, however, it appears that the process was reversed in that a tentative, 'universal' practice of international criminal justice emerged as diverse domestic practices encountered one another in the courtroom. This confirms that such 'norms are constituted by their agents, rather than the opposite ... it is international criminal lawyers who create international criminal justice, not the other way round' (Mégret, 2016: para 9). An ALO described this process to me in the following terms:

> There's no legal culture here that everyone recognizes. For example, that this is an 'obvious' case that this document can be entered as evidence or 'how do you write a subpoena?' There is a lack of consensus on what is valid and acceptable, therefore, everything has to be litigated.

Disagreements had to be resolved and a shared, working solution forged (see Mégret, 2011: 1016; Byrne, 2010: 252). A prosecution lawyer explained this process to me 'What we would normally take for granted, we would never even discuss it, but here, every tiny thing has to be discussed. We're actually creating law.' A defence lawyer described the process in similar terms:

> In a domestic jurisdiction there is a systemic structure. Each case is different, but that structure works to contain and guide each case. But, at the tribunal that does not exist. An innovation has to be made to account for something particular. A lot of the time it's a gut-check, we take something out of our pocket and see how it fits. The judiciary may give the impression that there is a standard guiding them, but the idea found in common law of centuries of practice, that's not there. There's no systematic structure, we're literally bringing it into existence in the courtroom.

This creative flexibility is seen in the openness to change in the episode above. While the defence lawyer demonstrates a parochial attachment to his home practice ('Maybe it's my national practice that I'm betraying knowledge of'), the prosecution lawyer rejects parochialism ('there's nothing in our rules that require disclosure of a witness's own memoranda'). In contrast to Rosemary Byrne (2010: 261) who suggests that international criminal lawyers 'cling to romanticized memories of their professional homelands', Frédéric Mégret (2016: para 26) suggests that while lawyers may draw on domestic experience as 'validators of their expertise', they also 'seek to emancipate themselves from them in an effort to deprovincialize their credentials'. Such openness was something I encountered regularly, for example, 'Practising here makes you think about what you are doing, how you do things. It makes you open to the fact that just because we have one way of doing something doesn't mean it's better' (defence lawyer) and 'you can be very creative in an institution in which there is no set way of doing things' (prosecution lawyer). This attitude was summed up by a judge, 'Who the hell cares how things are done in the old country.' For some legal practitioners, the transition in 'transitional justice' was a matter of reflection on prior assumptions and reformulating their procedural and performative preferences.

To accommodate the evolving practice ('we're literally bringing it into existence in the courtroom'), judges engaged in a constant process of rewriting the ICTR's Rules of Procedure and Evidence (RPE or RPEs). As an accelerated form of what happens in domestic jurisdictions, the experience at the ICTR directs our attention to the fact that the creation of law is always an exercise in (temporarily) ossifying arbitrary, situated, contingent responses into impersonal, universal principles by means of 'the cult of the [legal] text' (Bourdieu, 1987: 851). While the text (RPE) evolved and responded to day-to-day practice in the courtroom, this evolution was denied because the RPE were meant to control day-to-day practice and not the other way around.

Solely directing our attention to the RPE as a means to resolve the encounter between different legal systems (common and civil law) would be to ignore the fact that not all that happens in the courtroom is determined by written rules. As discussed in the Introduction, Peter Zoettl (2016) in his ethnography of German and Portuguese courtrooms, indicates that in domestic jurisdictions legal practitioners share both a publicly codified script (such as the RPE) and a hidden script born of practice, the latter only being revealed 'when something goes wrong' requiring a judge to 'verbally express a rule that, from the court's perspective, goes without saying' (Zoettl, 2016: 4). These rules 'are usually left unspoken as long as they are observed, being rendered explicit only when disregarded' (Zoettl, 2016: 7). These are the 'unwritten laws' of the judicial field (Bourdieu, 1987: 831, 820). Of special significance for the latter part of this chapter, Zoettl (2016: 6) notes that 'unwritten rules' concerning standing and sitting are part of this 'hidden' script. For Zoettl (2016: 10), such seemingly superficial details of courtroom practice are essential to 'producing and reproducing a legal system'. The ICTR provided an ideal opportunity to investigate these rules because lawyers and judges did not, necessarily, share assumptions on 'unwritten rules', given their diverse provenance from common and civil law jurisdictions.

This chapter will employ Zoettl's (2016) notion of codified vs. hidden rules to explore the ways lawyers and judges adapted to unfamiliar practices at the ICTR. First, the chapter will explore the way in which habitual practice was infringed by the demands of simultaneous interpretation, forcing lawyers to modify or surrender habitual practice. The chapter will then explore the ways in which, as noted by Zoettl (2016), embodied behaviours are a prominent element in any courtroom's 'unwritten rules'. I will argue that attention to such behaviours is revealing with regard to the encounter between practitioners drawn from common and civil law. Finally, the chapter will reflect on the way in which the 'codified rules' of the ICTR's RPE were deployed as a fixed regulator of courtroom practice even though they were constantly modified to reflect evolving practice (clashes of 'hidden rules') in the courtroom. The chapter ends, therefore, by demonstrating the concealed, mutually constitutive relationship between the 'hidden script' of courtroom practice and the 'codified script' of the RPE.

SIMULTANEOUS INTERPRETATION AND 'TRIBUNAL MODE'

While the working languages of the ICTR were French and English (United Nations, 1994e: Art. 31; ICTR, 2005[1995]: Rule 3a), the accused had a right to use his or her own language (Rule 3b), as were witnesses who had insufficient knowledge of the two working languages (Rule 3d). This reflects the same right at the Nuremberg (International Military Tribunal, 1945: Art. 16(c) and Tokyo (International Military Tribunal for the Far East, 1945: Art. 9(b)) Tribunals and corresponds to Article 14(3)(f) of the International Covenant on Civil and Political Rights (1966: 'To have the free assistance of an interpreter if he cannot understand or speak the language used in court').

Despite the official parity of English and French, judges were predominantly anglophone, although English was a second language for many. The dominance of English is alluded to in a report by the ICTR's President to the UN Security Council and General Assembly (United Nations, 1999b, UN Doc. S/1994/1125: para 92):

> Another positive development worth noting is the introduction of English language classes for the detainees in order to facilitate

communications between them and the Tribunal in the two official languages. The classes take place in the [UN Detention Facility] and are paid for by the Tribunal.

Initially, consecutive interpretation was used at the ICTR (the interpreter waits for the speaker to finish a sentence or an idea, and then renders the speaker's words into the target language). In 2001, simultaneous interpretation was introduced (the interpreter renders the speaker's words into the target language while he or she is speaking). This interpretation was provided by interpreters in soundproof booths, who, having received the source language via headphones (trial participants had to speak into a microphone) relayed an interpretation of the target language to participants via headphones attached to a wireless receiver with four channels (0 = floor, 1 = English, 2 = French, 3 = Kinyarwanda). It was reported that this innovation reduced the amount of time required for interpretation by 25 per cent (United Nations, 2003a, UN Doc. A/58/140: para 4). As an aside, I soon learned, in conversation, that there was a sensitivity among interpreters about being referred to as 'translators' (who work on written texts) (see Gaiba, 1998: 16) although lawyers and judges at the ICTR used the terms 'interpreter' and 'translator' interchangeably.

A 'relay' interpretation system, with three interpreters, was employed at the ICTR. Listening to channel 0 ('floor'), the French interpreter would interpret all English into French and a separate English interpreter would interpret all French into English. Both of these interpreters, whose interpretation was recorded as the two official transcripts by stenographers, followed the established practice of interpreting into their 'A' (i.e. native) language. The third, a Kinyarwanda interpreter, would, however, interpret from Kinyarwanda into English or French (depending on their second language) and from English or French back into Kinyarwanda. This meant that, depending on the Kinyarwanda booth, an anglophone lawyer would hear a witness testifying in Kinyarwanda either second- or thirdhand. In the absence of anyone speaking Kinyarwanda in the courtroom, only French and English were interpreted. While this reflected the two official transcripts (French and English) it also implied an assumption that any Rwandan in the Public Gallery would understand French or English.

The ICTR's transcripts (English and French) contain no systematic record of which language a person was speaking at any one moment, nor whether a Kinyarwanda speaker was interpreted immediately to English or via French. Although a judge impressed upon me that when 'investigators look at the transcripts in the future' they should ask 'In which language was the original?', this would not be possible in the absence of any systematic record. This is another example of the deficiency of the transcript to capture relevant detail (see the Introduction and Chapter 2).

Simultaneous interpretation was new to all of the judges and lawyers with whom I spoke. While some had experience of consecutive interpretation in asylum hearings in domestic jurisdictions, none had experienced wireless, simultaneous interpretation. I encountered praise for interpreters. Anglophone defence lawyers described them as 'very, very good'; that 'The Kinyarwanda boys in our trial are very good' and one reported that his client could not fault the Kinyarwanda interpreter. There was also sympathy for interpreters; that they had 'the most stressful job' (anglophone prosecution lawyer) and that after a shift 'their brains are coming out of their ears' (anglophone defence lawyer). There was also, however, negative assessment. An anglophone prosecution lawyer used the example of how the question 'What is your name?' having passed through English to French to Kinyarwanda and back again, would elicit the reply 'Yes'. Others complained there was a great deal of mistranslation. An anglophone prosecution lawyer explained to me that:

> We always had a Kinyarwanda speaker on my team. They just sat in court and would scribble when there was a problem with the interpretation. Almost every hour she would say there was a problem and the Presiding Judge would say 'what's the problem now?' Because of that, the defence lawyer went and got his own Kinyarwanda speaker to sit next to him.

Such independent monitoring of interpretation was not, however, available to all. An anglophone judge, for example, describing interpretation as 'very frustrating', noted that, despite evidence that French to Kinyarwanda interpretation was not correct, he was a member of an entirely 'English Bench', which meant there was 'no way to determine independently whether the interpreter is correct'. This sense of desiring, but lacking, independent assurance was summed up by another anglophone judge, 'If an interpreter says the witness said Friday afternoon but they said Thursday afternoon, we'd be misled, but there's no one in between to make it into Thursday afternoon.' The same judge expanded on his sense of unease:

> I can read the mind of the prosecution because they speak in my working language, English. In contrast, when the [francophone] defence speak I have to wait and the translators may not translate the correct nuance of the language. Therefore, no one is 100 per cent sure that the judges have understood definitely, because we're hearing it secondhand. This impacts on my mind, on the mind of a judge.

His phrase the 'mind of the judge' and the image of reading the mind of lawyers implies a habitual ease of communication in his home jurisdiction that was lost due to his reliance on simultaneous interpretation.

Such disruptions to habitual practice caused by simultaneous interpretation, and attempts to adapt, were in constant evidence as I watched ICTR trials. As discussed in Chapter 2, assessment of demeanour played a central role in how lawyers and judges interacted with witnesses, a judge commenting in the courtroom that in assessing a witness's testimony the judges would 'look at the totality of the picture, his behaviour, his demeanour in the witness box'. Lawyers also impressed upon me the importance of assessing demeanour in the moment-by-moment choices they made in examining a witness:

> You need to watch the demeanour of the witness for strategic reasons. I watch to see how he has answered. Is he sure or unsure? I'll be nice when he's sure, but more aggressive when he's unsure. Sometimes you can tell from the voice, but you also need to watch them (anglophone prosecution lawyer).

Lawyers, however, complained that simultaneous interpretation impeded this habitual component of their courtroom practice ('you can tell from the voice'):

> When it comes to judging credibility you rely on the inflection in the voice. But, this person is not saying anything to you. In English or French you can make it out. But if they're testifying in Kinyarwanda you can't make out whether they're angry or whatever (bilingual, French/English, defence lawyer).
> If they hesitated you'd hear that in the voice of the translator, but it would be highly dangerous to extrapolate causes. It's true that in most cases, the tone, vocabulary, repetitions, hesitations and so on are simply not available (anglophone defence lawyer).

Judges also commented on how simultaneous interpretation deprived them of habitual ways of assessing demeanour:

I have no idea when it comes to assessing demeanour. In any case, the translation comes afterwards, therefore, their demeanour is now different to what it was when they spoke. As far as I know they appear nice but are telling lies etc. or appear nasty, but they're speaking the truth (anglophone judge).

If the accused is asked an embarrassing question you cannot catch them on their demeanour, are they hesitating or is it because of the translation? A clever witness can use translation as pretence. If they get caught they can hesitate, in the meantime he has thought of an answer. So, you cannot judge demeanour as effectively as if there was no translation issue (anglophone judge).

A key adaptation required of lawyers and judges to simultaneous interpretation was the need to recalibrate their estimations of time. Asked by a judge how long a witness re-examination would take, an anglophone prosecution lawyer responded, 'It's difficult to gauge. If I was at home, it would be 15 minutes. So I guess that might mean an hour.' Not only did the rate of questions and answers slow down because of the delay caused by interpretation, lawyers were also required to slow their delivery. At every trial session I attended, judges would admonish witnesses and lawyers for speaking too fast. The sense that slowing down was counter-intuitive for experienced lawyers was illustrated by an anglophone defence lawyer who, after a recess of five days, apologized for speaking too fast and explained 'I have to remember to speak slowly. I have to get back into Tribunal mode. I have a post-it here on my desk that says "Speak slowly!"'

The counter-habitual 'Tribunal mode' involved other adjustments. In conversation, an anglophone judge explained that lawyers had to avoid 'being pompous, use easy words, avoid any kind of ambiguity'. For him, and other judges, 'brevity and simplicity' were needed to facilitate interpretation. This requirement was illustrated by a francophone defence lawyer who complained to me that simultaneous interpretation meant that 'All subtleties, all nuances are lost.' His bilingual colleague confirmed how, when speaking French, the same lawyer was 'a pleasure to listen to, beautiful and eloquent', but that all the inflection and 'beautiful emphasis' was lost in interpretation. As a consequence, the defence lawyer had adapted his sentences to be 'simple so they can be easily translated because the judges are English-speaking. You have to simplify.' Fearing that his eloquence and subtlety (developed over decades of domestic practice) were hampering his ability to convince anglophone judges, he abandoned these qualities in favour of simplicity.

Lawyers complained that this need for simplicity deprived them of habitual advocacy tools, especially in terms of cross-examination. An anglophone defence lawyer observed that 'You are forced to be a lot clearer in cross-examination. You reduce it to the bare essentials for clarity, but, it loses the punch', while his anglophone colleague complained that she needed to 'be monosyllabic for the judges' which meant that 'it's difficult to control the courtroom'. Lawyers felt that simultaneous interpretation had robbed them of such habitual 'control', an anglophone prosecution lawyer complaining that 'an experienced advocate cannot get a grip of a witness' because the tone of his voice when questioning a witness was important to 'control the witness'. Given that this particular lawyer told me that he always wanted to elicit a 'yes' from a witness under cross-examination, the lawyer habitually posed his 'question' (e.g. 'You were going down the road') as a statement of fact to which there could be only one possible answer ('Yes'). Different inflection added by an interpreter, however, transformed statements into questions thereby, in his opinion, substantially reducing his habitual 'grip' on a witness (see Atkinson and Drew, 1979; Dunstan, 1980). As Byrne (2010: 262) notes, 'the advanced art of cross-examination that plays with language, tempo and pace may appear as a series of tepid queries' when transmitted through multilingual interpretation.

As discussed in Chapter 4, in the examination and cross-examination of witnesses, only lawyers can ask questions and witnesses can only answer the question that is posed. Michael Conley and William O'Barr (2005: 21) note that these rules 'have the consequence of empowering lawyers linguistically over the witnesses they examine' and that this is most extreme in cross-examination. Drawing on Gregory Matoesian's (1993) research on rape trials, Conley and O'Barr (2005: 22–38) identify a number of ways that lawyers control witnesses in cross-examination. For example, by prematurely cutting into the silence after having asked a question a lawyer can imply hesitation on the part of the witness or by leaving a silence after a witness has answered a question the lawyer can imply a lack of credibility. Sandra Beatriz Hale (2004: 96–104), however, demonstrates that because interpreters omit pauses and hesitations, lawyers are denied the strategies described by Conley and O'Barr (see Jönsson and Linell, 1991: 438). Simultaneous interpretation robbed lawyers of these habitual tools in cross-examination, giving a sense of no longer being able to 'control the witness'.

While interpretation deprived lawyers of habitual tools, it also introduced novel tasks. In the midst of examining a witness, for example, lawyers would have to remember to indicate the document to which they were referring so that the interpreter could use a hard copy of the document to expedite interpretation. Documents provided to interpreters by lawyers included lists of questions the lawyer planned to ask and 'spelling lists' of individuals' names and places in Rwanda. A lawyer would pause and say 'I'm speaking to the interpreters. I'm asking question 87' or 'That's number 10 on the spelling list.' The regular complaint from interpreters that a lawyer had not indicated the document to which she was referring or had failed to distribute the document before the start of the trial session indicated that this novel competency had not been universally adopted.

The headphones and microphones essential for simultaneous interpretation also required a new competency. James Parker (2011: 973) notes that at the ICTR the 'acoustic experience' of practitioners was 'radically personalised', that 'participants in the judicial soundscape' were required to 'both occupy and arrange their own private acoustic worlds'. Lawyers had to ensure that they spoke into a microphone, remembering to turn it on and off. If they failed to do so, the transcript would read '(Microphone not activated)'. Interpreters would often intervene with, for example, 'The President's microphone please.' Because the system only allowed one microphone to be active at any one time, it was essential that microphones were turned off or interpretation channels would be 'blocked'. Again, this was something presiding judges had to remind witnesses and lawyers to do (although interpreters themselves occasionally forgot to turn their microphones off, the stenographers waving at them to do so). Parker (2011: 975–6) also notes that participants had to learn how to 'play' their microphones in terms of the right proximity and volume, requirements which, in themselves, altered the way that practitioners spoke and acted.

A further, novel, task was the need to 'observe the pause' between two people speaking. This is necessary because simultaneous interpretation involves a seven to eight second lag (the *décalage*) between the interpreter hearing a word in the source language and speaking it in the target language (Gaiba, 1998: 16). Failure to observe the pause was recorded in the transcript as '(Microphones overlapping)'. At every session I attended, either an interpreter or the presiding judge admonished a lawyer or witness for failing to observe the pause. This disrupted habitual practice because it required lawyers to 'break the rhythm' (anglophone defence lawyer) and made 'cross-examination completely different because you can't have sparing exchanges' (bilingual defence lawyer).

One consolation of the microphones was that they assisted in respecting 'the pause'. By paying attention to the small red ring that lit up at the base of the interpreter's microphone when it was being used, participants could see when the interpretation was complete. A francophone defence lawyer, for example, commented 'my lead counsel is telling me that I should look at the red light in the English booth' and presiding judges would often instruct witnesses to watch for the red light so 'you can observe the pause' (see Chapter 2 for discussion of the need 'to see and be seen' in the courtroom). While this practice facilitated respect for 'the pause', the need to watch for the interpreter's light interfered with lawyers' habitual practice of concentrating on witness demeanour (see above).

The novel requirement of observing 'the pause', was particularly demanding if the lawyer and witness were speaking the same language. An anglophone prosecution lawyer explained to me that:

> The real problem for me is when I examine a witness who testifies in English and the judge is English speaking, because there's a tendency to move ahead to the next question as soon as the witness answers. But if you go directly on, you will be speaking into the French and Kinyarwanda translation of the previous question. It's a novel experience. You have to have self-censorship, you have to learn a new technique.

The counter-intuitive demands that required 'self-censorship' and 'a new technique' were even greater if the witness was bilingual. A bilingual (English and French) defence lawyer recalled:

> I prepared a witness in English and examined her in English, but she testified in French although she obviously understood English. I told her 'Wait for the French translation before you answer. Live in French, because you're speaking in French. Don't answer when you hear the English question even though you understand it.

In this example, both lawyer and witness were required to act in a counter-intuitive manner, maintaining the pretence that they did not immediately understand what the other had said.

Given the challenges generated by the need to slow delivery, simplify content, observe a pause, and speak into microphones, anglophone lawyers considered lawyers bilingual in French and English (as many Canadian defence lawyers were) to have an advantage. An anglophone defence lawyer, for example, recalled how in her trial a bilingual defence lawyer had been able to ensure, by monitoring the transcript, that the interpretation of *barrière* at the entrance to a hospital in the French transcript reflected the English transcript in referring to a car park barrier rather than a roadblock manned by *Interahamwe* militia.

The supposed advantage of being bilingual was also seen in rapid language switches that allowed direct communication with anglophone judges. For example, while examining a witness in French a bilingual lawyer would respond in English to a judge's question, asked in English (e.g. Judge: 'Which date?'; Lawyer: 'April 11th') and would speak English when 'housekeeping' (discussing estimated time for examining a witness; the distribution of documents etc.). The feeling among monolingual lawyers was that bilingual lawyers benefitted from this dual competence. An interpreter explained to me, however, that such rapid language switches 'screws up the way the interpreters work, because the French booth would have been directed towards that lawyer'.

The advantage of being a bilingual lawyer was not, however, entirely straightforward. Not only did they, like monolingual lawyers, lose habitual tools (because of the need to slow delivery, simplify content etc.) and take on additional tasks (speak into microphones; observe a pause etc.), they also imposed on themselves an additional, non-habitual burden of monitoring the interpretation on LiveNote – a transcript management software program which allowed all in the courtroom (except the witness) to monitor the transcript instantaneously in 'real time' on laptops (see Chapter 2), as in the interpretation of *barrière* discussed above. In addition, bilingual lawyers would examine a French-speaking witness in English, but simultaneously monitor the French translation (through the headphones). While conducting a cross-examination in one language, these lawyers were aurally monitoring the interpretation of what they and the witness were saying.

All of these changes altered the habitual practice (and control) of lawyers and judges. It was not, however, simply that simultaneous interpretation diminished habitual control, but there was also a transfer of control from lawyers and judges to interpreters. Writing in the context of the US legal system, Susan Berk-Seligson (1990: 156) detects a belief that the court interpreter:

should not exist as a distinct verbal participant in her own right . . . she is meant to speak solely in place of the other participants in the courtroom, those considered to legitimately hold the right to speak: the attorneys, witnesses, plaintiffs, defendants, and the judge.

In the context of international criminal justice, the ICTY's code of ethics for interpreters (there was no such code for the ICTR) stated that 'Interpreters and translators shall not exercise power or influence over their listeners or readers' (ICTY, 1999: Art. 5 (3)). To fulfil this, interpreters were required to convey the interpretation with 'the greatest fidelity and accuracy, and with complete neutrality' (Art. 10 (1a)), including interpreting 'any non-verbal clue such as the tone of voice and emotions of the speaker, which might facilitate the understanding of their listeners' (Art. 10 (1b)) and 'shall not embellish, omit or edit anything' (Art. 10 (1c). While they were required to alert the judge to any 'lexical lacuna' encountered (Art. 6 (2)), the essence of the requirement that interpreters should not 'exercise power' corresponds with the requirement that they should only ever speak on behalf of another speaker and 'should not exist as a distinct verbal participant in her own right' (Berk-Seligson, 1990: 156; see Parker, 2011: 987).

This supposed invisibility was expressed in the fact that while the names of stenographers were recorded in ICTR transcripts and Case Minutes, the names of interpreters were not. And yet, interpreters were not passive participants. As already discussed, interpreters would interrupt lawyers to request that they spoke more slowly; that they observe a pause between speakers; turn microphones on or off; and demand that lawyers supply copies of documents to which they were referring.

Interpreters also played an active role in censoring protected witnesses (see Braverman, 2007: 255; Chapter 4). An English interpreter, for example, interjected, when the witness had just mentioned an organization of which the witness was a member, 'Sorry, I don't know whether to censor the witness or not' and later 'The witness is actually giving the name of the *cellule* [a local administrative unit] where he lives.' On another occasion, an English interpreter interjected over a witness's answer that 'The witness has mentioned the country [of asylum] again' and, a few moments later, 'The Kinyarwanda booth points out that the witness has pointed out the country twice.' On another occasion, listening on headphones in the public gallery I heard a prosecution lawyer ask a witness 'Can you tell us, what was the ethnicity of the two persons who were struck?' and the start of the witness's reply 'I know the ethnicity . . . ' which was then interrupted by the English interpreter 'The witness mentioned the name of one of the two persons. The Kinyarwanda interpreter doesn't deem it fit to mention the name of the said person.' This censoring role was actively encouraged by judges. For example, on one occasion a prosecution lawyer complained that the 'interpretation booth' was overstepping its assigned role in choosing not to interpret something, to which the presiding judge responded 'We expect the interpreters to exercise discretion when they're aware that protected information is accidentally uttered. We expect them not to translate it so it doesn't get onto the record.'

Such censoring, in addition to instructing witnesses, defendants and lawyers to speak more slowly; observe the pause; or repeat themselves, 'fundamentally alters the nature of [the interpreter's] prescribed role in court' as they became an 'active verbal participant in the interaction' (Berk-Seligson, 1990: 170; see Elias-Bursać, 2015: 74, 84–8, 121–30). Writing on the role of interpreters in criminal trials in Jerusalem, Irus Braverman (2007: 243) likewise notes that although interpreters are not normally perceived as active participants, the task of interpretation 'although conceived as solely mechanical . . . engages highly normative decisions'.

The enhanced role of interpreters further weakened lawyers' and judges' habitual control of witnesses (see Braverman, 2007: 257). This was particularly apparent when interpreters would ask a lawyer to clarify/repeat a question or ask a witness or a defendant to clarify/repeat an answer (see Berk-Seligson, 1990: 173–88). Berk-Seligson (1990: 199) suggests that through such 'clarification procedures' the interpreter 'unwittingly usurps some of the power of the interrogating attorney'. And yet, as the discussion above suggests, the lawyers and judges with whom I spoke appeared more conscious of the power that they had lost ('it's difficult to control the courtroom') than to whom that power may have been devolved. This did not alter the fact that the conventional four-way distribution of (differentiated) power in the courtroom (prosecution, defence, witness and judge) was now distributed five ways to include interpreters.

The discussion so far has reviewed adaptation in response to the novelty of simultaneous interpretation. It should be noted that simultaneous interpretation is, in fact, 'the child of international law' (Parker, 2011: 983), having been first developed for the Trial of the Major War Criminals before the International Military Tribunal at

Nuremberg (see Gaiba, 1998). Many of the adaptations judges and lawyers were required to make at the ICTR were experienced by their predecessors at the inception of international criminal justice. Lawyers and judges who practised at the International Military Tribunal (IMT) complained that 'cross-examination was ineffective when performed slowly' (Gaiba, 1998: 101); that when witness and lawyer spoke the same language they did not observe the pause (Gaiba, 1998: 103); and that German lawyers insisted on using 'long and complex sentences' (Gaiba, 1998: 104). The replication of all of these at the ICTR demonstrates, it can be argued, the failure to learn lessons from Nuremberg and Tokyo (see Elias-Bursać, 2015: 5).

The introduction to this chapter drew attention to how lawyers and judges responded to the lack of consensus on issues that they would normally take for granted as part of a 'hidden script' of habitual practice ('here, every tiny thing has to be discussed'; 'we take something out of our pocket and see how it fits'). I then discussed how the demands of simultaneous interpretation required lawyers and judges to accept that elements of their 'hidden script' of habitual practice (e.g. the control of witnesses in cross-examination) could not be sustained and they had to 'learn a new technique' and adopt 'Tribunal mode'. The next section further explores challenges to the 'hidden script' of habitual practice, but in a way in which the awareness of lawyers and judges of what they had lost and what had to be learned anew was far less explicit.

COMMON LAW VS. CIVIL LAW

As noted earlier, the ICTR's Statute and RPE have been described as a 'hybrid' of common ('adversarial') and civil ('inquisitorial') practice (see Ellis, 1997; Nice, 2001; Tochilovsky, 2004), even if the distinction between the two systems is open to debate (see Byrne, 2010: 256). Civil law features of the RPE included the provision that a presiding judge could order a party to shorten the estimated length of the examination-in-chief of witnesses (Rule 73bisC and 73terC); that a judge could question a witness at any time (Rule 85B); that presiding judges could summon their own witnesses or order a party to produce additional evidence (Rule 98); and that judges could admit any relevant evidence which they considered to have 'probative value', including hearsay evidence (Rule 89). Despite these provisions, the RPE remained essentially adversarial, trials taking a form almost identical to that in the United States, the UK and other Commonwealth countries (see

Apuuli, 2009: 15–17). This is not surprising given that the ICTY RPE, on which the ICTR RPE were modelled, were written by officials from the US State Department (see Cassese, 2004: 594; Wilson, 2011: 55). Lawyers and judges who practised law at the ICTR were, however, drawn from both legal systems, the ICTR Statute requiring that judges represent the 'principal legal systems of the world' (United Nations, 1994f, UN Doc. S/PV.3453: Art. 12c).

As with simultaneous interpretation, the need for practitioners from common and civil law backgrounds to adapt to each other's habitual practice was also a feature of the ICTR's predecessor at Nuremberg. Airey Neave (1978: 252), Assistant Secretary of the IMT, recalled:

> The defence suffered from their ignorance of Anglo-American Court procedure. In Continental Courts, the presiding judge is not an impartial referee. In Germany, especially, he examines and cross-examines the witnesses. It was a long time before the anxious and often hostile men understood the practice laid down by the Tribunal.

Likewise, Norman Birkett, the British Alternate Judge, wrote in his diary during the IMT trials that the 'ineffectiveness of most of the German counsel' was because they were 'unaccustomed to cross-examination and certainly do not shine in examination in chief' (Hyde, 1964: 519).

In contrast to this experience at the IMT, Kai Ambos (2003: 34) has argued that at the 'level of international criminal procedure, the common-civil law divide has been overcome' (see United Nations, 1999a, UN Doc. A/54/634: para 82). This upbeat assessment was borne out in conversations I had with ICTR judges:

> The most fascinating and challenging aspect of working here is the various backgrounds of the judges: the common law and civil law approaches. When we first started in 1996, when there were deliberations, one could see that each person brought their own baggage, their own background. But, there was a give and take element when we gave each other the opportunity. This was most surprising, we approached an issue differently, but the end results were the same. I cannot really explain it, you have to live through it. I don't even think about it now (common law judge).
>
> It's astonishing, there's so little tension. People are coming from different legal, cultural and linguistic backgrounds, it's amazing. What people say about the civil and common law traditions, that it's a war, is myth. In all my time here, none of the difference of opinion [between judges] was

based on where we came from: a civil or common law background. You have to leave your baggage at the doorstep and go through that door with an open mind (civil law judge).

Alongside the common idea of jettisoning 'baggage', judges impressed upon me that it had been an enriching process:

> One of the fascinating and enriching aspects of working here is working with people from various jurisdictions, with different backgrounds in life and in professional life. It's very, very enriching and useful. It's not easy to perceive for an outsider, you have to be in the process (common law judge).
>
> You have an Italian lawyer with that dead cat on his shoulder, a French lawyer with his *Légion d'honneur*, an American without a robe and a QC with that wig. It's a mixture, but we're all playing the same game. It's the differences that create the richness (civil law judge).

Such perspectives reflect views mentioned earlier in the chapter, regarding openness to different approaches rather than a parochial defensiveness. A civil law judge told me that:

> You know, as a boy I used to watch Perry Mason and he would say 'objection' and the judge would say 'sustained' or 'overruled'. Now I do it, even though it's not part of the civil law system of my country and it gives me great pleasure. There's an objection and there are those two catchphrases, 'sustained' and 'overruled', it's very efficient so why not use it? It's liberating.

Common law lawyers expressed to me a similar, liberating openness to alternative ways of doing things, that through practising at the ICTR 'I've learnt to think out of the box of common law, a new way of doing things. People from different systems can learn a lot if they are flexible and willing to learn' (defence lawyer); and 'Things that I assume are challenged here, which is good' (prosecution lawyer). The pragmatic benefit of this openness is borne out in an observation by a common law prosecution lawyer:

> For a common law lawyer, when the presiding judge is common law and so are the defence – although everything in that configuration is entirely common law – as I stand on my feet and I want a decision, when I have an objective, what drives me is not common law, but what I can do in a hybrid system to obtain my objective. A common law lawyer will try to find something in the civil law aspects of the Rules of Procedure and Evidence to help him and the civil law lawyer will try to find something

in the common law aspects of the Rules. Advocacy is about persuasion. I'll use any instrument available without qualms. It's purely practical. It's the same for a civil law lawyer in court. What is important is persuasion. Whatever is available, you'll use it.

A civil law prosecution lawyer made an identical observation that 'You have to decide what is best, what's efficient. You need to be less attached to personal preference, you need to adapt.'

Alongside this openness to alternatives approaches offered by the 'hybrid' system, lawyers impressed upon me the differences within common law, as illustrated in the opening episode when the prosecution lawyer states 'I think in that regard it must be a Californian practice because I practiced in New York and I've never heard an application quite like this one.' Although one US defence lawyer implied limited differences 'We speak the common law with a different accent', the dominant observation among lawyers was the diversity of common law practice, as illustrated, for example, by a US prosecution lawyer:

> [Name of English prosecution lawyer] and I are very different in the way we practise law. In the US we're aggressive, litigious, it's not elegant, it's in your face. Whether the judges like you is not important. We insult the Bench all the time in the USA. In contrast, [name of English prosecution lawyer] is very gentle, solicitous of the Bench.

His English prosecution colleague to whom he is referring had the following to say about the difference:

> Among American lawyers, there's a lack of due deference towards the judges, a feeling of trying to get around them, rather than defer to them, not in some English obsequious way, but to realize that they make the decisions and if you push them they will push back. You must find the right tone or it sounds like you're treating them like idiots. You say something like 'Your honour may have thought', goes down better to show that it was their idea. It has more elegance, adds to the sanctity of the proceedings.

Common law judges, drawn from Commonwealth countries (excluding Canada) drew attention to the behaviour of North American lawyers. A judge contrasted barristers trained in England, which he described as 'brethren', for whom 'it very rarely gets personal' with Canadian lawyers who 'have come here not to prosecute or defend, but to fight'. Another common law judge described as 'disgraceful' American lawyers yelling at one another 'you're a liar', behaviour which he maintained would lead to a lawyer being struck off by the Bar Council in his home jurisdiction. An English prosecution lawyer recounted an American lawyer standing up in court and said 'I'm really proud to represent my client who is the victim of a wrongful prosecution' noting that such behaviour in the UK would lead to a summons to the judge's chamber to be asked 'What are you doing?' because 'The question of guilt or innocence is of no importance for a British barrister.' An African common law prosecution lawyer praised the 'decorum' in his home jurisdiction in contrast to 'Canadians who do as it pleases them. They have no regard for the Bench or their colleagues.'

While common law lawyers reflected on differences within common law practice, the supposed disadvantage suffered by civil law lawyers in the predominantly adversarial, common law context of the ICTR was also a subject of discussion (see Byrne, 2010: 281). On one hand, a common law defence lawyer, commented that 'The skills of civil law lawyers in cross-examination are abysmal. Many don't get the difference between leading and non-leading questions.' Illustrating this, a common law prosecution lawyer described how in his trial 'the notion of cross-examination' was unknown to the two civil law defence lawyers and that they had asked the judges whether they could have a second cross-examination after the prosecution's re-examination. The prosecution lawyer approved of the fact the judges granted this request, that they had a 'second bite of the cherry'. The lawyer continued:

> You could see that they are at a disadvantage by the lack of their understanding of cross-examination. A common law lawyer learns not to ask questions that will incriminate their client. Common law lawyers will not ask questions because that could open a Pandora's box. But civil law lawyers do. They ask the question and then say they don't want the answer on the record! It raises the difficult question which touches on fair trial not because of the inadequacy of the counsel, but because the Tribunal recognizes lawyers from other jurisdictions.

While common law lawyers often expressed sympathy in this way, civil law defence lawyers spoke of rising to the challenge of the novel experience of cross-examination, relishing the opportunity to engage in something new:

> What excites a civil law lawyer here is that you can go at it. It's very stimulating and good criminal lawyers are absolutely up to the task.

> Those from civil law, they like it, they like the challenge. It's boring to
> do the same job all your life.
> All continental lawyers are excited by cross-examination because they
> are not normally given the time. They love investigating. They feel that
> as lawyers they have more to do.

Another civil law defence lawyer noted how 'You learn when you listen
to good common law lawyers.' This sense of civil law lawyers adapting
through observing common law practice in the courtroom was borne
out by common law practitioners, that 'Some civil lawyers are very
good, once they've seen another person they can attach it to their own
style' (judge); that 'those who are naturally good advocates adapt'
(defence); and that 'Quite a few have picked up cross-examination
swiftly' (prosecution) (see Byrne, 2010: 283–4). As a common law
prosecution lawyer suggested:

> The civil law lawyers quickly pick up what's needed. For example, they
> realise that cross-examination is simply a series of questions. Any advo-
> cate is used to asking questions, even a judge in a village. During
> examination-in-chief you may falter and ask leading questions, but
> examination-in-chief is the opportunity for the witness to tell their
> story and a smart lawyer will pick this up.

The idea of the 'smart lawyer' and her ability to adapt was often
explained to me as being a matter of 'personality':

> You should see [name of civil law lawyer]. He's brilliant and he's from
> a civil law background. It's more to do with personality than whether
> someone has a common law or civil law background, it's about personal
> skill, it depends on the individual (common law defence).
> There are good and bad cross-examinations from both the civil and
> common law systems. It's a matter of personality, the individual person
> (common law judge).
> It's more about the person than the system they come from. It's not in
> the training, but a good lawyer has good reflexes, the ability to look at
> both perspectives (common law prosecution).

In the discussion above, lawyers and judges are conscious of, reflect
upon and narrate the adaptation required in the presence of novel
procedures emanating from civil and common law. Such experiences
required externalizing what was habitual and 'taken for granted'
('Practising here makes you think about what you are doing, how you
do things.'). Assessment of that externalization was, for many, marked
by an openness to adapt ('I'll use any instrument available without

qualms. It's purely practical.'); a rejection of parochial chauvinism ('Who the hell cares how things are done in the old country?') and a celebration of diversity ('It's the differences that create the richness.'). The claim that the ICTR represented a successful hybrid of common and civil law (see Ambos, 2003: 34) appears to be borne out by the fact that some civil law lawyers adapted through experience and it depended on personality rather than background. This illustrates Elena Baylis' (2008: 377) observation, that while relevant knowledge for international lawyers and judges is assumed to be restricted to 'a limited set of authoritative legal documents and texts', other forms of knowledge, including 'relational skills ... to work successfully with a diverse set of international co-workers from numerous legal back-grounds' (Baylis, 2015: 273; see Introduction) was an important form of knowledge. Such apparent accommodation fails to take account, how-ever, of elements of the courtroom's 'hidden scripts' that defy conscious description, principally the embodied elements of 'legal *habitus*'.

EMBODIED COMPETENCE

The use of the term 'personality' to describe civil law lawyers who successfully adapted implies an intangible quality that cannot be ade-quately captured by reference to formal training. As discussed above, practitioners in domestic legal systems operate according to both codi-fied and hidden scripts (see Zoettl, 2016), the 'written and unwritten laws' of the judicial field (Bourdieu, 1987: 831). The suggestion here is that the 'hidden script' encompasses a spectrum of habitual expecta-tions ranging from those which can be easily described to those that are more intangible such as 'personality'.

Jerome Bruner (1990: 48) reminds us that in every context 'we take for granted that people behave in a manner appropriate to the setting in which they find themselves'. This is the case for lawyers and judges, Meierhenrich (2013: 51, 33) observing that 'a substantial part of every-day lawyering rests on habitual, routinised, ritualistic, repetitive or mundane behaviour', much of which remains unreflected upon because it is 'part and parcel of [the lawyer or judge's] being'. As in any established order, the practice of the courtroom (re)produces the 'nat-uralization of its own arbitrariness' (Bourdieu, 1987: 164). In other words, the rules of behaviour are arbitrary, but what is 'taken for granted' is treated as if it were 'self-evident, transparently normal' (Bourdieu, 1987: 812). For Bourdieu (2003[1977]: 72n71) *habitus* is this internalized, taken-for-granted, habitual way of understanding and acting in a given context according to disposition:

> The word disposition seems particularly suited to express what is covered by the concept of *habitus* . . . a way of being, a habitual state (especially of the body) and, in particular, a predisposition, tendency, propensity, or inclination.

Here, Bourdieu (2003[1977]: 72n71) emphasizes embodiment ('especially of the body'). Writing on the composition of professional groups (lawyers, academics, medical practitioners), Bourdieu (1984: 56) argues that the 'fee for admission' to such a group is 'a corporeal *hexis*' which he describes as 'a style of expression and thought, and of all those "indefinable somethings," pre-eminently physical, which we call "spirit"'. This corresponds with Goffman's (1959: 23, 27) idea of the 'social front' associated with a profession which includes 'posture; speech patterns; facial expressions; bodily gestures' which are institutionalized as 'abstract stereotyped expectations'. 'Corporeal *hexis*' is, therefore, the part of *habitus* which allows communication between people to take place through fine-grained body language (see Chapter 2). Bourdieu (2003[1977]: 94) acknowledges Goffman's (1991[1968]: 1–124) notion of the 'total institution' in which the 'insignificant details of dress, bearing, physical and verbal manners' are impressed upon new members. This implies that a 'corporeal *hexis*' can be learned in the 'educational apprenticeship' through which lawyers pass.

On one hand, some of this competency will be conscious. Research on legal training indicates that appropriate forms of dress and movement are acquired through imitation during 'training contracts' for English solicitors (see Sommerlad, 2007: 212, 213) and 'pupillage' for English barristers (see Pirie and Rogers, 2012). Other forms of competency will, however, be less amenable to explicit description. For Bourdieu (2003[1977]: 87) 'practical mastery' is 'transmitted in practice . . . without attaining the level of discourse'. Such principles embodied in this way are 'placed beyond the grasp of consciousness' (Bourdieu, 2003[1977]: 94) and 'cannot even be made explicit'. Practical mastery, therefore, is embedded in the very perceptions and dispositions of the body and hence is known only in practice as the way things are done (Bourdieu, 2003[1977]: 91) as a form of 'ritual mastery' (Bell 1992: 107).

Just as Bernard S. Jackson (1990: 42) argues that how judges and lawyers act in a courtroom is not 'adequately represented in doctrinal

textbooks' but depends upon the 'internalization of observed behaviour' (see Morison and Leith, 1992: 3), so Bourdieu (1984: 59)
observes that the 'fee' of embodied competence required for entry to
professional groups, including lawyers, is all the more powerful if it is
'less objectified, less formalized' more of an 'art', that 'can only be
acquired in the long term, and at first hand'. This implies it cannot
be taught or formalized in a teaching text, contributing to the difficulty lawyers may have in describing their elusive 'artistry' (Bourdieu,
2003[1977]: 94). Erving Goffman (1959: 108; see also Bourdieu, 1990:
91) notes the difficulty that actors have in describing elements of their
habitual practice, that they 'tend to take many of these standards for
granted, not realising they have done so until an accident, or crisis, or
peculiar circumstance occurs'. This corresponds with Pierre
Bourdieu's (2003[1977]: 94) notion of 'legal *habitus*' in which principles are embodied in a way that resists explicit description and with
Zoettl's (2016: 7) observation that the 'hidden rules' of the courtroom
'are usually left unspoken as long as they are observed, being rendered
explicit only when disregarded'. Such (embodied) 'artistry' is part of
the non-codified, 'extra-legal knowledge' discussed by Morison and
Leith (1992: 17; see Introduction) and a component of the 'extratextual and subtextual language' of the courtroom (Martin, 2006:
10–11; see Chapter 2).

Common law practitioners at the ICTR attested to the way the
'apprentice insensibly and unconsciously acquires the principles of
the "art"' (Bourdieu, 2003[1977]: 88), reflecting again Zoettl's
(2016) distinction between a publicly codified script and a hidden
script:

> In a national jurisdiction everyone knows the procedure and what
> etiquette is needed. A lot of court etiquette in the UK is not statutory,
> but is observed by custom and habit over the years. In the good old days
> you'd eat dinners in the Inns of Court and what have you, you'd gone
> through it, you'd know what was expected, you just do it (judge).
> In the UK, hobnobbing with the judges is part of the training, you go to
> dinners where they regale you with their boring stories. It's an osmotic
> process; you get to know how they think (prosecution lawyer).

All legal practitioners at the ICTR possessed a legal *habitus*, composed
of what they took for granted, including appropriate 'posture; speech
patterns; facial expressions; bodily gestures' (Goffman 1959: 23, 27).
Each *habitus* imposed different ideas of what were 'natural or reasonable'

or 'unthinkable or scandalous' practices (Bourdieu, 1987: 78). Furthermore, given that Bourdieu (1992: 133) maintained that *habitus* was 'durable but not eternal', each practitioner's *habitus* was open to both reinforcement and/or modification in the novel context of the ICTR.

When describing one particular common law defence lawyer, common law lawyers spoke in a manner redolent of Bourdieu's 'corporeal *hexis*' in the sense of a 'style of expression and thought ... of all those "indefinable somethings", pre-eminently physical, which we call "spirit"' (Bourdieu, 1984: 56):

> In our trial, the Americans and French have adopted Crown Court etiquette. Part of the reason was [name of a English defence lawyer]. He imposed it by doing it with authority and attractively rather than by dint of commanding it. If you try to operate to high standards with a few demonstrations, by dint of influence and example, you can affect the people around you (defence).
>
> The whole feeling of the courtroom was different when he was there, the way in which his behaviour, his way of acting had an effect on the whole defence, even on the prosecution and the judges themselves. Everyone responded to the way he acted (defence).
>
> Those sorts of people, they have the ear of the court. There's a social dynamic, others watch someone who has the ear of the court, it brings everyone else's game up. It's like playing with a great footballer. People follow the game of a good person (prosecution).

These comments substantiate the sense of an embodied artistry that resists adequate description. The comments also demonstrate the desire to emulate ('Everyone responded to the way he acted') suggesting that elements of habitus were modified and that the durability of dispositions taught at law school (see Good, 2004: paras 53–9) and through experience is not as intransigent as some writers suggest (Tochilovsky, 2004: 324; Ellis, 1997: 525–6).

The embodied elements of legal *habitus* indicated by the description of this particular lawyer ('Everyone responded to the way he acted') are best explored through the seemingly mundane practice of standing. The regulation of standing and sitting was an essential feature of the 'hidden script' at the ICTR just as Zoettl (2016: 5–6) found that it was 'meticulously enforced by the presiding judge' in Portuguese courts as if the least deviation from the regulations would rob the proceedings of their character and make them worthless. Such regulation contributed to designating the courtroom as a 'play-ground' in which the rules of ordinary life were suspended; where an 'absolute and peculiar order reigns' (Huizinga, 1949: 10, 12, 19; see Chapter 2). The rules of sitting and standing it could be argued are 'the most visible and at the same time the best hidden (because most natural) manifestation of submission to the established order' precisely because they 'extort the essential while seeming to demand the insignificant' (Bourdieu, 2003[1977]: 95; see Carlen, 1976: 20). Apparently insignificant, standing and sitting down, were, in fact significant because 'a single note off key can disrupt the tone of an entire performance' (Goffman, 1959: 56).

At the ICTR, everyone in the courtroom and public gallery had to stand when the judges entered (see Chapter 2); witnesses made the oath standing; defendants entered a plea standing and had to stand when the judgement was delivered. The concern here, however, is with the standing and sitting of lawyers, its relationship to legal *habitus* and what it indicates about the issues discussed earlier in this chapter: divergence within common law and the relationship between common law and civil law practitioners.

At the first trial I attended in 2005, a defence lawyer was in the process of cross-examining a prosecution witness. The prosecution lawyer stood up to object to a particular question. The defence lawyer refused, on this occasion, to yield, remained standing and said 'I am not going to talk across the court' at which point the common law presiding judge said 'I will not have two counsel on their feet at the same time.' A common law defence lawyer explained to me that 'There's a fairly strict rule in English courts that only one person should be on feet at the same time.' Having witnessed this, I assumed, the practice of 'English courts' has been adopted, that lawyers were only allowed to speak when standing and only one lawyer could stand at any one moment (lawyers also stood up when they were spoken to by a judge). I witnessed a desire to enforce this rule in the courtroom, for example, an English defence lawyer chastised an African (Commonwealth) prosecution lawyer, saying 'I was on my feet first and in courtroom etiquette whoever is on their feet first continues and he knows that and he knows that he should not interrupt counsel on their feet.' In conversation, common law judges were keen to impress on me the need to enforce this element of common law's 'hidden script':

> Generally, in Commonwealth countries, two counsel are not on their feet at the same time. An English barrister will expect to sit down when someone else rises to speak. But the French will continue to stand and

even address the court sitting down. You never address the court if not on your feet, the court would never hear it. The French counsel do not have that etiquette. In court one expects good manners, to listen to one person at a time, otherwise you don't know who to pay attention to (common law judge).

Etiquette is very important in the common law tradition I am used to. For examples, we have to tell lawyers that when their opposite is speaking you must sit down. These are important etiquette matters. It looks offensive to us (common law judge).

As for people standing at the same time, we can only hear one person at a time, otherwise it's difficult to hear. One at a time is most ideal. There are other practices elsewhere, in other jurisdictions, but that's what normally happens. All are free to speak here, but one after another (common law judge).

Other conversations further established in my mind that the common law principle by which standing simultaneously indicates the desire to speak and grants permission to speak once a speaking opponent sits had been widely adopted at the ICTR. As a common law defence lawyer observed 'In the trial I was in, the presiding judge came from civil law, but despite that, she seemed to have a very, very clear common law approach to court etiquette regarding standing.' I also witnessed a civil law defence lawyer make this explicit in the courtroom, commenting 'I see my learned friend is on his feet' before sitting down. When I asked an English lawyer about this, he replied 'Yes, they've learned to do that in our trial.' The example of the unwritten rule of standing appeared to illustrate the embodied nature of legal habitus and the adoption by civil law lawyers indicating that 'legal *habitus*' is 'durable but not eternal' (Bourdieu and Wacquant, 1992: 133).

Over time, however, it became apparent that the issue was not necessarily one of common law vs. civil law practice. In the example used above, in which the judge said 'I will not have two counsel on their feet at the same time', three of those involved, the presiding judge, prosecution lawyer and defence lawyer, were all barristers who had trained in England. This admonition was not of a civil law lawyer, one of those who 'do not have that etiquette' (common law judge), but of those who described themselves as 'brethren'.

This issue was driven home to me on another occasion. The two co-judges were both from Commonwealth (common law) countries, while the presiding judge, although from a civil law country, had, on previous days, acknowledged a lawyer's desire to speak by saying 'Mr [name] is on his feet.' While this implied adoption of the speech/standing nexus, the US prosecution lawyer, who had examined a prosecution witness over the last couple of days, had never sat down when the Canadian defence lawyer rose to make an objection. Today, it was the Canadian defence lawyer's turn to cross-examine the same prosecution witness. After a few minutes, the defence lawyer's co-counsel (also Canadian) rose to assist his colleague, at which point:

Co-Judge: Mr [name], just for good order, courtroom order, isn't it possible that when you want to stand up, you let Mr. [name] sit down and when you want to sit down, you let . . .

Defence Lawyer: No. No. Let me explain . . .

Co-Judge: I mean, if you are sharing it question by question, that's fine. But let us know who is on their feet.

Defence Co-Counsel: [explains he is assisting his colleague].

Co-Judge: I have grown up in the common law tradition, and there courtroom practice requires that there is always one counsel on his feet, never two counsels.

While this censure was clearly inconsistent given the earlier behaviour of the common law (US) prosecution lawyer, the real significance of this statement is that the judge should make it at all. The very act of explicitly articulating the principle suggests a consciousness of a breakdown in habitual practice, an anxiety to re-establish a norm, a 'hidden rule' that was 'being rendered explicit only when disregarded' (Zoettl, 2016: 7).

All involved in this, and the previous, incident were Commonwealth-trained lawyers (the two Canadian defence lawyers and the co-judge); this was not a confrontation between common and civil law. The norm was rendered explicit among those for whom it was supposedly habitual. The examination of standing/sitting at the ICTR indicates three things. First, that the supposed confrontation between common and civil law must acknowledge that the former is diverse ('Canadians do as it pleases them') and that practitioners from the latter are adaptive ('The civil law lawyers quickly pick up what's needed.'). Second, that lawyers are willing to disregard habitual practice ('just because we have one way of doing something doesn't mean it's better'). Finally, the novel conditions of the ICTR required judges to articulate what normally remained unsaid ('let us know who is on their feet'), thereby revealing the central role played by 'unwritten', often embodied 'hidden rules' in ordinary, domestic courtrooms.

LEGAL ACCRETION (RULES OF PROCEDURE AND EVIDENCE)

The theme of this chapter has been the way in which the ICTR challenged the habitual practices of lawyers and judges. This final section continues that theme by exploring the way in which the 'codified script' of the ICTR's RPE were deployed as a fixed regulator of courtroom practice while simultaneously being modified to reflect evolving practice (including clashes of 'hidden rules') in the courtroom. In the Introduction to this book, I discussed how references by lawyers and judges to 'the Tribunal' created an image of 'transcendent justice' that is not 'confined totally to persons' (Garapon, 2001: 28) but is 'somewhere else, always out of reach' (Feldman, 2004: 193). Here I suggest that the RPE played a similar role as all in the courtroom were required to submit to an impersonal text (that of the RPE), even if that text was modified to reflect evolving practice in the courtroom.

Appeals to the RPE were a prominent feature of courtroom exchanges. A prosecution lawyer, for example, contested the alleged non-disclosure of documents to the defence by referring to 'Rule 66' or when a presiding judge asked a defence lawyer whether a document was a 'judicial record', the prosecution lawyer referred to 'Rule 98'. Especially prominent were debates concerning Rule 89 ('Rules of Evidence'):

> The Chambers shall not be bound by national rules of Evidence ... a Chamber shall apply rules of evidence which will best favour a fair determination of the matter before it and are consonant with the spirit of the Statute and the general principles of law. A Chamber may admit any relevant evidence which it deems to have probative value.

This Rule required significant adaptation from common law lawyers. In domestic common law jurisdictions, lay juries are the 'triers of fact' and are protected from inappropriate testimony by rules of evidence that determine admissibility. In the absence of a jury, the ICTR judges were 'triers of law' (made legal rulings) and 'triers of fact' (decided whether/how an event happened). As 'professional judges' it was assumed that they did not need to be 'protected' by exclusionary rules of evidence and they should admit any 'relevant evidence' they considered had 'probative value' (Rule 89(C)) and then decide on relative 'weight' as they deliberated the judgement (see Good, 2007: 144–5; see Chapter 4). For this reason, hearsay, that is reporting what someone else witnessed, could be admitted at the ICTR if it was considered relevant and to have probative value. This freedom also reflects the civil law system in which there are no equivalents to common law rules that exclude hearsay because judges 'may draw inferences from any factual information submitted to them' (Weinstock, 1986: 19).

Whereas a common law judge described admissibility of hearsay as 'the major difference' from his home jurisdiction and that it still jarred with him, he argued that 'you get used to it'. Likewise, another common law judge argued that despite hearsay being contrary to his common law background, its admission was necessary because the length of time that had passed since the crimes had been committed meant that 'witnesses are unavailable and you need to get evidence from other sources'. Common law defence lawyers were, however, more vociferous in their condemnation, describing the admissibility of hearsay as a 'negation of justice'; an 'erosion of the rules of evidence in civilized communities'; and that 'no system of law in the world would accept hearsay evidence in crimes as serious as these'. Despite such views regarding elements of the RPE, lawyers had to simply live with or pragmatically use the RPE whether or not they corresponded to their habitual practice at home, as summarized by the common law prosecution lawyer quoted earlier in the chapter: 'I'll use any instrument available without qualms. It's purely practical. It's the same for a civil law lawyer in court.'

As discussed in Chapter 2, the courtroom is established through ritualization that establishes a distinct set of rules that differentiate the activities therein (see Huizinga, 1949: 10, 12, 19; Bell, 1992: 90). David Parkin (1992: 13) notes that while participants (and observers) in a ritualized space remain 'united by a sense of the occasion as being in some way rule-governed and as necessarily so in order to be complete, efficacious, and proper', ritualization is always 'an arena of contradictory and contestable perspectives – participants having their own reasons, viewpoints, and motives [a ritual] in fact is made up as it goes along'. Applied to the ICTR, Parkin's observation suggests that whatever the misgivings lawyers and judges may have had about the RPE, submission to them was necessary. And yet, to only acknowledge that submission would be to privilege the first feature noted by Parkin ('rule-governed') and obscure the second feature ('made up as it goes along').

Right from the start, the RPE were designed to evolve. The ICTR Statute (United Nations, 1994e: Art. 14) stated that the ICTR judges would adopt the RPE of the ICTY 'with such changes as they deem necessary'. Writing three years later, Rod Dixon (1997: 82) suggested the 'generality' of the RPE indicated that they 'deliberately invite an expansive interpretation to fill in the missing spaces' although he believed it would not be 'feasible to continuously amend and add to the rules'. The ICTR's RPE were, however, continuously amended and added to by the ICTR judiciary at an annual 'Plenary Session', the proceedings of which were confidential because, as an ALO explained to me, there was a concern that lawyers would exploit the knowledge that an individual judge disagreed with a particular rule. While representatives from the prosecution were invited to suggest rule changes, the same invitation was not extended to the defence.

Although the number of rules remained constant at 126 the English translation expanded from 11,000 to 25,000 words from 1995 to 2014.[1] These amendments were justified as expediting proceedings, modifications being made in response to omissions and contradictions encountered in the daily practice of the court (see Dieng, 2001; Moghalu, 2002: 34; United Nations, 1999a). An ALO summarized this justification:

> Changes arise from what the judges consider inconvenient things, a rule that means that trials will run more how they want to run them. However, the rules weren't written especially well, they didn't contemplate things that came up. It's a system where there's a lot of uncertainty. If judges adopt a position in practice regarding a rule they put them into the RPEs as soon as possible.

When I asked the ALO why there was no commentary on why a Rule had been modified, he explained that 'every change is the outcome of an actual case' which meant that 'when a change is made, everyone understands the context of a rule change, everyone is aware of the past experience which has led to a change in the rules.' He added that there was a strong argument that 'if judges have discretion in the courtroom, then why not write a rule that reflects the practice?'

In practice this meant that lawyers were required to adapt their habitual, domestic practice to the RPE (in relation, for example, to 'hearsay'), while the RPE were simultaneously being adapted to the courtroom practice in which the same lawyers participated. Such a dialectic, symbiotic relationship sat uneasily with the need for the

---

[1] See http://unictr.unmict.org/en/documents/rules-procedure-and-evidence.

RPE to be independent from courtroom practice in order to regulate it. The 'codified script' of regulations such as the ICTR's RPE were designed to enable judges' resolutions to appear not as 'naked exercises of power', but as the 'necessary result of a principled interpretation of a unanimously accepted' text immune from the vagaries of individual arbitrariness (Bourdieu, 1987: 818; see Woolford, 2010). Such rules were required to maintain an appearance of implementing neutral, impersonal principles.

The RPE at the ICTR correspond (in accelerated microcosm) to all legal systems which claim adherence to independent regulation (judicial precedent or legal code), but are, in reality, constructed from a continuous, adaptive, piecemeal process of accretion (see Falk Moore, 2000: 9, 11; Humphreys, 1985: 253). As Bourdieu (1987: 828) notes, the 'elasticity of texts' allows judges to discover 'new possibilities in them' through a form of 'sublimation' which enable the appearance that a 'decision expresses not the will or the world-view of the judge but the will of the law'. This maintains the same principle discussed in the Introduction to this book, that references to 'the Chamber' and 'the Tribunal' are used to imply that the law 'cannot be ... confined totally to persons' (Garapon, 2001: 28).

From this perspective, revising the RPE was a sleight of hand whereby emergent, contingent practice was transformed to impersonal, authoritative regulation. Recasting day-to-day practice as ossified text ('If judges have discretion in the courtroom, then why not write a rule that reflects the practice?'):

> removes norms from the contingency of a particular situation by establishing an exemplary judgement ... in a form designed to become a model for later decisions. This form simultaneously authorizes and fosters the logic of precedent upon which specifically juridical thought and action are based (Bourdieu, 1987: 845).

By revising the RPE everyone in the courtroom could treat them as if they were static, autonomous and authorless, when, in reality, they contained codifications of their own courtroom practice, formalized by the same judges who evoked the Rules as if they were entirely autonomous. The judges needed an autonomous referent, but it was accomplished by the (re)constructive work of the judges themselves. This process was facilitated by an appeal to 'core principles' in order to preserve an aura of consistency so that revised rules attained legitimacy by giving the impression that 'all new rules are somehow logically related to old ones, either consciously or unconsciously playing out certain themes throughout ... The whole then becomes as apparently logical as if it had been intentional' (Falk Moore, 2000: 10; see Sarat and Kearns, 2002: 4–9).

Pragmatic modifications of the RPE were, therefore, portrayed not as creations, but as clarifications, not as innovations, but revelations of immanent principles. The Rules were treated as a consistent whole that existed prior to any amendment, a comprehensive logic awaiting discovery. This systematization created the appearance of a transcendental basis obscuring the degree to which it was 'made up as it goes along' (Parkin 1992:13).

Lawyers at the ICTR did 'care about what happens in the old country', the rejection of 'hearsay' by some for example, and they did refer to practice in their home jurisdictions ('Isn't that common practice in every jurisdiction?'). Ultimately, however, they had to adapt to the 'codified script' of the RPE, both resigning themselves to what was contrary to their familiar practice and adopting new alternatives ('I'll use any instrument available without qualms.'). However, we should not let the image of lawyers adapting to the RPE obscure the fact that the RPE were simultaneously an adaption to courtroom practice in which lawyers played an integral part. While revealing the particular nature of adaptation at the ICTR, this process also reconfirms the general observation that law is claimed to be an expression of transcendent principles but is, in reality, the codification (in text) of personal, contingent practice (see Falk Moore, 2000: 9–10).

CONCLUSION

This chapter began with considering Peter Zoettl's (2016) discussion of the distinction between a public and a hidden script in the courtrooms. Every courtroom and every legal practitioner in the world follows (often embodied) scripts, learned through an 'osmotic process' of emulation so that these scripts become 'self-evident, transparently normal' (Bourdieu, 1987: 812) in ways that are 'placed beyond the grasp of consciousness' (Bourdieu, 2003[1977]: 94). These scripts 'are usually left unspoken as long as they are observed, being rendered explicit only when disregarded' (Zoettl, 2016: 7). It is normally laypersons, strangers in the 'play-ground' (Huizinga, 1949: 10) who provoke the need to be explicit.

In the exceptional case of the ICTR, however, it was legal practitioners who, faced with a series of impediments (simultaneous interpretation, unfamiliar procedure), were required to make explicit to themselves that which they had previously taken for granted ('Practising here makes you think about what you are doing, how you do things'). In so doing, many lawyers and judges did not display precious, parochial adherence to what they were used to and suggested the existence of an adaptable, common legal 'personality type' ('It's not in the training, but a good lawyer has good reflexes, the ability to look at both perspectives').

This process made explicit what had previously been implicit, whether it be controlling witnesses in cross-examination or the relationship between standing and speaking. And yet, there were still elements of habitual 'artistry' (Bourdieu 2003[1977]: 94) that resisted simple description as in the attempts by lawyers to describe the colleague ('The whole feeling of the courtroom was different when he was there.'). This suggests that there was much that remained elusive, beyond the grasp of description.

The discussion above contributes to the call in the Introduction to move away from the domination of texts in the study of trials and recognize that the lawyer is 'fully social individual' (Morison and Leith, 1992: 19) and law a 'necessarily flawed human process' (Morison and Leith, 1992: vii). Such a call, however, always encounters resistance, as seen in the way that the constant revision of the codified RPE served to obscure the 'flawed human process' of the courtroom which gave rise to the need for the revisions in the first place.

4

'THEY DON'T SAY WHAT THEY MEAN OR MEAN WHAT THEY SAY'

Courtroom III, 9am. A protected, Rwandan prosecution witness is being cross-examined and is speaking in Kinyarwanda. The anglophone defence lawyer returns to parts of the witness's testimony discussed the previous day. The witness complains 'We shouldn't be going back to issues that have already been dealt with.' The judge gently explains to her that 'lawyers' questions assist the Court in evaluating the quality and accuracy of your testimony and it is sometimes necessary to revisit issues'. Asked where in a photograph of the crime scene she was standing in 1994, the witness tells the lawyer to consult her statement 'I think everything is written therein.' The defence lawyer then refers to a list of names the witness had been asked to write on the previous day of people present on a specific day in 1994. The lawyer asks her why she has never mentioned the presence of a particular person before in two statements to the ICTR, three statements made to the Rwandan authorities and testimony in another ICTR trial. 'Listen, Counsel', replies the witness, 'When you give accounts of all the events that took place during the war, you cannot mention all the details. I am not a computer. Don't be surprised that even today I could give you some new information' (during this exchange the English interpreter interjects to indicate that she has chosen not to interpret a name the witness has just mentioned).

The lawyer shows the witness a statement the witness gave to the ICTR eight years earlier and asks if she can see her signature, 'I cannot speak French. I do not know French. You must forgive me. I am not educated.' The lawyer then reads another statement (given two years earlier) and asks 'It's a different story, isn't it, that you are telling in this statement?' Confronted with different statements the witness explains 'If I had known that the matter was going to continue, I would have written things down. I have told you that I did not retain everything in my memory. I'm not a computer. But as we keep talking, some information comes back to mind.' When challenged by the defence lawyer about times given for events in 1994, the witness replies 'you know when you are waiting to die at any moment, you can't retain information concerning hours, night or day'. Unable to account for differences in her statements, the witness continues 'I should like to tell you that when one loses someone one is so shocked, so affected, that one forgets.' Exasperated by the lawyer's line of questioning, the witness says 'Don't you understand what I am saying or am I the person who is not understanding what is being said through the interpreter?'

Over 3,000 witnesses gave testimony at the ICTR from 1996 to 2014 (United Nations, 2011a, UN Doc. S/PV.6678: 8). Most were Rwandan, around one-third were women and 80 per cent were 'protected'. Flown to Arusha under supervision; accommodated in safe houses; hidden behind curtains in the courtroom; referred to by pseudonyms such as FE13 and CF23, their sensitive testimony was heard in 'closed session' and any identifying information redacted from public transcripts. Given that it is a criminal offence to reveal the identity of protected witnesses it is difficult to directly access their experience of the trial (see African Rights & Redress 2008: 55–71).

Scholars reflecting on the participation of African witnesses in international trials have argued that 'culture' is an impediment (Almqvist, 2006; Bostian, 2005; Combs, 2009; Kelsall, 2009). Nancy Combs (2009: 252), for example, writes that '[c]ultural differences between the witnesses and Western court personnel [are] an additional impediment to accurate fact-finding'. While some of the judges and lawyers with whom I spoke at the ICTR supported this position, others placed emphasis on other impediments unrelated to Rwandan culture, Examples of these appear in the episode recounted above, including the issue of memory ('I am not a computer'), especially under extreme circumstances ('When you are waiting to die') and after personal loss ('when one loses someone ... one forgets'). In addition, there is tension between an assumption that a witness statement is comprehensive ('I think everything is written therein') and recognition that each time testimony is elicited new information may emerge ('even today I could give some new information'). These impediments to testimony are compounded by the requirements of the Court, including the unfamiliar practices of the courtroom that need to be explained by the judge ('lawyers' questions assist the Court'); the restriction of the ICTR's official languages of French and English ('I cannot speak French'); the suspicion that interpretation may be impeding the exchange ('am I the person who is not understanding what is being said through the interpreter?') and the need for lawyers, judges, interpreters and the witness to censure themselves in order to preserve the witness's anonymity (the interpreter chooses not to repeat a name mentioned by the witness).

This chapter will interrogate the role assigned to 'culture' by scholars by evaluating these other impediments that could have been misinterpreted as being 'cultural'. The chapter begins by considering the way in which 'culture' is 'demonised' (see Merry, 2003) as a backward attribute of hapless victims that can be 'saved' by international criminal tribunals (see Schwöbel-Patel, 2016). Acknowledging that some judges and lawyers at the ICTR did consider Rwandan culture to be an impediment, the chapter then considers the alternative impediments (simultaneous interpretation, the question and answer format of witness examination, protection orders and the consequences of multiple testimony). The chapter ends by asking whether the blame placed on witnesses' 'culture' should in fact be placed on 'legal culture'.

DEMONIZED CULTURE

A number of scholars have argued that witnesses' 'culture' has impeded their ability to give credible testimony in international trials. In her review of transcripts from the ICTR, the Special Court for Sierra Leone and the Special Panels in the Dili District Court in East Timor, the legal scholar Nancy Combs (2009: 239–40; 251–61) observes that testimony is often vague, that witnesses are unable to answer questions clearly, read maps, comment on photographs, recall dates and times, estimate distances or quantities; and that there was inconsistency between different statements and testimony. Combs (2009: 252) suggests that intentional dishonesty on the part of the witness cannot be ruled out and that education and translation are also possible causes, but concludes, that 'an inability to answer certain questions may be driven less by educational factors than by cultural factors' (see Bostian 2005).

Echoing these observations, the political scientist Tim Kelsall (2009: 183) states that much of the testimony in the trial (2004–6) of leaders of the Civil Defence Forces at the Special Court for Sierra Leone was ambiguous and vague and that witnesses 'often gave accounts of events that were disjointed, entangled or contained small or large inconsistencies or ellipses'. Kelsall (2009: 184, 200) acknowledges this may have been caused by 'trauma, imperfect perception and memory lapse', simultaneous interpretation or the 'sheer unfamiliarity of the setting'. Kelsall (2009: 175), also states, however, that 'Indirectness, obliqueness, dissembling and circumspection are practiced arts' and that these were 'culturally grounded strategies of concealment' (Kelsall, 2009: 3). While Kelsall's observations draw on his research in Sierra Leone, he extends them to Rwanda, stating that 'rather like Uganda and Rwanda, Sierra Leone is a society with a number of cultural features that contributed to making the application of international justice a fraught affair' (Kelsall, 2009: 17). Although acknowledging other explanations for the difficulties encountered in trials (trauma, memory, simultaneous interpretation, education) Combs and Kelsall suggest that African 'culture' was a key impediment. This chapter assesses whether such a suggestion is justified.

Kelsall's (2009: 3) argument that 'culturally grounded strategies of concealment' are also present in Rwanda finds support in commentary on Rwandan culture. Drawing on the work of Aloys Rukebesha (1985), Cornelis-Marinus Overdulve (1997: 275), a Presbyterian missionary who spent 25 years in Rwanda, suggests that in pre-colonial Rwanda, communication was determined by strategies for survival and that, as a consequence, a speaker's goal was not 'to provide objectively correct information, but to consolidate his own social position and the positive disposition of his superior towards him'. According to Overdulve (1997: 279), in Rwanda an interlocutor's goal is not to communicate truth, but rather to ask 'what is it that he would like to hear? How can I keep him happy and avoid him having a bad opinion of me?' Overdule (1997: 275) argues that such evasiveness has 'become a part of daily life skills' and is seen as a sign of 'wisdom and prudence' (Overdulve, 1997: 282; see Sibomana et al., 1999: 78).

Even though Overdulve supports his argument with reference to work by Rwandans (Rukebesha, 1985) there is a need to be cautious about essentializing views of culture that propose that 'a group is defined by a distinctive culture and that cultures are discrete, clearly bounded and internally homogeneous' (Cowan et al., 2001: 3). In contrast to essentialism, contemporary anthropologists consider it is 'more illuminating to think of culture as a field of creative interchange and contestation . . . and continuous transformation' (Cowan *et al.*, 2001: 5). As a consequence, culture is 'marked by hybridity and creolization rather than uniformity or consistency' (Merry, 2003: 67). The notion that groups (including the citizens of whole nations) can be characterized by a 'culture' remains rife, however, particularly within the field of human rights. In her research on the international human rights system and its approach to violence against women, Sally Merry (2003: 63, 71) notes a general tendency displayed by UN human rights bodies to 'culturalize problems' and 'demonize' culture so that it emerges as an obstacle'. Merry (2003: 60) notes how culture is typically talked about as a 'barrier to progress' and that this critique 'builds on imperial understandings of culture as belonging to the domain of the primitive or backward, in contrast to the civilisation of the coloniser'. Such approaches both essentialize culture (as in Overdulve's description above) but also (in contrast to Overdulve) demean that culture. Women's subordination, for example, is blamed on 'cultural practices' rather than economic or political conditions. Regarding issues as diverse as child marriage in Kenya (Archambault, 2011): child prostitution in Thailand (Montgomery, 2001); and female genital circumcision (FGC) in East Africa (Koomen, 2014b), anthropologists have demonstrated how 'culture' is employed as a convenient explanation for practices that have far more diverse explanations (child marriage and prostitution are responses to socio-economic insecurity, contemporary forms of FGC are a response to attempts at eradication etc.).

The deployment of essentialized, demeaned 'culture' strengthens the sense of a gulf between 'ourselves, rational observers of the human condition, and those other people, enmeshed in their traditional patterns of belief and practice' (Ingold, 1993: 212). This contributes to the perception of an 'other' who is often portrayed as being in need of 'enlightenment' (see Abu-Lughod, 1991), a move that re-asserts a 'dominant-subordinate' relationship with hapless 'locals' in need of rescue (see Nader, 1969: 289; Introduction). Alexander Hinton (2016: 263) detected this relationship at the ECCC, where the trial of Duch was portrayed as the action of a 'saviour' (the 'international community') rescuing 'a backward society by bringing democracy, justice, the rule of law, and human rights'.

This tendency to essentialize and demean 'culture' has also been detected in court proceedings. Miriam Ticktin (1999: 27, 30) reflecting on the case of Kiranjit Ahluwali (an Indian-born women whose life sentence for killing her husband in the UK was overturned due to 'diminished responsibility') notes how Ahluwali was presented at her appeal according to 'neo-colonial views of pitiable Asian women', in which an essentialized, culture 'external to oneself, as something frozen, quantifiable, alienable' was pathologized to partly explain her 'mental abnormality'. This reaffirmed a 'colonial discourse that defines Asians as abnormal, as Other' (Ticktin, 1999: 30). In a similar vein, writing on asylum cases in the United States, Michelle McKinley (1997: 71) notes how those advocating for asylum seekers 'have to present the persecution of refugee women in the most tragic and convincing light – which, inevitably deploys stereotypical notions of the alien, the Orient, the African etc.' illustrated with 'cultural practices' like FGC and arranged marriages.

Sonia Lawrence (2001: 113) found the same tendency among legal practitioners in Canadian trials involving violence against women from ethnic minorities. Lawrence suggests that there is a 'cultural racism' in courtrooms which claims to be a 'sensitive recognition of difference', but in reality 'recognises difference only to decry its existence and to imply the superiority of White mainstream norms'. Lawrence (2001: 117) suggests that this 'cultural racism' both constructs the 'Other' and shores up an idea of the 'mainstream' supposedly free from 'culture'. This corresponds with the way UN human rights lawyers demonize 'culture' while positioning themselves as 'representing modernity and law, a culture-free zone' (Merry, 2003: 70) and the broader trend by which 'marginalised groups are regarded as mired in culturally specific ways, while members of dominant groups are unmarked and individual' (Kahane, 2003: 11). Christine Schwöbel-Patel (2016: 256) detects the same tendency among international criminal law practitioners who perceive themselves as 'neutral, measured, professional' compared to victims who are 'partisan, emotional and unskilled'.

Lawrence, McKinley, Merry and Schwöbel-Patel detect an assertion of superiority whenever a culture is essentialized by legal practitioners which, on one hand, amplifies the image of the 'unskilled', benighted witness (see below), but also obscures the fact that 'outsiders' also possess a 'culture', the myriad practices and assumptions that lawyers and judges take so much for granted (see Bourdieu, 2003[1977]: 94; Chapter 3).

All of this is accentuated further in the context of sub-Saharan Africa. It has been argued that Africa is not really a place but 'a category through which a "world" is structured' (Ferguson, 2006: 5; see Asad, 1973; Comaroff and Comaroff, 1991: 86–125). Described as a 'paradigm of difference' by V. Y. Mudimbe (1994: xii), the alterity (otherness) of

Africa enabled the 'colonial dialectic' by which Europeans constructed a civilized Self (see Hardt and Negri, 2000: 127; Said 2003[1978]: 332). As Achille Mbembe (2001: 2) writes, 'Africa as an idea, a concept, has historically served, and continues to serve, as a polemical argument for the West's desperate desire to assert its difference from the rest of the world', a sentiment echoed by Chinua Achebe's (1988: 17) observation that 'the West seems to suffer deep anxieties about the precariousness of its civilization and to have a need for a constant reassurance by comparison with Africa'.

Such portrayals of Africa as a 'paradigm of difference' are alive and well in international trials. Gerhard Anders (2011: 938) has demonstrated how stereotypes of Africa as a place of 'savagery and magic' opposed to the 'rational and modern West' featured in trials at the Special Court for Sierra Leone. Anders (2011: 941–2) describes how Joseph 'ZigZag' Mazarh, an associate of Charles Taylor (former President of Liberia), gave testimony in Taylor's trial in which he claimed to have committed acts of cannibalism and ritual murder. This, Anders observes, portrayed Africa 'as a place of horror and absolute evil' which 'spoke to a deep-seated Western fascination for Africa's "savagery" and "primitivism"'. Given that Mazarh's testimony was not relevant to the indictment against Charles Taylor and the events he described took place outside the territorial jurisdiction of the Special Court, Anders (2011: 958) concludes that the prosecution had called Mazarh to demonize Taylor and attract international media attention and that, in the process the prosecution had 'tapped into Western images of Africa as a dark continent . . . representing Africa as the primitive Other of Western modernity'.

RESCUERS

So far I have argued that to posit that Rwandan witnesses at the ICTR were impeded by their 'culture' essentializes Rwandan 'culture' in a manner rejected by anthropologists and which may (inadvertently) perpetuate representations of 'Africa as the primitive Other of Western modernity' (Anders 2011: 958) while serving to obscure the fact that legal practitioners also possess a 'culture', which could also be considered an impediment to witnesses. The dangers of this approach are further heightened when one considers the way in which witnesses at international criminal tribunals have been portrayed as victims in need of salvation.

Kieran McEvoy and Kirsten McConnachie (2013: 2) argue that an 'imagined victim' is required to justify the financial and political cost of international trials and that without such a victim more abstract justifications such as 'justice', deterrence and upholding the 'rule of law' might appear 'just too intangible' (see Fletcher and Weinstein, 2002). According to McEvoy and McConnachie (2013: 2), the 'imagined victim' supposedly served by international tribunals is an instantiation of a 'notion of global victimhood' that has emerged over the last 60 years. Drawing on Didier Fassin and Richard Rechtman's (2009: 29) observation that 'The victim's word can no longer be doubted', Thomas Bonacker (2013: 115, 101) talks of an infallible, 'charismatic victim' whose 'perspective has become the normative basis for dealing with past atrocities' and that, as a consequence, the justifications for creating transitional justice institutions like the ICTR 'are always in reference to the victims'.

Although this victim may be 'charismatic', she is abject. Kamari Clarke (2009: 13–15) suggests that international criminal tribunals require a 'tragic spectacle of suffering – the spectre of a victim representing the condition of oppression in need of salvation' and that without such a 'victim', the 'moral – and thus institutional – power' of institutions like the ICTR would be weakened. Christine Schwöbel-Patel (2016: 248–50) also argues that international criminal tribunals employ the image of the benighted victim in ways that simultaneously disempower the 'victim' while legitimizing the projects of powerful, international 'rescuers' (see Abu-Lughod, 2002; Galchinsky, 2010; Kennedy 2002; Mutua 2001: 227; Spivak, 1988: 297). Schwöbel-Patel (2016: 256) notes that victims in international trials have been spectacularized (where spectacle 'naturalizes stereotypes for the public gaze in order to secure the domination of those already privileged'; see Debord 1967) whereby international courts, Schwöbel-Patel argues, employ the already naturalized 'fundraising image' of abject victims employed by humanitarian NGOs in order to portray the 'saviours' of international criminal law as 'neutral, measured, professional' compared to victims who are portrayed as 'partisan, emotional and unskilled' (Schwöbel-Patel, 2016: 256). Sara Kendall and Sarah Nouwen (2014: 241) talk of an abstract: 'The Victims' (grammatically plural but treated as singular) which 'transcends all actual victims and corresponds to no individual victim in their particularity'. 'The Victims' then becomes a 'placeholder for the agency of others', as the 'helpless mirror image of international actors who must act in its name' thereby enhancing these actors' 'own resources, power and status' (Kendall and Nouwen, 2014: 259–61). In other words, the agency of 'The Victims' is 're-assigned to the institutionally powerful in their name' (Clarke, 2009: 4; see McEvoy and McConnachie, 2013: 2). The implication is that international legal practitioners employ 'geopolitical and institutional privilege' to reinforce their status 'as the authoritative knower who is ordained to teach, civilize and rescue the benighted, hapless victim' (Madlingozi, 2010: 210).

The discussion above suggests that not only were Rwandan victim-witnesses at the ICTR in danger of being considered impaired by Rwandan 'culture', but also as abject, 'partisan, emotional and unskilled' (Schwöbel-Patel, 2016: 256) victims in need of salvation. The ICTR Statute (United Nations, 1994e, UN Doc. S/RES/955 (1994)) implies that being a witness and being a victim would be synonymous. Article 21, entitled 'Protection of Victims and Witnesses' reads 'Such protection measures shall include, but shall not be limited to, the conduct of in camera proceedings and the protection of the *victim's* identity' (emphasis added). The shift from 'Victims and Witnesses' in the title, to just 'victim' implies a presumption by the statute's drafters that witnesses would inevitably be victims. The irony, however, is that many of those who gave testimony at the ICTR were not 'victims', but 'detained witnesses' i.e. perpetrators. Defence lawyers complained to me, for example, that 'The prosecution all rely on murderers' and that 'The prosecution witnesses are confessed murderers, confessed killers from Rwanda.' The prosecution's assessment of their own witnesses was hardly more complimentary. During a break in proceedings an exasperated prosecution lawyer described the prosecution witness he had been examining as 'a dirty, lying, murdering bastard'. But, the lawyer smiled, 'the thing is that he tells tales on the other lying, murdering bastards'.

As will become clear in the following section, some lawyers and judges spoke in terms redolent of Overdulve's assessment of Rwandan culture. Such a perspective applied to all Rwandan witnesses, whether perpetrators or victims. Having said that, while the image of the abject victim would, obviously, apply primarily to Rwandan witnesses who had survived the genocide, I would argue that just as Kendall and Nouwen's (2014: 241) abstract 'The Victims' 'transcends all actual victims and corresponds to no individual victim in their particularity', the double impairment of culture and being 'partisan, emotional and unskilled' (Schwöbel-Patel, 2016: 256) was applied to an abstract category of 'The Rwandan Witnesses', irrespective of whether they were victims or survivors.

RWANDAN CULTURE FROM THE PERSPECTIVE OF ICTR LAWYERS AND JUDGES

In conversation with me, some lawyers and judges at the ICTR spoke in terms redolent of Overdulve's position and supportive of the emphasis placed on 'culture' by Combs and Kelsall. A judge, for example, told me that 'the culture here is don't provide information unless asked' and a prosecution lawyer explained to me that 'there's an element of caution in their culture. They don't say everything at once. It's their culture not to reveal everything immediately.' Some lawyers and judges told me that Rwandan witnesses were incapable of providing a narrative. A prosecution lawyer, for example:

> Rwandans are not used to narrative storytelling. In Europe, we're used to a story with a beginning, a middle and an end with some factual observations in between. This is not the same with Rwandans. Maybe it's because there's a reluctance to say anything too definite, they don't want to engage in a conflict. This causes a lot of problems. Evidence goes around the houses.

Problems associated with evasiveness were, in the minds of some lawyers, compounded by additional 'cultural' tendencies. These included the prevalence of unintentional 'hearsay' among Rwandan witnesses, a defence lawyer telling me that 'if they hear something they'll say it's happened to them'.

In addition to 'cultural' evasiveness, lawyers also noted, like Combes (2009: 243–5) and Kelsall (2009: 171), that witnesses had problems with numbers, one prosecution lawyer boldly informing me that 'there's no concept of numbers in Rwanda'. A fellow prosecution lawyer described how witnesses would say that there were tens of thousands of people in a particular place, 'You'll then ask, "Well, was it the same as the number of people at church on a Sunday morning?" They'll say "Yes." Well, that can be no more than 600. So, there's a tendency to inflate.' Similarly, an interpreter explained to me that the 'notions of time and of distance are very different', that if a lawyer were to ask "How far is it from here to there, is it 25kms?" a Rwandan would respond that it was a three-hour walk. The above statements by judges, lawyers and other ICTR practitioners appear to confirm the observations of Combs, and Kelsall that Rwandan 'culture' was an impediment to trials at the ICTR.

Other judges and lawyers, however, told me that the impediment caused by 'culture' had been exaggerated. This was particularly the case among judges and lawyers from Africa who, for obvious reasons, were sensitive to positions that questioned the capacity of Rwandans. They did not deny that there were differences, but argued that they could be easily surmounted. Discussing the possibility of misunderstanding, an African prosecution lawyer, explained to me that 'in Africa the term "my husband" has a myriad of meanings. It can be a term of endearment, an economic expression or conjugal relations. So, my mother may call me "my husband" indicating an economic position.' His African colleague made a similar observation:

> Someone will say that 'the person in front of me is my son'. I'll ask 'You are his father?' They reply 'No, he's my brother's son, but not my nephew.' He's not a 'nephew', but a 'son', 'because they call me papa'. Therefore, you must understand this before branding witnesses as liars.

Here, the lawyer is making the point that such an example could be (mis)understood as 'cultural' evasiveness (resulting in 'branding witnesses as liars') when, in reality, it is matter of contextual knowledge. Judges and lawyers from Africa, therefore, impressed upon me that such misunderstandings could be easily rectified in the courtroom. An African prosecution lawyer explained, for example:

> A witness may say 'his house' for where he lives and 'his house' when he talks about his uncle's house. I call my uncle's house my house at home. In Africa, we do this. But, Canadians make the distinction: 'It wasn't your house, why are you lying?' I could understand it perfectly, but if you don't have that common ground, it leads to a whole series of arguments that don't make much difference. If you're looking for inconsistency you'll jump on them. But are these really inconsistencies?

The lawyer's comment regarding 'arguments that don't make much difference' implies that misunderstandings such as this may have been seized upon by lawyers, but that the relevance of those issues to the overall credibility of a witness in the eyes of the judges may have been minimal. The lawyer also draws attention to differentiated knowledge in the courtroom ('I could understand it perfectly') indicating that he was in a position to rectify such misunderstandings. This parallels Anthony Good's (2007: 170, 173) observation that many of the misunderstandings seized upon by lawyers in UK asylum hearings as credibility-damaging discrepancies can, in fact, be swiftly resolved if lawyers and judges possess the necessary elucidation. The lawyer's comments suggest that such elucidation was often available in the ICTR courtroom.

The length of trials (an average of four years) meant, in addition, that non-African ICTR practitioners could acquire elucidation over time (see Byrne, 2010: 288–9). For example, a prosecution lawyer explained to me how he had adapted to the fact that when the French *lendemain* was translated into Kinyarwanda it changed from 'the next day' to 'the following days'. Likewise, a French to English interpreter explained to me that she had learned that Rwandans will answer a negative question with a 'yes' where a Westerner would answer 'no'. For example, 'If you ask them "Have you not eaten today?", they will answer "Yes"' (see Berk-Seligson, 1990: 179). While the interpreter spoke of her ability to adapt, she also noted that because 'the majority of lawyers are Western or Westernized, they are not aware of this and it can take them a very long time to get the answers they want'.

So far I have suggested that while some lawyers and judges made comments in line with the assertion that Rwandan 'culture' impeded testimony; others, especially those from Africa, implied that such impediments could be easily overcome. Uncertainty on whether 'culture' was a significant impediment can also be detected in ICTR judgments, including the ICTR's first judgment of Jean Paul Akayesu in September 1998. During the trial, Dr Mathias Ruzindana, a Rwandan linguist, had appeared as an expert witness for the prosecution (see Eltringham, 2013a). Under the title 'Cultural Factors Affecting the Evidence of Witnesses' the judgment summarized his testimony:

> According to the testimony of Dr Ruzindana it is a particular feature of the Rwandan culture that people are not always direct in answering questions, especially if the question is delicate. In such cases, the answers given will very often have to be 'decoded' in order to be understood correctly. This interpretation will rely on the context, the particular speech community, the identity of and the relation between the orator and listener, and the subject matter of the question. ... cultural constraints were evident in their difficulty to be specific as to dates, times, distances and locations. The Chamber also noted the inexperience of witnesses with maps, film and graphic representations of localities, in the light of this understanding, the Chamber did not draw any adverse conclusions regarding the

credibility of witnesses based only on their reticence and their sometimes circuitous responses to questions.
> (ICTR, *Prosecutor* v. *Jean Paul Akayesu*, Case No. ICTR-96-4-T,
> 2 September 1998, para 156).

On one hand, the judges appear to support the presence of 'culture' as
an impediment in line with Overdulve ('cultural constraints were
evident'). But the judges also note that when it came to 'maps, film
and graphic representations of localities' it was 'inexperience' that was
the impediment rather than 'culture'.

The hesitancy of judges to attribute problems solely to 'culture' is
more pronounced in the following extract from the judgement of André
Rwamakuba in 2006 in which judges reflect on how they assess
a witness's credibility:

> The Chamber will use various criteria in its assessment of the evidence,
> such as internal discrepancies in the witness' testimony, inconsistencies
> with other witnesses' testimony, inconsistencies with the witness' prior
> statements, relationship between the witness and the Accused and other
> witnesses, the criminal record of the witness, the impact of trauma on
> a witness' memory, discrepancies in translation, social and cultural
> factors, and the demeanour of the witness.
> (ICTR, *Prosecutor* v. *André Rwamakuba*, Case No. ICTR-98-44C,
> 20 September 2006, para 40).

The judges hedge their bets. Alongside 'cultural factors' are a range of
other issues that the judges believe may obstruct evidence such as
trauma and simultaneous interpretation (see Chapter 3). The relative
weight given to each factor is left unquantified. The same refusal to
assign 'culture' a determining role can be seen in the judgement of
Georges Rutaganda in 1999:

> The Chamber has also taken into consideration various social and
> cultural factors in assessing the testimony of some of the witnesses.
> Some of these witnesses were farmers and people who did not have
> a high standard of education ... the Chamber also notes that many of
> the witnesses testified in Kinyarwanda and as such their testimonies were
> simultaneously translated into French and English. As a result, the
> essence of the witnesses' testimonies was at times lost. ... In some
> instances it was evident, after translation, that the witnesses had not
> understood the questions.
> (ICTR, *Prosecutor* v. *Georges Rutaganda*, Case No. ICTR-96-3,
> 11 December 1999, para 23).

In the three judgments quoted, judges propose a number of causes other than 'cultural factors' for the difficulties encountered by Rwandan witnesses, including lack of experience of the courtroom, low standard of education, trauma and simultaneous interpretation. In my observation of trials and in conversation with judges and lawyers, the four main impediments to witness testimony I observed were the effect of interpretation; the fact that witnesses could only respond to the question asked by a lawyer or judge; the impact of protection orders that anonymized witnesses; and that many witnesses had given multiple testimony in multiple fora. I will assess each of these impediments in turn.

SIMULTANEOUS INTERPRETATION

The effect of simultaneous interpretation on the practice of lawyers and judges was discussed in Chapter 3 and many of the observations made there are also applicable to witnesses, including the need to slow delivery, simplify content and observe the pause. Under the RPE (ICTR, 2005[1995]) the working languages of the ICTR were English and French (Rule 3A); the accused had a right to use her own language (Rule 3B) and those appearing before the ICTR with insufficient knowledge of the two working languages could use her or his own language (Rule 3D). The problems interpretation caused in relation to whether witnesses were understood was acknowledged in the first judgment at the ICTR:

> the syntax and everyday modes of expression in the Kinyarwanda language are complex and difficult to translate into French or English. ....
> Most of the testimony of witnesses at trial was given in the language, Kinyarwanda, first interpreted into French, and then from French into English. This process entailed obvious risks of misunderstandings in the English version of words spoken in the source language by the witness in Kinyarwanda.
> (ICTR, *Prosecutor* v. *Jean Paul Akayesu*, Case No. ICTR-96-4-T, 2 September 1998, para 145).

The concern that interpretation led to misunderstanding was voiced in other judgments (see ICTR, *Prosecutor* v. *Georges Rutaganda*, Case No. ICTR-96-3, 6 December 1999, para 23) and was a frequent topic in conversation with lawyers and judges, for example, 'If one word is changed, the credibility of the witness can go down' (prosecution lawyer); that 'precise wording becomes important and may lead to a measure of doubt' (prosecution lawyer); and that 'If an interpreter says the witness said Friday afternoon and they said Thursday afternoon we'd be misled' (judge). These comments could be interpreted as displaying unrealistic expectations, as a defence lawyer explained to me, 'There is a danger that you read too much in to the interpretation. The interpretation is off the wall, loose, and general. One could put too much weight on what is said.' Court interpreters in other contexts have acknowledged this tension between interpreting 'word-for-word' and 'the spirit of the words' and that the latter may be mistaken for the former (Braverman, 2007: 249; see Stern 2011). The fact that simultaneous interpretation is never 'word-for-word' (even if it is considered to be) was compounded at the ICTR where interpreters interviewed by Jonneke Koomen (2014a: 587–8) reported making subtle changes for reasons of cultural sensitivity, such as replacing offensive words (e.g. references to genitalia) with alternatives. A lawyer or judge holding the expectation of 'word-for-word' would be liable to place the fault of misunderstanding with the witness (and her 'culture') rather than the interpreter.

When I asked a judge whether he thought Rwandans had difficulty forming a narrative he replied, 'Maybe, but pre-testimony sessions really assist the witness. Counsel tell the witness what they have to explain. My impression is, therefore, that witnesses can follow a chronological narrative.' The judge is referring to the practice at the ICTR for the lawyer who would be examining the witness in the courtroom to go through the questions beforehand (see Jordash, 2009: 513; see Chapter 5). Based on this practice of pre-trial witness preparation, a prosecution lawyer with whom I spoke was certain that it was interpretation that was at fault, not the ('cultural') incapacity of the witness:

> The translation from Kinyarwanda to English is atrocious. We prepare the witness before they give testimony with an assistant who speaks Kinyarwanda. But what we say as we ask questions in court does not correspond to what the witness hears. Likewise, the witness is not saying what the witness actually says. We know it is Tuesday 14th April but it comes out a different day, month and year. The witness was able to answer questions in preparation and the witness was consistent, but it's different in court. It must be the translation because I know what the witness knows.

Drawing on pre-testimony preparation, this lawyer was certain that the fault lay with simultaneous interpretation and not with his Rwandan witness. Lawyers and judges observing discrepancies of dates in this testimony may, however, have placed the blame on the witness (and her 'culture') rather than the interpretation process. In addition, the reason for discrepancies between questions and answers may have lain with the way the question was posed, as the next section will explore.

QUESTION/ANSWER FORMAT

While the lawyer in the example discussed above was certain that simultaneous interpretation was the problem, other lawyers were more indecisive on whether the problem lay with interpretation or 'culture'. Having asked a prosecution lawyer what effect simultaneous interpretation had, he absolved the witness stating that 'the directness of questioning is muted. It's not a function of the witness but how it's translated.' However, having initially placed the blame on interpretation, he continued:

> They're not used to narrative storytelling as a cultural thing in Rwanda. In Rwanda, they don't say what they mean and mean what they say. They want to know what you want to hear so as not to offend. They don't want to disappoint me. They're doing something they're not used to. It's culturally different to Northern Europe where there's an expectation of knowing how to tell a story.

The lawyer displayed indecisiveness as he oscillated between blaming interpretation and blaming 'culture'. What is most telling is his use of the phrase 'narrative storytelling' and his statement 'knowing how to tell a story' given that there are 'fundamental contradictions between everyday storytelling . . . and the expectations and interpretations of storytelling and retelling in court' (Eades, 2008: 210). Drawing on research in trials involving Aboriginal people in Australia, Diana Eades (2008: 210) notes that 'the ways in which you tell your story in the legal process is very strange' because it is delivered in 'very short bits, segmented by lawyer questions'. It is the lawyer's questions that 'organise the story, deciding which parts can be told, and in what order, as well as what parts can't be told'. All of this relies on an arrangement that limits some speakers (lawyers) to ask questions, while others (witnesses) may only answer questions they are asked.[1] As Michael Conley and William O'Barr (2005: 21) observe:

---

[1] The only questions a witness can refuse to answer are those that would incriminate him or herself and the RPE (Rule 75D) required that judges controlled the manner of questioning to avoid any harassment or intimidation.

133

> The special rules of the courtroom are highly unusual from a conversational point of view. From an everyday perspective, it would be very peculiar to limit some speakers so that their only type of turn is asking questions, while restricting others to giving answers to whatever questions they are asked.

Research has also shown that a large number of questions put to witnesses in trials require a minimal response and narrative answers are often avoided (in both examination-in-chief and cross-examination) with the result that 'witnesses can hardly be thought to tell their stories in their own words' (Luchjenbroers, 1997: 501; see Danet et al., 1976). Furthermore, given that a witness can only speak when answering the question that has most recently been asked of them and that only lawyers and judges are permitted to ask questions, witnesses are prevented from 'participating in meaningful negotiation on anything but the smallest point of clarification on this most immediate question' (Eades, 2008: 212). What this means is that witnesses cannot 'tell their own story in their own way' (Eades, 2008: 212) irrespective of whether they originate from a different 'culture' to the lawyer posing the question.

Put bluntly, Rwandans at the ICTR were not asked to provide a narrative in the everyday sense, so we cannot know whether or not they were 'used to narrative storytelling' and, because they were not asked to tell their own story in their own way, we cannot know whether or not they knew 'how to tell a story'. The narrative sought by lawyers, the narrative Rwandans are not supposedly 'capable' of providing, does not correspond to the unmediated narrative witnesses would tell given the opportunity (see Baines and Stewart, 2011), but to the stilted, antiphonal process of question and answer that is specific to the courtroom (see Chapter 3). As a defence lawyer made clear to me 'There's a difference between answering questions and forming a narrative'. Furthermore, any witness possesses only limited knowledge of the part they play in the (counter)narrative a lawyer wishes to construct, which means that a witness's story is 'rarely a narrative with a beginning, middle and an end' (Gewirtz, 1996: 7).

Rather than unfamiliarity with narrative storytelling as a 'cultural thing' as the prosecution lawyer asserted, Rwandans may just have been unfamiliar with the question/answer format of the courtroom. In fact, the prosecution lawyer admitted as much, 'They're doing something they're not used to.' That unfamiliarity was, of course, further compounded by the problems associated with simultaneous interpretation (see Chapter 3). This raises the question of whether lawyers and judges misinterpreted as 'cultural' the witness's resistance to the exceptional way in which stories were elicited in the ICTR courtroom.

It is not only the way in which a witness' narrative is elicited that is exceptional, but the restricted focus of that narrative, as a prosecution lawyer commented:

> We only need ten or fifteen minutes out of their whole lifetime. We're only interested in a tiny little part. We're not interested in the before or the after. They can't understand why this miniscule incident is so important. For example, a woman who was gang raped at four different locations. At the final location she became a 'kept woman'. When she came to give evidence we tell her that the benevolence of that final person vs. the horrific nature of previous events doesn't really matter because we want her to talk about being a kept woman against her will. We tell her 'We just want you to talk about that little bit.' But, they don't really want to talk about that, the least of the experiential issues. They want to talk about other things. Therefore, they're frustrated, they're not fulfilled because they haven't told their story.

From the perspective of this prosecution lawyer, it is not 'culture' but the fact that the lawyer pursues what seems, from the perspective of the witness, to be an unimportant part of their narrative, that leads the witness to behave contrary to the lawyer's wishes (see Koomen, 2013: 264). Witnesses may want to tell 'whole stories' that reflect their whole lives which would be 'complex and messy stories' (Crosby and Lykes, 2011: 476; see Theidon, 2007: 465, 468), interweaving the actual event with the emotional aftermath (Henry, 2010: 1106). But, as discussed in Chapter 5, a defining feature of legal procedure is the 'skeletonisation of fact' (Geertz 1983: 170) into a form to which rules can be applied, that 'Whatever the law is after it is not the whole story.' 'Truth', is, in this way, 'immaterial in legal representation'; what is important is the way a lawyer assembles the witnesses' answers into a 'persuasive and intelligible format for the judiciary' (McKinley, 1997: 70). If the lawyer's strategy did not make sense to a witness, the witness's incomprehension could have been misinterpreted by lawyers and judges as evidence of 'cultural' impairment.

Commenting on this issue, an ALO described the judge's leniency with victim-witnesses, that 'The judges let the witnesses talk, but you can't get these people to concentrate on the important facts, they're not used to a legal culture, they don't know what's important.' The legal officer draws attention to the fact it may not be Rwandan's 'cultural' incapacity that is the problem, but the incapacity of 'legal culture' to make itself accessible to lay persons (see Merry, 1986; Conley and O'Barr, 1990). The exceptional manner in which stories are elicited in the courtroom is so contrary to how storytelling works in everyday conversation that this can cause 'problems for any witness who is unfamiliar with the ways of thinking, believing and acting that are part of legal culture' (Eades, 2008: 223). Such unfamiliarity is inevitable for witnesses, as a judge explained to me 'I ask myself, is it easy or difficult being a witness? It's not a profession. It'll probably be their first and last time as a witness.' Unfamiliarity with 'legal culture (common to all witnesses) could have been misinterpreted by lawyers and judges as evidence of 'cultural' impairment.

The prosecution lawyer's reflexive critique above – which placed the responsibility on his imperatives ('We're only interested in a tiny little part') rather than the witnesses' 'cultural' incapacity – was reflected in the response of a European judge when I asked whether Rwandan witnesses were able to provide a narrative:

> It depends on the lawyer who leads the witness and it depends on the judges, whether they interfere. Some witnesses are very concise and precise. But, it depends on their education and the circumstances and traumas. There are different scenarios. For example, a witness who had a narrow escape testifies that he was trapped under dead bodies and that's why he wasn't finished off. But, his testimony is concise and to the point even though there is trauma. Others, who have not had such experiences, give testimonies that are too long. The obligation of the lawyer is to ask clear questions and to interrupt when the witness is too long.

The judge suggests that Rwandan witnesses could provide a concise narrative (even if they were traumatized) and that it is lawyers who were at fault, unable to frame their questions appropriately, all the more necessary in a context of simultaneous interpretation (see Byrne, 2010: 292; Good, 2007: 159; Chapter 3). Another judge complained that lawyers were choosing inappropriate questions:

> Two thirds of what witnesses say is irrelevant. What I need to know is whether someone committed acts with the intention 'to destroy, in whole or in part, a national, ethnical, racial or religious group'. What I want to hear is that this member of the *Interahamwe* was called up by this specific person on 8th April who gave them car keys and guns and

said 'go to this place and this place and kill Tutsi'. How hard can that be? Instead of this, they ask this illiterate person to come and describe the structure and the hierarchy of the *Interahamwe*. What's the point of asking a peasant what the internal structure was? How would they know that and what has it got to do with the crime that the person is accused of?

Similarly, a defence lawyer who had examined 12 Rwandan witnesses, while acknowledging that they had to be 'closely led' because they had a lot to say, was adamant that 'our witnesses tell their story very clearly. The perception that they don't "tell it straight" is because of the quality of the questions they are asked.' This suggests that witnesses answering poorly phrased questions could have been misinterpreted by lawyers and judges as evidence of 'cultural' impairment.

The discussion so far has suggested a number of issues that must be taken into account when assessing the argument that 'Rwandan culture' impaired testimony by Rwandan witnesses at the ICTR. First, while some lawyer and judges were able to make simple adjustments that avoided irrelevant misunderstandings, others may have failed to acquire such knowledge and interpreted such issues as evidence of 'cultural' impediment. Second, eliciting stories through question and answer in court would be artificial and unfamiliar to laypersons and even more difficult to follow in a context of simultaneous interpretation. Third, witnesses were only asked to narrate a 'tiny part' of their experience and the reasons for that choice may not have been clear from their perspective. Fourth, judges suggested that it was lawyers that were at fault in their questioning, not witnesses. Taken together, these observations suggest caution is necessary before suggesting that 'Rwandan culture' impaired testimony.

THE IMPACT OF PROTECTION ORDERS

It has been suggested above that before one assesses the performance of Rwandan witnesses at the ICTR by reference to 'culture', one must take into account the effect of simultaneous interpretation and the forms of storytelling required by 'legal culture'. In addition to these factors, one must also take into account how witness protection impeded communication between the lawyer and the witness at the ICTR.

According to Rule 75 of the RPE, lawyers (prosecution or defence), the witness or the Witnesses and Victims Support Section (WVSS) could ask a Trial Chamber to 'order appropriate measures to safeguard the privacy and security of victims and witnesses, provided that the measures are consistent with the rights of the accused'. Members of the WVSS explained to me that in practice it was the party calling the witness who would submit such a request. The Trial Chamber would consider this motion in closed session and could, according to Rule 75[2], adopt a number of options, including, expunging from the ICTR's public records the witness's name and any information that may identify him or her; allow the witness to give testimony through 'image- or voice-altering devices or closed circuit'; assign a pseudonym; or hear testimony in closed sessions. Around 80 per cent of witnesses were granted some form of protection.

Lawyers expressed a significant amount of cynicism about such protection orders. Defence lawyers impressed upon that the 'whole place is infiltrated anyway' by Rwandan government spies, while a prosecution lawyer told me that 'when we give a name to the defence it's shared around among the accused'. I encountered similar cynicism among judges. One worried that it was a licence for perjury, that 'my view is come forward and testify publicly or don't' while another felt that it was 'taken too far', that anyone from Rwanda could claim to be in danger and that it 'puts the judges in a very hard position because if we say no, they say that we're preventing justice'. Irrespective of the value of such protection, the impact in the courtroom was clear.

This can be illustrated by the case of a Rwandan female witness (called by the prosecution). Given that she testified in Kinyarwanda and both the defence and prosecution lawyers were Anglophone, all of the impediments associated with simultaneous interpretation discussed above were applicable (see Chapter 3). The examination-in-chief passed without incident, confidential information being written on a piece of paper which, at the end of the examination, was placed under seal by order of the judge.

The next day, the witness was cross-examined by a defence lawyer who produced a list of names. It transpired that this was a list of names of prosecution witnesses in the trial. The defence lawyer stated that the list included 'pseudonyms as well as names for ease of reference'. A copy of the list was given to the witness and the defence lawyer told the witness 'I'll remind you that we're in open session, and so please don't speak the names out loud; but where you need to, you can refer to them

---

[2] Protection measures were found in Rules 69 and 75 of the ICTR's RPE: 'Rule 75Bi (a) Expunging names and identifying information from the Tribunal's public records; (b) Non-disclosure to the public of any records identifying the victim'.

by way of the number that appears against the name'. The witness, therefore, was confronted with a list on which each individual entry was identified in three different ways; by number, by name and by pseudonym.

The defence lawyer began, 'So looking at number 1, you see the name there. Is that someone you know?' The witness answered in the negative. Asked about name number 2 on the list, the witness stated, twice, her place of employment. The presiding judge ordered the removal of the place of employment from the transcript (so that it read 'By order of the Court, this word has been extracted and filed under seal.'). A few moments later, the defence lawyer asked about name number 3 and the witness said the person's name. Again, the presiding judge intervened, telling the witness 'to be careful that in your answers, that you don't make disclosure which could identify where you work, which could be traced back to your identity'. A minute later the presiding judge had to intervene a third time to order that something the defence lawyer had said about the witness's place of work should also be removed from the transcript.

I observed episodes like this on almost every occasion that a protected Rwandan witness gave testimony (see Byrne, 2010: 300). Behind such interactions a network of censoring was at play in the courtroom. Most obviously, judges censored lawyers. For example, when a prosecution lawyer challenged the authenticity of a defence document, the presiding judge responded 'I think you just mentioned the witness's name', and ordered the redaction of the name from the transcript.

While judges had to be alert to such censoring, lawyers were required to censor on three levels. Lawyers had first to censor witnesses they were examining by reminding them that they were testifying in open session and instructing them not to divulge names of people, places or other identifying information. Lawyers also had to be ready to censor witnesses being examined by others. For example, a defence lawyer interrupted the cross-examination of a defence witness by a prosecution lawyer (the examination-in-chief of the witness had begun in closed session):

Defence Lawyer: Mr President, we are in open session, and the witness just stated where he worked, so I think we have to seal that.
Presiding Judge: I didn't hear it in English.
Defence Lawyer: I heard it in my headphones.
Prosecution Lawyer: Mr President, I agree.

And, of course, lawyers had to consciously censor themselves:

Presiding Judge: I think you just mentioned the witness's name.

Prosecution Lawyer: I crave your indulgence. I am sorry, Mr President. Since the curtains were drawn, I was under the impression that we are in closed session. I do acknowledge it is an error on my part, and I am sorry for it.

Presiding Judge: It does happen from time to time. I'm just concerned to make a proper order for redaction.

Finally, of course, witnesses were required to censor themselves. When a witness revealed where he was working in April 1994, the presiding judge addressed him:

Presiding Judge: Mr Witness, we thought you had understood. You haven't. Are you able to avoid mentioning specifics concerning your professional activities or do we have to go into closed session?

Witness: In order that I may be at ease in my statements I believe we can go into closed session.

Presiding Judge: Yes, we will do that.

Similarly, on another occasion, when a witness mentioned the name of the organization of which he was a member, the presiding judge ordered the name to be redacted from the transcript and, with some annoyance, addressed the witness:

Presiding Judge: Mr Witness, do you understand? This is connected with your protection order to conceal your identity.

Witness: I understand, Mr President, but it's really difficult to answer bearing that in mind spontaneously one might reveal one or another aspect that could lead to revealing my identity.

On one hand, protection orders required all in the courtroom to modify their behaviour (see Chapter 3). However, the two statements above indicate the particular impact on witnesses. One witness fears 'spontaneously' revealing his identity, the other says he will not be at ease testifying if he must constantly censor himself. Witnesses who already could not 'tell their own story in their own way' (Eades, 2008: 212), due to the question/answer format and that only parts of their story were required, were also asked to censor themselves or risk being censored. Again, the difficulties this gave rise to may have been be wrongly attributed to the witnesses' 'culture'.

THE IMPACT OF MULTIPLE STATEMENTS AND TESTIMONY

As mentioned at the start of the chapter, having reviewed transcripts from the ICTR, the Special Court for Sierra Leone and the Special Panels in the Dili District Court in East Timor, Combs (2009: 247) observes that 'a substantial proportion of witnesses testify inconsistently with their written statements or with their in court testimony in previous cases'. Many of the Rwandan witnesses who gave testimony at the ICTR had, indeed, testified in multiple trials, not only at the ICTR but also in Rwanda, giving numerous statements in the process. The opposing party very often used previous statements to identify contradictions in order to discredit the witness. The degree to which such a process dominated the proceedings was captured by a judge:

> A witness may have given a written statement, once, twice, three times, four times, five times, to the prosecution or the defence. When a witness is shown his own statement, or his statement is read out to him, a statement he has signed etc., they often say 'I never said that.' To me it's strange, that they can't acknowledge what they have said.

Inconsistency between multiple witness statements is illustrated by a protected Rwandan prosecution witness who gave testimony at the ICTR while on provisional release awaiting trial in Rwanda. In cross-examination the defence lawyer noted that the witness had given a number of statements regarding the case against him: two to Rwandan prosecutors in 2000; two to the ICTR prosecutor in 2002 and 2004; and one to the Rwandan authorities. It also transpired that he had given statements in relation to other accused in Rwanda.

The defence lawyer indicated that he believed that the witness 'essentially told the truth' when he was first arrested by the Rwandan authorities in 1998, but that 'after having languished in prison for six years, you came to Arusha in April of 2004, and you decided that it was in your interests to tell a different story'. The defence lawyer suggested that only after 2004 did the witness write a letter implicating the accused in meetings at the start of the 1994 genocide, meetings about which the witness had testified in his examination-in-chief. In other words, the defence lawyer argued, that because the witness's testimony at the ICTR contradicted earlier statements, it should be discounted. When asked why he did not mention the presence of the accused at the meeting in the earlier 2002 statement to the ICTR prosecutor, the witness replied 'I agree with you that I did not mention that meeting, but it really depended on the questions that were put to me, because as you can see, this document is a sort of summary.'

Embedded within this example are two interrelated features of multiple testimony that could contribute to the appearance of inconsistency and may, in turn be interpreted as indicating an evasive 'Rwandan culture'. First, that a statement is a product of the questions that are asked; and second, that a statement can never be comprehensive. Before considering those two features it is necessary to reflect on the witness's description of his statement as a 'sort of summary' (see Koomen, 2013: 260). Legal statements can take two forms: a full, dialogical record of every question and answer in an interview or a monological, narrative summary. Although the former question/answer format was described to me by ICTR practitioners as coming from 'civil law' and the monological, narrative statement originating with common law (see Chapter 3), some civil law jurisdictions do employ the narrative form in police reports (see Jönsson and Linell, 1991; Komter, 2006).

The difficulty with narrative statements is that judges did not know what questions had been asked (see Rock, 2001: 47). As a common law judge explained to me, 'When witnesses are brought here, the lawyer says that everything is in the statement, but they do not say what questions were asked and the statement is in a narrative form.' When I asked a civil law judge which form of statement was used at the ICTR, he explained that at the start of the ICTR's operation statements had been in the narrative form, but that this had been changed to the question and answer form by an Appeals Chamber judgment in 2004 which states that 'A record of a witness interview, ideally, is composed of all the questions that were put to a witness and of all the answers given by the witness' (*Prosecutor* v. *Niyitegeka*, Case No. ICTR 96–14-A, Appeals Chamber Judgment, July 9, 2004, para 31). The judge explained to me that the question/answer format was superior because with the narrative/summary statement when confronted with an inconsistency the witness can simply say 'I understood something very different from what was written.'

Linda Jönsson and Per Linell (1991: 431–4) discuss transformation of a dialogical interview to narrative statement in police interviews. Jönsson and Linell note that whereas storytelling in an interview may be rambling, repetitive, incoherent and not always chronological, the edited, narrative/summary will be chronological and coherent, repetition and irrelevant side-remarks will have been removed and 'coherence creating material' will have been inserted. Furthermore, the sequence of events will have been portrayed as being much more dependent on decisions by the accused, a perspective strengthened by the removal of any expressions of uncertainty during the interview. One of the reasons for this is that witness statements are written in a way so that legally relevant features stand out clearly and contain all the information required so that they can be understood by any reader (Jönsson and Linell, 1991: 436; see Geertz, 1983: 170). Given such transformations, it is not surprising that ICTR witnesses had said 'I understood something very different from what was written' when confronted with a narrative/summary of an interview.

Co-production may be another reason why a witness may say 'I never said that.' While oral testimonies have been described as allowing 'survivors to speak for themselves' (Hartman, 1995 192) as a '"pure" utterance and "authentic" transmission of experience' (Douglass, 2003: 56), research demonstrates that narrative is a co-produced artefact of the interviewee and interviewer and their dialogical encounter (Clark, 2005: 296; see Eades, 2000: 213; Eastmond, 2007; Gelles, 1998: 16; Greenspan and Bolkosky, 2006: 432; Jackson, 2002: 22; Langfield and Maclean, 2009; Laub, 1992: 57; Portelli, 1981: 103; Stier, 2003: 67–109; Vansina, 1965; 2006[1961]: 29). In other words, what 'transpires in a dialogue is a collective construction by the dialogue participants; what gets said in a given contribution by one person is dependent on the partner's prior contributions and her projected forthcoming reactions' (Jönsson and Linell, 1991: 434). This active 'co-construction' is seen in the 'choice of words in the propositions of questions, the order in which topics are introduced, the ways in which topics are linked, and the topics which are omitted or which the witness is prevented from talking about' (Eades, 2008: 215). Research on police statements in domestic jurisdictions demonstrates, however, that this co-construction (the part played by the interviewer) is erased so that the statement reads as if the witness was speaking alone (see Eades, 2008; Jönsson and Linell, 1991; Komter, 2006; Rock, 2001). Under such circumstances it is not surprising that when confronted with (pre-2004) narrative/summary statements, witnesses at the ICTR responded 'I never said that', as reported by the judge above.

Despite these problematic features of their production, statements tend to be 'given supremacy above spoken information directly from witness's themselves' (Rock, 2001: 47). This leads to a 'strange relation-ship' in which the statement becomes an 'authoritative text against which even the witness, the original source of the information con-tained in the statement, is assessed' (Rock, 2001: 47). This is another example of the proclivity of law to privilege a text above all else (see Introduction, Chapter 2 and Chapter 5).

The main consequence of the 2004 Appeals Judgment requiring question/answer statements rather than narrative/summary statements is that the former can reveal that it may be an interviewer who has failed to ask particular questions rather than a witness lying or being evasive. This point is made by the prosecution witness quoted above, 'it really depended on the questions that were put to me'. On another occasion, when a prosecution witness was asked by a defence lawyer why it had taken him almost a year to reveal a crucial piece of informa-tion the witness responded, 'I was not the one asking the questions. The investigators had their own plan of questioning. When they asked me questions, I answered.' The fact that particular questions may not have been asked was acknowledged by judges in a judgment:

> witness statements from witnesses who saw and experienced events over many months which may be of interest to this Tribunal, may not be complete. Some witnesses only answered questions put to them by investigators whose focus may have been on persons other than the accused rather than volunteering all the information of which they are aware. (*Prosecutor* v. *Theoneste Bagosora, Gratien Kabiligi, Aloys Ntabakuze, Anatole Nsengiyumva*, Case No. ICTR-98-41, Decision on Admissibility of Witness DBQ (TC), 18 November 2003, para 29).

The importance of questions asked applies to both question/answer and narrative/summary statements. Martha Komter (2006: 222) notes that while the narrative/summary statement produced from a witness inter-view would be viewed by legal professionals as 'the suspect's own words' (see Rock, 2001: 44), most of what the suspect said was in response to the interrogator's questions (see discussion of 'co-production' above). The problem for the witness is that it is difficult to prove with a narrative/summary statement that a question was not asked. With a question/answer statement, however, the witness can respond with confidence, as a prosecution lawyer explained to me, by referring to the statement 'I didn't volunteer that information because I wasn't asked, but now I'm asked, I'll answer.'

Being able to prove that a question was not asked is important because, as a judge explained to me, an omission (easily detected in a question/answer statement) would be treated leniently, in that 'To use against a witness that which they did not say is something we do, but not volunteering information is a counter argument against giving that a lot of weight.' In other words, this judge accepted that witnesses may not know what is relevant and cannot, therefore, be penalized for not volunteering information. As noted earlier, a witness possesses only limited knowledge of their part in the (counter)narrative an investigator wishes to tell (Gewirtz, 1996: 7). This was made clear by another judge:

> Some discrepancies can be attributed to memory, but others can be attributed to how the questions were put by the person taking the statement. A witness, for example, is interviewed by a prosecutor in Rwanda. Suddenly, in 2004, the witness mentions the accused, that the accused was at a particular meeting or whatever. The question is whether the witness has suddenly decided to lie or was always telling the truth, but what he had said was determined by the questions that the person taking the statement asked. Obviously, one wouldn't talk about everything one knows, that would just be too lengthy and dull.

The judge's comment that what a witness says in an interview is 'determined by the questions that the person taking the statement' asks raises the point that interviewers themselves may not know what is relevant at the time a statement is taken (Rock, 2001: 48). The final sentence of the judge's comment ('one wouldn't talk about everything one knows, that would just be too lengthy and dull') raises the additional fact that a statement can never be comprehensive. This is illustrated by an example of a non-protected Rwandan prosecution witness responding to a question from a defence lawyer:

> I would like to tell you that even today I have not said everything that I know in this statement. If I had to do that, I would have written a whole biography for myself. Here, I only responded to what I was asked. I was not asked to compile a biography or give the details of all that I knew. But when it came time to answer a specific question, I did answer that question.

Evaluation of statements given by Rwandan witnesses should, therefore, take account of the fact that statements can never be exhaustive and are the product of questions asked.

It was suggested to me that many of the pre-2004 narrative/summary statements were of poor quality. A prosecution lawyer explained to me that they were full of discrepancies because they were 'not a contemporary record, the person is illiterate, it's been translated by an untrained interpreter, taken in shorthand and then typed out and expanded upon'. In this lawyer's opinion there had been a 'tendency to over-summarize, to paraphrase such as "all hell broke loose" when the person did not say that'. The prosecution lawyer's reference to paraphrasing and testimony being 'expanded upon' resonates with research in other contexts. In her exploration of asylum cases in the United States, Michelle McKinley (1997: 72) suggests that there are 'insuperable barriers' in the process of 'translating' personal experience into a framework intelligible to lawyers and judges and she doubts whether the subjective definition of a witness's experience can ever be reconciled with a lawyer's objective definition of that experience. McKinley (1997: 74) illustrates this with case of a Zimbabwean asylum seeker who, although able to recount her experience of rape with 'emotional detachment', her lawyers wanted her to inhabit the subject position of a 'deeply disturbed and traumatised' person in order to present a story of persecution. Working on the case as a law student, McKinley (1997: 75) admits that in order to create a statement that the judge would believe she found herself '"editing in" sentiments of resentment, vulnerability and loss which *completely* contravened everything [the asylum seeker] said and certainly contradicted her attitude'. The asylum seeker was initially furious when the statement was read back to her, although she eventually conceded and was given asylum. This demonstrates that lawyers repackage testimony according to 'stock stories' that they assume judges will respond to more positively (see Dershowitz, 1996).

Examples of such 'editing in' and embellishment were a frequent occurrence in the ICTR courtroom:

Witness: [Referring to statement] You can see that that the muzungu [i.e. 'foreigner'] who took my statement has put militiamen in parentheses after the word '*Interahamwe*'. That is his interpretation, his construction.

Prosecution Lawyer [GT]: Did he add this after?

Witness: Yes, he must have done it on his computer.

This example not only indicates subjective embellishment on the part of the statement taker, but also implies that this witness had not been given the opportunity to read, or have read to him, his statement in order to make any corrections, all of which was required by the later 2004 appeals judgment that prescribed question and answer statements (*Prosecutor* v. *Niyitegeka*, Case No. ICTR 96–14-A, Appeals Chamber Judgment, July 9, 2004, para 32).

It was apparent, however, that pre-2004 statement taking had not always followed this procedure. Cross-examining a protected Rwandan prosecution witness in 2005 a defence lawyer asked whether she recognized her signature on the last page of a statement taken eight years earlier in 1997, to which the witness replied 'let me have confidence and say that it is indeed my signature'. The defence lawyer then asked the witness 'The statement was read to you, after you had made it. You had the opportunity to correct it. And you then signed a solemn declaration that what you had said was true. Do you accept that procedure took place?' Before the witness could answer, the prosecution lawyer interjected, asked that the witness take her headphones off so she could not hear the interpretation of what he was about to say, and stated 'Prosecution accepts her signatures appear. But it's not right to go so far as to say the Prosecution formally accept all the proper procedures were adopted. We don't know.' This demonstrates that having not been present when the statement was taken, the prosecution lawyer was not prepared to guarantee that the procedure had been followed. Again, it is not surprising that witnesses may have responded 'I never said that' when confronted with a statement.

There is an additional issue that applies to statements. In a narrative/summary statement, there can be a 'blurring of source distinctions' i.e. 'one cannot know from reading [a police statement] under what conditions a given piece of information had been introduced' (Jönsson and Linell, 1991: 434). This can refer to the incorporation by the witness, over time, of 'foreign material' (Levi, 1986: 130) into their testimony; material that they have encountered *post facto* (see Douglas, 2001: 142). Hannah Arendt (1994[1963]: 224), for example, notes that almost none of the witnesses in the Eichmann trial possessed the 'capacity for distinguishing between things that had happened ... more than sixteen, and sometimes twenty, years ago, and what [the witness] had read and heard and imagined in the meantime' (see Eltringham 2013a). The way in which 'foreign material' is incorporated into a testimony is continuous and evident in the course of the trials: For example, a protected Rwandan prosecution witness:

Prosecution Lawyer: Is there anything about any aspect of your testimony over the past two weeks that you wish to correct or amend?

Witness: Thank you. Regarding my testimony, what I would like to correct is what I said regarding the rally at Ruhengeri. I thought I said that I had seen [the accused] in Ruhengeri, but when the video footage of that rally was shown to me [in the courtroom] I realised that I had been mistaken. I saw somebody else, but he was not the one.

From that moment on, the witness's testimony would have been altered by exposure to the video and it is unlikely that the reason for that alteration (viewing a video as part of giving testimony at the ICTR) would be acknowledged if the witness were to give testimony in the future.

Julie Stone Peters (2008: 185) describes law as the 'ultimate institution' of Richard Schechner's (1985: 36) 'twice-behaved behavior' (see Chapter 2). Discussing theatrical performance, Schechner discusses how 'strips of behavior' (slices cut from a stream of ongoing behaviour) are performed having been rearranged in rehearsal. Such 'strips of behavior', which includes texts such as witness statements, take on a life of their own that is independent of the original 'source' of the behaviour (such as when the statement was taken). In the context of law, testimony given in the courtroom 'disguises itself as a restoration of actual events when in fact it is a restoration of earlier performances' (Schechner, 1985: 54). These earlier performance include the taking of the original statement, pre-trial witness preparation and any number of performances by a witness to 'survivors in the local community, perpetrators in the local community, the dead, national government officials, and international human rights advocates' (French, 2009: 98; see Rock, 2001: 51). It is these earlier performances that become the reference point, rather than the original event (Schechner, 1985: 52).

Witness testimonies, therefore, are particular 'synopses on experience, told at given times for specific audiences and located in distinct spatial and temporal contexts' (Ross, 2003a: 102). Likewise, Diana Eades (2008: 213) notes that storytelling involves 'different emphases for different audiences' and changes, including different choice of words and expressions and the 'omission of details from the original telling of the story, or inclusion of details not found in its original telling'. In other words, 'as an experienced and performed event, any story is like Heraclitus' river, differently realized each time it is told and differently signified in the minds of individual listeners' (Jackson, 2005: 358). Taking this all into account, the recovery of an original narrative free from 'foreign material' will be very difficult, as a defence lawyer acknowledged:

> Let me give you an example, 'Hutu Power' can be a rallying cry for a party to unite the Hutus and represent their interests or as incitement [to genocide]. But your interpretation of what you saw in 1994 mixes with layers of other accounts and new points. Therefore, what did it originally mean to a witness? You don't know, the person can't know.

While 'foreign material' may be added, other material may be excluded. Writing in the context of the trial of Duch by the ECCC, Alexander Hinton (2016: 264, 272) notes that all accounts (whether witness testimony or judgments) invariably have gaps as we 'selectively edit, foreground, background, frame, push that which is discordant out of sight', that we 'redact as we weave together our narratives'.

The incorporation of new, *post facto* 'foreign material' or the redaction (exclusion) of material, therefore, reflects a universal process rather than something particular to Rwandan 'culture' as seen in Michael Jackson's (2002: 22) observation that stories:

> are *nowhere* articulated as personal revelations, but authored and authorised dialogically and collaboratively in the course of sharing one's recollections with others. . . . That is why one may no more recover the 'original' story than step into the same river twice. The fault is not with memory *per se*, but an effect of the transformations all experience undergoes as it is replayed, recited, reworked and reconstrued in the play of intersubjective life.

A European judge noting the particular features of testimony at the ICTR acknowledged this *universal* process:

> So many years have passed. The story is not the same as ten years back. If you narrate a story ten times, there will be differences. So, how do you assess? You will have erased some parts, time has passed, the events confused them etc. Even for us, we can't say the same story ten times in the same way.

The judge indicates that this is a universal disposition ('Even for us') rather than something specific to Rwandan 'culture'.

This process of (innocent) reworking and reconstruing is difficult to detect. When investigators (working on behalf of the defence or the prosecution) took the statement of a witness there would have been no traces that the witness's memory had already been 'reworked and reconstrued' (Jackson, 2002: 22) in her imagination, in dialogue with others and augmented with information she did not possess at the time ('foreign material'). And yet, such *unintentional* revision is continuous and would have taken place between the giving of one statement and the next. This was particularly acute in the context of the ICTR where, as a judge described, there are 'recycled witnesses' who have 'been talking about the same events for more than a decade'.

The fact that witnesses may change their minds or introduce additional material was formally acknowledged in the phenomenon of a 'Will say'. As indicated in the discussion above, witnesses at the ICTR were 'prepared' before giving testimony in the courtroom. If in the process of preparation an addition or alteration in their testimony emerged, this would be contained in a 'Will say', described by a prosecution lawyer in the following way:

> Preparation may lead to new things coming out, to added information. That's when you use a 'Will say'. This is to avoid prejudicial surprises because it's not considered fair to spring surprises. In the process of preparing, new facts may emerge. If there are too many, the other party must make an objection and say this is new, we'll have to go and investigate and we need an adjournment. We try to minimize that, so when limited additional new facts come out during the preparation, they're put in a Will say. All of this is to prevent 'prejudicial surprise'.

The intention behind the 'Will say' was to expedite trials by avoiding requests for adjournments in order to investigate new evidence that appeared in testimony (Møse, 2005: 930). But the phenomenon of the 'Will say' also demonstrates an acknowledgment by judges that statements were inherently unstable even if they were treated, especially by lawyers, as an 'authoritative text' (Rock, 2001: 47). As the witness discussed at the start of the chapter says, 'Don't be surprised that even today I could give you some new information.'

Inconsistency between witness statements and testimony at the ICTR has been seen as evidence of either intentional dishonesty or 'culture', including a culture of evasiveness (see Combs, 2009: 252; Kelsall, 2009: 3). However, as the above section has indicated, there are numerous reasons other than 'culture' why statements or prior testimony may be contradictory, including that questions were not asked (undetectable if narrative summary statements are used), the tendency for narrative, summary statements to be embellished; and the innocent incorporation of 'foreign material'.

CONCLUSION

The discussion above suggests that simultaneous interpretation, the question and answer format of adversarial trials, protected witnesses and multiple statements/testimony all caused substantial problems as lawyers and judges tried to elicit testimony from Rwandan witnesses. These problems could, I have argued, been mistakenly attributed to 'culture'.

On one hand, challenging arguments that 'Rwandan culture' was an impediment to witness testimony is also a challenge to the tendency, noted by others, that African witnesses have been portrayed as 'emotional and unskilled' (Schwöbel-Patel, 2016: 256) and as representing a 'condition of oppression in need of salvation' (Clarke, 2009: 15). In addition to the need to challenge such portrayals, I would also argue that ICTR trials were also instructive on the nature of (adversarial) law wherever it is practised. While some of the issues identified in this chapter are particular to international criminal justice (simultaneous interpretation; the length of time that has passed since the crimes were committed; that witnesses have given multiple statements/testimony in multiple contexts), other features are general to common law (the question and answer format; testimony as 'twice-behaved behaviour'). This suggests that impediments to testimony, including the artificial question and answer of witness examination; that witnesses only state what they are asked about; that witness testimony is a co-production; and that 'foreign material' will inevitably incorporated are all present in domestic jurisdictions, but have been become naturalized and unremarkable. However, once made apparent in the exceptional context of the ICTR, the blame was placed (by some judges and lawyers) on to the alien 'culture' of the witness rather than an alien 'legal culture' that all witnesses, wherever they testify, have to negotiate.

5

'WE ARE NOT A TRUTH COMMISSION'

Presiding Judge: [Our] real objection has to be the number, 174 exhibits that we have to read. Now, the witness has admitted [he made a mistake] so what's the purpose for the document? . . .

Defence Counsel: . . . we are trying to make a historical record of exactly what happened in Rwanda during this time, and we think we are entitled to rely on authentic documents as well as oral testimony . . . I don't see the harm to anybody if the document is in evidence. This is the way we've been proceeding in the trial throughout, to document what happened in Rwanda through official records, as well as oral testimony.

Prosecution Counsel: . . . I'm not opposed to allowing official documents on the record, but [if] we are adopting the approach that all official documents should come in because they help us to reconstruct the history, then that approach has to be even handed . . .

Presiding Judge: Gentlemen, please. We are trying to cut out this type of argument. We are running a trial now. We are not a truth commission. That's the point. There is nothing to contradict this witness anymore because when shown the document he admitted that he had made an error . . . So there is no reason for entering it at this point . . . And I think that it is time for us the draw a distinction between the truth commission and a trial where we are trying to focus on the issues that are really important . . .

Defence Counsel: I think it is a mistake not to admit documentary evidence when it is relevant in a trial. Those of us researching the Nuremberg trials . . . would look at that type of material. . . . And for historical purposes, it is not necessarily a truth commission but it is not a very good way of dealing with a trial of historical significance to let documents be referred to then not be available as part of the record.

For James Clifford (1988: 290), the courtroom may be a 'theater of dramatic gestures' (see Chapter 2), but it is also a 'machine for producing a permanent document'. The exchange above raises the question of whether the 'permanent document' should also contain historical material that is not required to convict or acquit an indicted individual (see Sarat and Kearns, 2002: 11; Turner, 2008: 535). This question reflects Frédéric Mégret's (2011: 1035) distinction between an '"internal" or "forensic" vision of international criminal justice' focused solely on the determination of guilt or innocence of an individual and an '"external" or "strategic"' vision concerned with the re-percussions of trials beyond the courtroom, including establishing history. Such a distinction gives rise to two primary questions which will be considered in this chapter. First, did judges and lawyers at the ICTR conceive of preserving an 'historical record' as an intentional, strategic objective of trials, or as an incidental by-product? Whether or not it was a strategic objective, is it not the case that the documents and exhibits preserved in the ICTR's archive may be used in future to promote alternative findings to those of the judgments?

In the opening episode, the defence lawyer refers to the ICTR's predecessor, the Trial of the Major War Criminals before the International Military Tribunal at Nuremberg (1945–6) ('Those of us researching the Nuremberg trials'). Judges and lawyers who participated in that trial appear to have considered the 'historical record' as an important strategic feature. Robert M. W. Kempner (Assistant US Chief Counsel during the IMT trials) described Nuremberg as 'the greatest history seminar ever held in the history of the world' (Buruma, 1995: 144–5; quoted in Douglas, 2001: 266n265). Airey Neave (1978: 356–8), Assistant Secretary of the IMT, reflected that 'Without the trial, the scene of horror would have taken years to reproduce in all its dreadful detail. … Historical research has since produced more detail, but the trial was the original testimony to the terrible Final Solution.' Sir Hartley Shawcross (British Attorney General and Chief Prosecutor for the United Kingdom) stated that the trial would provide 'an authoritative and impartial record to which future historians may turn for truth and future politicians for warning'

(International Military Tribunal, 1947: 594) and speaking to the American Bar Association less than a month after the execution of ten of the Nuremberg defendants, Norman Birkett (British Alternate Judge of the IMT) stated that 'the fate of the individual defendants was perhaps the least important result of the Nuremberg trial', more important was the record of 'the dreadful consequences which come to a great nation when the rights of the individual are disregarded' a record that was 'now available, not merely for the present generation, but for all generations to come' (Hyde, 1964: 529).

The contrasting position, that trials should only be concerned with the guilt or innocence of the accused and not seek to intentionally contribute to historical interpretation, is exemplified by Hannah Arendt's (1994[1963]) comments regarding the trial of Adolf Eichmann (German Nazi SS-*Obersturmbannführer* and a key organizer of the Holocaust) in Jerusalem in 1962. The prosecutor Gideon Hausner (1967: 292), argued that in 'any criminal proceedings the proof of guilt and the imposition of a penalty ... are not the exclusive objects' and called witnesses whose testimony was only marginally related to the alleged actions of Eichmann. Hausner ensured that the trial became a 'didactic drama' (Douglas, 2001: 128) which would 'represent a traumatic history' (see Bachmann, 2010: 110). Having witnessed the Eichmann trial, Arendt (1994[1963]: 5 253) argued:

> Justice demands that the accused be prosecuted, defended and judged, and that all the other questions of seemingly greater import – of 'How could it happen?' and 'Why did it happen?' ... be left in abeyance. Justice insists on the importance of Adolf Eichmann. ... On trial are his deeds, not the sufferings of the Jews, not the German people or mankind ... the purpose of the trial is to render justice, and nothing else: even the noblest of ulterior purposes – 'the making of a record of the Hitler regime which would withstand the test of history' ... can only detract from the law's main business: to weigh the charges brought against the accused, to render judgement, and to mete out due punishment.

The historian Henry Rousso (2001) recognized the same problem at the 1997 trial of Maurice Papon (accused of deporting Jews in Vichy France during the Second World War). Rousso (2001: xiv) argues that the court's objective to pronounce on Papon's guilt or innocence came into tension with public opinion which 'wanted to see the history of Vichy on the accused bench at least as much as it wanted to see a highly placed collaborator on trial'. Rousso and Arendt agree, therefore, that a trial should only concentrate on individuals, in contrast to the historian who will place the 'decisions of the leaders and their interventions into the framework of broader, more complex interactions' (Ricoeur, 2004: 324; see Hinton 2016: 292; Koskenniemi, 2002: 12; Stahn, 2012: 272).

Richard Wilson (2011: 1) notes that it is because of this tension between the individual and broader frameworks that it is often argued that 'the justice system should not attempt to write history at all, lest it sacrifice high standards of judicial procedure' and that a consensus has emerged in the literature on legal responses to mass atrocity crimes that 'courts of law produce mediocre historical accounts of the origins and causes of mass crimes'. Based on his research at the ICTY, ICTR and ICC, Wilson (2011: 169, 220) argues, however, that the 'legal testing' that takes place in the course of a trial means that 'historical points of view are all aired openly and are all challenged robustly, thus illustrating their strengths and weaknesses and leading the court to search for new material to make sense of the past' (see Douglas, 2001: 265n264; Orentlicher, 1991: 2546n2532; Scharf, 1999: 513). For those reasons, Wilson (2011: 19) argues that 'there is a compelling case for rethinking the long-standing view that the pursuit of justice and the writing of history are inherently irreconcilable'. Regarding legal practitioners, Jenia Iontcheva Turner (2008: 368) found that defence lawyers at the ICTY, ICTR and SCSL also believed that a contested trial produced a more accurate historical record because it tested the prosecution's case. Kirsten Campbell (2013: 255) also celebrates 'legal testing' at the ICTY, arguing that:

> law 'acts as a historian' in its legal function of establishing and recording an objective history of the conflict. This 'objective' history is seen to include the legal testing of evidence during the trial process, and the judicial finding of facts and culpability.

In addition to arguments that law 'acts as a historian', there is a need to acknowledge that historians are embedded in international criminal trials. It is not simply the case that trials produce an archive consulted afterwards by historians, such as the use of the Nuremberg archive by Raul Hilberg (1961; see Douglas, 2001: 3). Rather, historians collaborated in the creation of the ICTR archive when they were called as expert witnesses or when extracts from their publications were submitted as evidence. As I have discussed elsewhere (see Eltringham, 2013a), historians also changed their positions over time in response to information emerging from the trials. For example, when a historian, called by the defence as an expert witness, was challenged by a prosecution lawyer on why he had changed his opinion, the historian explained, 'When I wrote my book of 1996, proceedings at the ICTR were still in their infancy. Today, 90 per cent of the documents on the basis of which we can have a contemporaneous vision of the situation, are based on documents produced by the ICTR.' On one hand, this statement indicates the value placed on the archive by historians, but it also indicates that trials and historical knowledge were mutually implicated rather than historians simply consulting an archive after the fact.

While acknowledging that historians were embedded in ICTR trials, it remains the case that that such trials 'produce a body of evidence that is invaluable for historians' so that the impact of trials 'as producers of history lasts long after the trials are completed' (Wilson, 2011: 18). This corresponds with Austin Sarat and Thomas Kearns' (2002: 12) observation that 'Law in the modern era is ... one of the most important of our society's technologies for preserving memory', that law 'materialises memory in documents [and] transcripts'. This suggests that trials contribute to history immediately (through 'legal testing') and in the longer term by preserving an archive ('a body of evidence that is invaluable for historians').

The materialization of memory referred to by Sarat and Kearns takes a number of forms. On one hand, international tribunals preserve a record of themselves as sites of the development of international criminal law and as bureaucratic institutions. There is, therefore, an 'archive of process' (the intricacies of procedure and evidence), an 'archive of jurisprudence' (interlocutory and final judgments), and an 'archive of an institution' (bureaucracy and best practice) (Kaye, 2014: 391–6; see Campbell, 2013: 255). For example, in 2015, the ICTR President, addressing the UN General Assembly, stated that 'the records generated over the last two decades provide not only an account of the Genocide, but also tell the story of the Tribunal' (United Nations, 2015 UN Doc. A/70/218). When lawyers and judges at the ICTR referred to the 'historical record', they were referring to the record of the 1994 genocide, not the record of the ICTR's operation or its legal advances, as a prosecution lawyer confirmed:

> The historical record is every record, every piece of oral evidence before a Chamber. There are also documents released from the US State Department, human rights groups, radio broadcasts etc., all sources recording the events, all are part of the historical record. Like

Nuremberg, we preserve everything because scholars have different interests. Therefore, this is the record.

This chapter will explore how judges and lawyers at the ICTR related to the longstanding tension (discussed above) between the creation of a 'historical record' and 'law's main business' of determining guilt or innocence (Arendt, 1994[1963]: 253). The chapter starts with a review of the opinions of ICTR judges and lawyers concerning the place they considered a 'historical record' should play in the ICTR's objectives. Having noted that their opinions relied on contrasting their work with that of truth commissions and historians, the chapter interrogates the extent to which such contrasts are legitimate. Finally, the chapter reflects on the 'after-life' of the 'historical record' created by the trials and the different uses to which it may be put. In so doing, the chapter asks whether judge's and lawyer's aversion to 'writing history' is naïve given that the ICTR's publicly available archives will inevitably be used to compile narratives of the 1994 genocide that both accord with and challenge the ICTR's judgments.

'TO DOCUMENT AS WELL AS JUDGE'

> Among the most basic and most important of the Tribunal's achieve-
> ments has been the accumulation of an indisputable historical record,
> including testimony of witnesses, testimony of victims, testimony of
> accused, documentary evidence, video recordings and audio recordings
> *(United Nations, 2008, UN Doc. A/63/209: 2)*

This statement by the President of the ICTR (the chief judge) illustrates a position promoted by those speaking on behalf of the ICTR, that a historical record was an important accomplishment (see Gallimore, 2008: 255; Moghalu, 2005: 204). In a similar vein, an ICTR Public Relations Officer explained to me:

> We are also recording a true history of the genocide, the archives are
> rich, the evidence and the judgments are very important for future
> generations and academics to learn and for there to be methods to stop
> these kinds of situations. This is the exercise of law, contributing to
> international criminal law and human rights and trying to record the
> history of Rwanda so that future generations will know what happened
> in Rwanda.

Such a statement refutes Arendt's requirement that 'law's main business' of determining guilt or innocence should be privileged and implies that an ICTR trial could be both an 'exercise of law' and record a 'true history of the genocide'. What exercised lawyers and judges, in conversation with me, was whether the accumulation of an historical record was an intentional objective of the trials or merely an incidental by-product. The judge who participated in the episode described at the start of the chapter reiterated, in private, the position he had adopted in the courtroom ('it is time for us to draw a distinction between the truth commission and a trial'):

> Both the prosecution and the defence want documents entered to 'preserve the historical record', but the question is what documents are central to the trial? People compare us with truth commissions. A 'historical record' is not a purpose of the Tribunal, even if it is an inevitable result. We evaluate the credibility of evidence and relate it to the nature of the crimes alleged, although an historical record is an inevitable result.

Here the judge's position corresponds with Arendt's position that 'law's main business' is the trial of the defendant with the historical record being a by-product. The judge's statement that both defence and prosecution lawyers were committed to preserving a 'historical record' should, however, be treated with caution. While I did encounter defence lawyers who promoted the historical record as a primary objective, having been instructed by their clients to put 'everything on the record for history' (see Chapter 1), other defence lawyers wished to distance themselves from such an approach:

> Only some advocates in the prosecution and defence introduce documents they consider of 'historical importance'. When parties are partisan – as the name implies – they do it in a partisan way that suits their case, but exclude other documents. If you want the truth, you look at all the documents. There are different formats for that, like a truth commission, but trials are not a good format.

I was told that the same kind of diversity existed among prosecution lawyers:

> As regards history, even at the level of the Office of the Prosecutor [OTP] there are different views. Some people believe that prosecution is intended to create an historical record. Others say that the prosecution should only be concerned with the particular case at hand, with the guilt of that particular person. For me, I'm concerned with proving the case, not establishing history.

Regarding those located in the OTP in favour of creating a historical record, a prosecution lawyer explained to me that under normal circumstances trials should only be concerned with the accused, but that the ICTR was exceptional:

> These trials are an opportunity to document as well as judge. I disagree that the only issue is that the accused receive a fair trial. I think it's much more broad, created to give victims and witnesses a voice. This was a reason to establish the Tribunal, to document the conflict. Therefore, due process should be one and two, document what happened. This is not common law, common law does not have a concern with history but only giving the accused their day in court. But what we have here is a theatre of history, the accused is incidental. The conflict, the what, why, the circumstances, that must come through the trial process as a means of healing society. There should be a middle ground.

A judge made the same point in terms of the general and specific, arguing that 'the ICTR performs more functions than a normal court' and that it would 'establish an historical record and individual guilt and innocence of an individual, the general and the specific'.

Despite being told of these competing views among both prosecution and defence lawyers I learned to be cautious about taking for granted what lawyers said regarding the historical record given that such opinions were entangled with courtroom strategy. In the episode at the start of the chapter, the defence lawyer appears committed to preserving an 'historical record' ('we are trying to make a historical record of exactly what happened in Rwanda during this time'). In a similar vein, I witnessed the same lawyer challenge a witness's protection order (see Chapter 4) by arguing that 'We are here for truth, reconciliation in Rwanda, an historical record that will outlast this witness and any of us here. Therefore, the witness should not be anonymous.' The lawyer appeared to be wholeheartedly committed to preserving a 'historical record'. And yet, in private, when I asked him whether he wanted to get everything on the record for the future, he responded 'No, I am not an archivist. I only submit documents that help me.' In a separate conversation, the prosecution lawyer who featured in the same episode gave the following assessment of his courtroom opponent:

> I want a full historical record. But it can be exploited by an interested party. The record is flooded with all of these documents. He's not really concerned with the 'historical record', but dumping all the evidence that he can so that he can use it to his advantage. Those documents don't go

to the point. He's trying to overwhelm the record so that he can wiggle through substantively.

Here we have a prosecution lawyer who, on the face of it, agrees with his defence opponent ('I want a full historical record'), but who denies this commonality because of his suspicion that the defence lawyer is exploiting his espousal of an historical record, a suspicion that turns out to be well-placed ('I only submit documents that help me'). This puts into question whether a lawyer's public promotion of an historical record as objective could be fully disentangled from strategic benefit. Keeping this caution in mind, the prevalent position among those with whom I spoke reflected the earlier statement by the judge that 'an historical record is an inevitable result' although not an intentional objective. Even judges who privileged 'law's main business' acknowledged this:

> We are not a truth commission. It's a different kind of body. The South African commission, Sierra Leone etc., these are there to establish an historical record, to fill in gaps. They are purely for history and gave people the opportunity to vent grievances. But, these tribunals do not have that objective as a primary purpose. We allow counsel to go into the historical record. But if not intrinsically related to the guilt or innocence of the accused they make the trial longer. Our primary objective is to determine the guilt or innocence of the individual. Counsel should only deal with history to the extent of delivering on the guilt or innocence of the client.

By implying that a historical record was not a 'primary purpose', the judge implies it is a secondary effect and one that judges did not obstruct ('We allow counsel to go in to the historical record'). Another judge also acknowledged an historical record was an inevitable by-product as long as it did not interfere with the efficacy of the trial:

> We are not historians. We need to deal with the case in the most effective manner and this means not letting in documents that are not related to the case. That would be inefficient. The historical record is created through the participation of each individual who participates before us. That's the historical record. We can assist in creating a record.

Among prosecution lawyers I also encountered this idea of the historical record as an inevitable, secondary result:

There's a divergence among prosecutors. Some want an 'historical record'. I believe it's a court, this was my view when I arrived and I'm still in that camp. But I recognize that part of the legacy is to have some account, but it's more of an incidental result than the primary purpose.

Another prosecution lawyer described the relationship between the objective of determining guilt or innocence and an 'historical record' as 'inevitable result' in the following way:

I see concentric circles. The outer circle: while acting as a court, it's also preserving evidence, cutting a path through a thicket. So, if the circle of law establishes truth, then it preserves history. As they say 'If it quacks and flaps like a duck ... '. So, the core is legal, but at the periphery there are other things. History is not the primary role, but the trials do it. No matter how you cut and dice it, the primary responsibility of the Tribunal is justice, but there are other secondary things including a factual, historical record.

Such a position maintained the primacy of establishing guilt or innocence ('the core is legal'), but also sought a tentative equality with establishing an historical record, envisaging the two as core and peripheral. This was reflected in the comments of a prosecution lawyer:

This is history. The Tribunal itself is history. Yes, punish the most responsible, but also an accurate historical record, the why and how. The Tribunal serves both purposes. It punishes, but it also has a wider historical importance, part of Rwandan history. You're going to have a version of history anyway, so better to have an accurate legal version rather than a watered-down version. That's why Nuremberg was such an important historical event. It established the Holocaust. If there had not been Nuremberg, it would just be 'things people said' with no proof.

Whereas Arendt's (1994[1963]: 253) position implies an either/or (granting primacy to either a historical record or individual prosecution), the lawyers and judges with whom I spoke implied that both could be pursued simultaneously. Likewise, Sarat and Kearns (2002: 13) suggest that while the purpose of the trial is not 'first and foremost memorial', there is always a 'relentless insistence on record keeping and remembrance'. While the position adopted by Arendt offers a stark choice, many legal practitioners at the ICTR suggested a 'middle ground' was possible, in which a historical record as inevitable (valued) by-product could exist alongside the 'core' objective of prosecution. Despite this concession, many judges and lawyers were keen to distinguish their endeavour from activities expressly dedicated to establishing history: the work of truth commissions and historians.

'WE ARE NOT A TRUTH COMMISSION'

Despite the concession from lawyers and judges that a historical record was a valued, albeit incidental, by-product, the discussion above also demonstrated how judges and lawyers frequently distinguished their work from that of truth commissions and historians. Such distinctions are, I will argue, open to challenge given that they rely on a caricature of the former and limited understanding of shared practices with the latter.

Lawyers and judges made the distinction that truth commissions prioritize the needs for those who testify ('They are purely for history and give people the opportunity to vent grievances') and that the breadth of what they consider is more extensive ('If you want the truth, you look at all the documents. There are different formats for that, like a Truth Commission.'). Both of these assertions are open to question, irrespective of the fact that 'truth commission' denotes institutions with substantial variation (see Hayner, 2010).

Before questioning the assertions by judges and lawyers that the ICTR was not a 'truth commission', it is important to recognize that the nature of the 'historical record' preserved in the ICTR archives changed over time. Having studied the ICTR transcripts, Henry Redwood (2017), notes that in early trials, such as that of Jean-Paul Akayesu (1997–8), witnesses appeared (when compared to later trials) to be 'offered more space to testify and tell their story'. With the imposition of a 'completion strategy' by the UN Security Council in 2003 (see Introduction) 'priorities changed' and judges began to exert greater control over witness testimony. Redwood (2017) observes that this meant that 'fewer, and arguably "thinner" accounts were to be produced for archives in later trials'. This suggests that the degree to which ICTR trials gave witnesses the 'opportunity to vent grievances' (a defining feature of truth commissions in the eyes of ICTR judges and lawyers) changed over time.

Regardless of this evolution, the judges and lawyers with whom I spoke frequently distinguished their work from that of truth commissions often on the basis that such bodies prioritize the needs of those who testify. Regarding the needs of those who testify, it has been argued that while in a criminal trial a witness tells her story in fragments in response to the lawyer's questions (see Chapter 4), a truth commission allows the witness to speak 'unimpeded and uninterrupted' (Cole, 2007: 173) in an environment characterized by 'empathic listening rather than an adversarial hermeneutics of suspicion' (Theidon, 2007: 456). Such characteristics were actively promoted by Commissioners at the South African Truth and Reconciliation Commission (SATRC). For example, at a hearing in Durban (Vryheid) on 16 April 1997, a Commissioner informed a testifier, 'Now, please be free. This is not a court of law, it's just a place where you want to come and ventilate your truth' (quoted in Verdoolaege, 2006: 67). The use of the term 'ventilate' corresponds with the ICTR judge quoted above, that truth commissions 'give people the opportunity to vent grievances'.

The SATRC Commissioner's claim that those testifying in truth commissions simply 'ventilated' a personal truth has been challenged. Those taking statements for the SATRC followed a pre-determined protocol which was deliberately designed to control the direction taken by testimony (see Langfield and Maclean, 2009: 204; Stier, 2003: 75–6). Lars Buur (2003a: 72ff) demonstrates how witness testimony was coercively framed in the process of statement-taking (see Wilson, 2001: 47; see Chapter 5). The 'controlled vocabulary' by which witness statements were collected and entered into the SATRC's 'Information Management System' (IMS) meant that:

> when the TRC went out and 'collected' information from people who suffered violations, it did not collect people's stories or narratives as they were told. Stories about violations became coded right from the outset and underwent changes so that they fitted the vocabulary or language of the IMS [which] retrospectively re-framed and re-ordered past experiences
>
> (Buur, 2001: 45–6).

In this manner, a 'new interpretive grid for giving the past meaning was ... imposed' (Buur, 2003b: 80). While Buur demonstrates coercive framing prior to public testimony at the SATRC, Annelies Verdoolaege (2006: 65) demonstrates how a discursive framework was imposed on witnesses at the oral hearings of the Human Rights Violation Committee (HRVC) of the SATRC whereby commissioners 'tried to elicit statements on reconciliation [but] seemed to ignore feelings of retribution hatred or revenge' in a context in which 'reconciliation' would serve the interests of a new political elite (see Wilson, 2001: 17). Verdoolage (2002: 11) demonstrates that 'the commissioners wanted to have full control over the testimonies, not only by asking certain questions and by interrupting the testifiers, but also by preventing them from talking about unanticipated topics' (see Blommaert *et al.*, 2007: 41). This control was enabled by the commissioners' possession of the witness's statement allowing commissioners to quote from the statement to elicit information they deemed relevant (Verdoolaege, 2002: 11–14, 22–3, 26–7). From this perspective, the claim of 'ventilating truth' ignores the fact that testimony was a 'product of dialogue between a testifier and a member of the HRVRC' (Ross 2003: 79). As discussed in Chapter 4, all testimony is a co-production/co-construction between interviewer and interviewee, wherein the former controls the 'the order in which topics are introduced ... and the topics which are omitted or which the witness is prevented from talking about' (Eades, 2008: 215). Seen from this perspective, Verdoolage's description of how commissioners used prior statements to control testimony at the HRVC corresponds with the way in which lawyers control witnesses in a criminal trial rather than an untrammelled 'opportunity to vent grievances' (see Chapter 2).

Regarding the second claim that the breadth of what truth commissions consider is more extensive than trials and, therefore, better suited to establishing an historical record it should be noted that the mandate of truth commissions is often relatively narrow. The SATRC, for example, was established to 'provide for the investigation and the establishment of as complete a picture as possible of the nature, causes and extent of gross violations of human rights committed during the period from 1 March 1960' (Government of South Africa, 1995). The term 'gross violations of human rights' was defined as 'the killing, abduction, torture or severe ill-treatment of any person' by 'any person acting with a political motive' (Government of South Africa, 1995) and resulted in 30,384 statements of which 2,400 were heard by the HRVC. Mahmood Mamdani (2000: 179) criticizes the emphasis on individual civil and political rights within the definition of 'gross violations of human rights' given that apartheid was 'aimed less at individuals than entire communities' and the violence was not just 'political' but designed to 'dispossess people of means of livelihood'. Mamdani (2000: 179) notes that the 3.5 million people who were forcibly removed between 1960 and 1982 did not count as victims under the SATRC's definition of 'gross violations of human rights'. Not only were the vast majority of the victims of apartheid thereby excluded from consideration by the HRVC, but the mandate of the SATRC meant that it 'wrote the vast majority of apartheid's victims out of its version of history' (Mamdani, 2000: 183).

The example of the SATRC suggests that while truth commissions may be relieved of the 'disciplining drama of judgement' (Douglas, 2001: 175) and determining the guilt or innocence of individuals, they can be equally restricted by idiosyncratic mandates that impose temporal, geographical and investigatory restrictions. Such restrictions question the distinction made by ICTR judges and lawyers between their work and that of truth commissions and that truth commissions were better suited to establishing a historical record because they allowed witnesses to 'ventilate their grievances' and capture a broader history. If the distinction between trials and truth commissions does not stand up to scrutiny, what of the claim that the work of judges and lawyers is distinct from that of historians?

'WE ARE NOT HISTORIANS'

The obvious difference between a criminal trial and the writing of history is the imperative of judgment in the former. As Paul Ricouer (2004: 320) notes, the judge, unlike the historian, 'has to pass judgement . . . Judges must come to a conclusion. They must decide.' In contrast, the writing of history is 'a perpetual rewriting' and that it is this 'openness to rewriting that marks the difference between a provisional historical judgment and a definitive judicial judgment' (Douglas, 2001: 175; see Sarat and Kearns, 2002: 3). The key distinction between the historian and the judge is, therefore, that 'the historian is under no obligation to make up his mind within any stated time' (Collingwood and Dussen, 1993[1946]: 268). Faced with multiple, contradictory versions of an event, a historian can refuse to make an unequivocal judgement (see Esmier, 2003: 40).

To claim, as the judge quoted above did, that 'we are not historians' on the basis that judges pass judgments risks, however, obscuring an assessment of those practices that lawyers, judges and historians share. After all, at a fundamental level, judges, lawyers and historians all work with the currency of narrative, they all seek to impose 'temporal causal sequencing [that] makes sense of action' and share an aspiration to 'produce a coherent narrative . . . that explains and interprets as well as records' (Maier, 2000: 271).

Law, it is argued, is the application of 'purportedly neutral principles' that transcend the details of any particular case (Conley and

O'Barr, 1990: 9). For Clifford Geertz (1983: 170) the defining feature of courtroom practice is the 'skeletonisation of fact' into a form to which these 'neutral principles' can be applied (see Christodoulidis, 2001: 223). Alexander Hinton (2016: 236), describes this process of 'disambiguation' in which 'the complexity of real-world details is edited down to a more singular narrative calibrated to accord with a framing set of abstract parameters (law)'. The organization of ICTR judgments reflected this: '1. Factual Section' and '2. Legal Findings' in which the former contains 'close-edited diagrams of [a past] reality' (Geertz, 1983: 173). The contents of the 'Factual Section' are generated by a trial process that claims to only apply legal norms to facts that exist independently of the process ('in the past') when, in reality, these 'diagrams of reality' are anticipated from the outset of the trial by the choice of charges in the indictment, rules of evidence, courtroom etiquette and advocacy techniques (Geertz, 1983: 173; see Gewirtz, 1996: 10). From the outset of a trial, it is not the 'the whole story' that is sought, but sufficient aspects of reality to which the 'neutral principles' of law can be applied. The paramount intention of lawyers and judges is, therefore, to stabilize 'facts' in a form that will allow the application of law. This is achieved by means of narrative because 'The event is not what happen[ed]. The event is that which can be narrated' (Feldman, 1991: 14) and it is 'not what happened, but what happens [in the courtroom], that law sees' (Geertz, 1983: 173).

As a consequence, a trial is 'not simply a procedure governed by rules, but a complex ritual which produces and suppresses narratives' (Douglas, 2001: 113). The trial is propelled by desire of the parties to have judges declare their narrative as 'what really happened', as the 'winning story' (see Eades, 2000: 210). A criminal trial, therefore, is characterized by 'fragmented narratives and narrative multiplicity' which means that the past is 'always disassembled into multiple, conflicting and partly overlapping versions ... each fighting to be declared "what really happened"' (Gewirtz, 1996: 8).

The centrality of narrative is apparent when one considers how a trial is brought into existence by an indictment:

> The Prosecutor of the [ICTR], pursuant to the authority stipulated in Article 17 of the Statute of the [ICTR] charges:
> [NAME OF ACCUSED]

With GENOCIDE; CONSPIRACY TO COMMIT GENOCIDE; and CRIMES AGAINST HUMANITY for MURDER and EXTERMINATION; offences stipulated in Articles 2 and 3 of the Statute of the Tribunal, as set forth below.

This is the endpoint of the prosecutor's narrative; this is the culmination to which all the stories that the prosecutor will call forth from witnesses will lead.

All narratives are constructed backwards from a culmination already known. Jean-Paul Sartre (1984[1965]: 62) observes that when conveying a narrative 'You appear to start at the beginning [when] in fact you have begun at the end.' In other words, the narrator knows (even if her listeners do not) what her end point will be (see Brooks, 1996: 19). In this way, the '"conclusion" of the story is the pole of attraction of the whole process' (Ricoeur and Thompson, 1981: 277). Conventionality, the narrator hides the conclusion, because 'There is no story unless our attention is held in suspense by a thousand contingencies' (Ricoeur and Thompson, 1981: 277). In a criminal trial, however, the prosecutor reveals at the outset the conclusion of a story she believes she can tell; it is a story that the judge who confirms the indictment believes the prosecutor may be able to tell (see Obote-Odora, 2001). The preceding narrative will be revealed through the testimony of each witness, but all these contributions 'are caught by the end of the story which attracts them and each of them in turn attracts the preceding moment' (Sartre, 1984[1965]: 62).

The narrative revelation of a conclusion already known is, of course, also central to the practice of the historian. The historian and prosecutor both begin with accomplished facts (the 'here and now') and seek to reconstruct a precursory process. Like the prosecutor, the historian, is forever under the sway of retrospective hindsight, knowing the conclusion of the story she is telling, but telling that story as a process of revelation so that the audience is 'held in suspense by a thousand contingencies' (Ricoeur and Thompson, 1981: 277).

In addition to a shared reliance on retrospective hindsight, the historian and the lawyer's narratives artificially integrate multiple 'fields of vision'. Eyewitnesses to an event do not experience it in its entirety (see Haidu, 1992: 294; Jay, 1992: 104). For the historian or lawyer to reconstruct a meaningful narrative of an event, or series of events, she must take a wider view than that accessible to any single eyewitness or participant (Passmore, 1974: 148). Historical and legal narratives assume a 'meanwhile': 'this eyewitness experienced this, meanwhile at the same moment, another experienced that' (Errington, 1979: 239). A historical narrative is more than any one eyewitness could have experienced. Both at a single moment in time and over time the historian and lawyer have access to a wider field of vision than the eyewitness. By occupying an artificial, all-seeing position that no single eyewitness could have occupied (acting as an 'omniscient' observer) the historian and lawyer are able to 'detect' structures and trends that were hidden from those who were 'actually there'. Thus, 'events seem more logical in hindsight that when the observer is caught in the middle of the confusion' (Hirsch, 1995: 19; see Lowenthal, 1985: 191). The *post facto* detection of 'structures and trends' is possible because the historian and lawyer can take a wider view than those 'actually there' and because (unlike eyewitnesses) the historian and lawyer know how the narrative ends. Hannah Arendt's (1998[1958]: 191–12) observation, independent of her views on the Eichmann trial discussed above, is as applicable to the lawyer as to the historian: 'Action reveals itself fully only to the storyteller, that is, to the backward glance of the historian, who indeed always knows better what it was all about than the participants.'

Possessing knowledge of an accomplished past, both the historian and lawyer employ this 'backward glance', both see retrospective significance hidden from the participants and it is that significance which determines what facts are chosen to populate the narratives the lawyer and historian choose to construct. E. H. Carr's (1987: 11) observation on the historian is just as applicable, therefore, to the lawyer:

> It used to be said that facts speak for themselves. This is, of course, untrue. The facts speak only when the historian calls on them: it is he who decides to which facts to give the floor, and in what order or context.

In addition to relying on the retrospective hindsight of narrative and artificially integrating multiple 'fields of vision', historians and lawyers both employ evaluative re-enactment to explore retrospective significance. Milner Ball (1975: 91) notes that in 'the playhouse, as in the courtroom, an event already completed is re-enacted in a sequence which allows its meaning to be searched out' (see Chapter 2). In order to have one's narrative declared as 'what really happened' it must be opened for inspection and this is done through evaluative re-enactment. Prosecution and defence lawyers select, formulate and sequence competing versions of an already accomplished event which is re-enacted for evaluative inspection. This reflects Paul Ricoeur's (1981: 292–3) argument that (re-)enactment of the past is not simply 'imitation'. Rather (re-)enactment involves a 'productive imagination [which] refers to reality not in order to copy it, but in order to prescribe a new reading'. Felix Cohen (1950: 242; quoted in Ball, 1975: 93) similarly notes that 'it is the function of lawyers, poets, historians and map-makers not to reproduce reality but to illuminate some aspect of reality'. In other words, evaluative re-enactment is not done to reproduce reality but to illuminate some aspect of reality for, after all, it was 'not what [actually] happened, but what happens [in the courtroom], that law sees' (Geertz, 1983: 173).

Regarding the fact that both lawyers and historians employ evaluative re-enactment, Alfred Schutz (1962: 20) suggests that we anticipate our future conduct by way of fantasizing, not about the process leading to the completion of a given project, but with the fantasized act having been accomplished and then retracing our steps to determine what action we should take to attain the desired end (reflecting Sartre's (1984[1965]: 62) 'You appear to start at the beginning [when] in fact you have begun at the end.'). In other words, we 're-enact' that which is not yet enacted in order to choose our actions:

> I have to place myself in my phantasy [sic] at a future time, when this action will already have been accomplished. Only then may I reconstruct in phantasy the single steps which will have brought forth this future act (Schutz, 1962: 20).

While historians and lawyers already know the end point of actions (the 'here and now'), they also engage in an evaluative fantasy to determine the steps that may have preceded that end point. I observed, for example, the cross-examination of a prosecution witness by a defence lawyer. The lawyer took the witness through what he described as the 'sequence of events':

Defence Lawyer: In your statement you say . . . 'I saw that he killed on the spot, five adult women patients with his axe. After seeing this I was scared and went out with my aunt pretending to go to the toilet.' Is that right? That you left pretending to go to the toilet?
Prosecution Witness: That is correct.
Defence Lawyer: And in your evidence you told us that you picked up your aunt, and am I right in having heard you say that you put her

over your shoulder? Is that right? Your 30-year-old aunt, you put her over your shoulder?

Prosecution Witness: Actually, I did not carry her on my shoulder. She leaned on to my shoulder and I helped her carry her drip.

Defence Lawyer: I had it interpreted as over your shoulder but you say she's just leaning on your shoulder. Of course, you've been macheted and injured in both your left leg and your left arm, your aunt is very seriously injured indeed. Is she still on a blood transfusion or not?

Prosecution Witness: I was injured – wounded on my left leg and my left arm, which means that when we left, she still had her drip but I held the drip and we exited.

Defence Lawyer: When you say you held the drip, did you hold the bottle or did you hold the stand that the drip was on? What do you mean by that?

Prosecution Witness: I took the drip bottle.

Defence Lawyer: And did you say, 'Excuse me, we're just going to the toilet'?

Prosecution Witness: Yes, that's what I said.

The defence lawyer here employs re-enactment to engage in evaluative fantasy. The witness's statement, on which the defence lawyer drew, was an account of the 'single steps' taken by the witness. These 'single steps', contained in the witness's statement, had already been re-enacted earlier in examination-in-chief, during which the prosecution lawyer had advised the witness: 'Please proceed stage by stage, so that we can follow.'

Now that the cross-examination is under way, the defence lawyer's choice of questions were a consequence of him having posed to himself subjunctive questions within a set of given circumstances: 'I want to get out of here. I could carry my aunt, but can I, given that I'm wounded and she's on a drip?' Such subjunctive stories are 'tried on for psychological size, accepted if they fit' (Bruner, 1990: 54). In each of the defence lawyer's questions, one can replace the 'you' with 'I' and 'your' with 'my'. The cross-examining lawyer (re)lives for himself, as fantasy, the steps taken by the witness to achieve a future state of affairs: the claim that she and her aunt had escaped from the hospital. In plotting vicarious steps and finding them inadvisable or impossible, the defence lawyer implies that these are not steps that will achieve a future state of affairs; they are not steps the lawyer should take; they are not, therefore, steps that the witness would/could have taken and, therefore, her testimony is not credible. The defence lawyer's imitation of steps taken, by means of steps envisaged, has nothing to do with the witness's own planning as it happened (given that 'Action reveals itself fully only to the storyteller' (Arendt, 1998[1958]: 191)). Spontaneous response by the witness at the time will, in retrospect, be portrayed as purposive action (see Collingwood and Dussen, 1993[1946]: 302–3 306–9; Chapter 4). And yet, it is through such subjunctive, vicarious re-enactment ('could one do that?'; 'would one do that?'), that the defence lawyer insinuates that the witness's narrative is not credible.

The 'historical imagination' employs the same evaluative re-enactment. In his classic account of the historical method, R. G. Collingwood (1993[1946]: 327) observed 'What makes [the historian] a qualified judge [is] that he does not look at his subject from a detached point of view, but re-lives it in himself.' As a consequence, the past activities studied by the historian 'are not spectacles to be watched, but experiences to be lived through in his own mind; they are objective, or known to him, only because they are also subjective, or activities of his own' (Collingwood and Dussen, 1993[1946]: 218). Supporting Collingwood's assertion, the Holocaust scholar Richard Evans (2002: 339) recounts being confronted by a survivor of Auschwitz and 'being told that we could never understand what they went through'. Evans reflects:

> if historians can never understand what prisoners experienced at Auschwitz, then they can never understand anything else in history either. . . . The whole discipline of history has grown up as an elaborate attempt to bridge the gap in experience through the exercise of the historical imagination, and there is no difference in principle between bridging this gap in the case of Auschwitz and bridging it in other any historical subject.

I would argue that both historical and legal narratives become persuasive because of evaluative re-enactment because they are 'organised by and filtered through individual minds, not in spite of the fact' (Lowenthal, 1985: 218). The historian, lawyer and judge are themselves evaluative devices. Further, each is aware that her account will, in turn, be judged in the same manner, on its re-enactable plausibility: the historian by her readership; the lawyer in her closing argument; the judge in her judgment. Given future scrutiny, each will employ vicarious re-enactment so that they can say with confidence 'this end required those events and that chain of action' (Ricoeur and Thompson, 1981: 277) because I have enacted them for myself.

Integral to the use of re-enactment through evaluative re-enactment is the use of 'normative plausibility' (Maier, 2000: 270–1; or 'common sense'). Thirty minutes into the first trial I watched at the ICTR, I observed the following exchange regarding the keys to a ward in Kanombe military hospital, Kigali during the 1994 genocide:

Prosecution Lawyer: So are you testifying that when you left the building to do whatever little chores you had to do, you went – opened the door or the gate; you went through the gate; you turned around; and you locked the gate as you were leaving, keeping the disabled soldiers locked up inside the ward?

Defence Witness: That is correct. I locked up before leaving.

Prosecution Lawyer: And what if there was a fire? You were hoping to kill them?

Defence Lawyer: Objection. This question is humiliating.

Prosecution Lawyer: I'll withdraw the last . . .

Presiding Judge: Wasn't it risky, Mr Witness, in case they needed to get out fast, the patients?

Here the prosecution lawyer does the same as the defence lawyer above who re-enacted the 'single steps' of the prosecution witness's narrative and applied 'normative plausibility' (Maier, 2000: 270–1). Given that evidence is assessed through an 'appeal to common experience' (Heydon and Ockelton, 1996: 7), such 'narrative typifications of behaviour' (Jackson, 1990: 30) or 'folk psychology' of normal descriptions/expectations of behaviour (Bruner, 1990: 35) are a key means at the lawyer's disposal. In their evaluative re-enactments lawyers, judges and historians all employ 'a sense of how normal people . . . are expected to behave' (Maier, 2000: 270–1; see Gluckman, 1955). A 'normal' person with 'common sense' would not lock patients in a hospital, thus the lawyer implies that the witness is not credible.

This section began with the judge's statement 'we are not historians' which, alongside the distinction drawn with truth commissions, was employed by judges and lawyers at the ICTR to draw a distinction between the 'main business of the law', determining the guilt or innocence of the accused, and the creation of an historical record. While I acknowledged that historians do not need to make a definitive judgment, I have argued that judges, lawyers and historians employ similar methods: narrative revelation of a conclusion already known; an omniscience that enables the detection of 'structures and trends' hidden from an eyewitness; and evaluative re-enactment. This is not to argue that the work of lawyers and historians is identical. However, recognition of these similarities bolsters the assertion made by Wilson (2011: 169, 220), Turner (2008: 368) and Campbell (2013: 255) that 'legal testing' means that law 'acts as a historian'. This suggests that we should be cautious when judges and lawyers argue that their work is distinct from that of the historian and that we should look elsewhere (such as truth commissions) for a historical record.

Given commonality in method, why would lawyers and judges wish to distinguish themselves in this manner? Research on historians acting as expert witnesses has implied that 'history and the law are in a state of perpetual warfare' (Tanner, 1999: 694) and that Anglo-American courts are 'predisposed to reject history' unless historians abandon the subtle, qualified and tentative quality of their knowledge (Kessler-Harris, 1986: 72–4; see Eltringham 2013a: 345; Evans, 2002: 330). Driven by the 'disciplining drama of judgement' (Douglas, 2001: 175) it could be argued that judges and lawyers cannot abide such forms of 'qualified and tentative' knowledge and the potential for 'perpetual rewriting'. Hence those who practise law must adamantly distinguish themselves from those who practise historiography and refuse to acknowledge the similarity in method. The irony, however, is that the 'historical record', acknowledged by ICTR lawyers and judges as something of value, could be the source for a 'perpetual rewriting' of the history of the Rwandan genocide as the next section will consider.

THE ARCHIVE

I noted earlier Wilson's (2011: 18) argument that courts 'produce a body of evidence that is invaluable for historians' so that the impact of trials 'as producers of history lasts long after the trials are completed'. The Prosecutor's former spokesperson (Gallimore, 2008: 255, 258) endorsed that claim:

> The records of the Tribunal will be useful for future generations of Rwandans and all peoples of the world. Researchers and historians may find the records useful for refuting genocide ideology while establishing an authentic public historical record against negationism and revisionism. Policymakers and political leaders may find the ICTR archives and records useful for national reconciliation by creating from them a new history and basis for the re-imaging of Rwanda. ... The

judicial records and ICTR Archives are perhaps the best historical narrative of the genocide and hold a great potential for re-imaging Rwanda based on the truth about the past. The Archives present a rich source for re-education in the recent history of the country and for reconciliation. The Tribunal can magnify the impact of its legal legacy to Rwanda by providing access to this invaluable national resource.

While laudable such aspirations do not acknowledge three practical considerations: the sheer enormity of the archive; the difficulty of locating material within it, and the possibility that the archive may be employed to write a history that is at odds with judgments. I will deal with these three issues in turn.

The sheer scale of the archive is seen in the estimate that the paper records would require one and a half miles of shelves (United Nations, 2009a UN Doc. S/2009/258: para 51). This reflected 26,000 hours of testimony, 900,000 hours of testimony produced by 3,200 witnesses over 6,000 trial days (United Nations, 2011a UN Doc. S/PV.6678: 8). The volume of material was often raised in conversation:

> In my trial, there are over 400 days of transcripts, the motions and submissions are 30,000 pages; there are 1,500 exhibits ... maybe twelve hundred. Someone may exhibit the 'UN Blue Book' [(United Nations, 1996b)], that's around 740 pages long alone. This means there are 600,000 to 700,000 pages of material. How do you manage all of that? (defence lawyer).

At the same time, there was a process of digitization (see Eltringham, 2009: 70–1) which while essential for the trials also allowed documents to be available to the 'researchers and historians' through the ICTR's website. On one hand, this implied a degree of mastery of the overwhelming amount of paper, as one defence lawyer explained to me:

> There's over 30,000 pages in my case. The Case File is a monster. When we hand things in they burn it on to a CD. Everything is just one click away. The judges know this. They say 'I'm surprised that Mr [lawyer's name] hasn't found it already!' So while the Registry official has to flick through a file, I have it all on my hard drive. Just one click and I have it.

Such a description of the benefits of digitizations, and what it means for future users of the 'historical record' is, however, deceptive. On one hand, scanned documents are available on a 'Public Judicial Records Database' website (http://jrad.unmict.org/), identical to the internal judicial database, with the exception of inclusion in the latter of confidential material (Adami, 2007: 218). However, 'researchers and historians' will experience the same problems described to me by lawyers. Although one can search within documents (Optical Character Recognition software was used in the process of scanning), there is no facility to search across documents. As an ALO explained to me, 'I've spent the morning looking for all Rule 89C decisions in transcripts. No such search facility exists, so I have to look at each transcript in turn and do a search' (see Donia, 2012). And there is a further archive: thousands of hours of audio-visual recording (see Eltringham, 2009: 72). Trials in courtrooms I, II and III were recorded on to VHS tape, Sony 148 DV Cam tapes, on 'For the Record' (FTR) software and C90 audio cassette (the preferred format of stenographers). While audiotapes of trials prior to 2001 (when FTR was introduced) have been digitized on to DVD, they are not all publicly available and the cost of redacting video tapes so they can be made publicly available is estimated at $1 million.

Future 'researchers and historians' will, therefore, have to contend with inadequate search facilities and the sheer volume of material. Perhaps more important, however, is the assumption, evident in the statement by the Prosecutor's spokesperson above, that the archive will only be used in ways that correspond with judgments. In Chapter 1, I discussed the ways in which defence lawyers celebrated the way the trials preserved 'the untold story of the Rwanda War' (Erlinder, 2009: 20) so that 'that our children's children will know the truth'. Given such statements, the response from an ALO when asked whether he considered the archive or the judgements to be the 'historical record' is naïve:

> A future researcher cannot just read an exhibit [in the archive] because they would be unable to assess credibility. The burden of proof is so high that only by looking at the judgment can one ascertain whether it is trustworthy or not. Future researchers should always read the judgments before they use any document.

The naivety is fourfold in that it assumes that judgments are immune from change; that the archive may contain multiple copies of the same exhibit that was used in contradictory ways in different trials; that 'future researchers' may not be so compliant; and that only bona fide 'researchers' would consult the archive. I will consider each of these in turn.

Contrary to the ALO's comment, judgments are not immune from change. They can be revised through judicial review if new facts are discovered (Rule 120 of the RPE) and appeal on the basis of issues of law (Rule 107ff of the RPE). Even if judgments are not challenged and remain unaltered, different trials at the ICTR may have come to different conclusions about the same events. As Douglas (2016: 46) notes, as 'prosecutors, judges, and other legal actors master the learning curve of complex crimes – atrocity trials typically come to frame a richer, more nuanced treatment of the larger historical complex'. Barrie Sander (2018: 554–68), notes that while in the judgment of Jean-Paul Akayesu (1998) and Clément Kayishema and Obed Ruzindana (1999) judges concluded in unambiguous terms that the 1994 genocide had been planned in advance, by the time of the judgment of Théoneste Bagosora et al. (2008), judges concluded that the prosecution had failed to prove beyond reasonable doubt that the four accused had conspired to commit the genocide before its commencement. This raises the question of which judgment should be consulted for the 'correct' history?

Furthermore, future trials in different courts may challenge ICTR judgments. Douglas (2001: 4) notes, for example, how the trial of Klaus Barbie (in 1987 for crimes committed while he directed the Gestapo in Lyon 1942–4) revisited and revised the Nuremberg judgement (see Rousso, 2001: 67; Sander 2018: 551–4). Douglas (2001: 4) observes that 'Individual trials must be staged to reach closure; yet, the discourse of legal judgement and the historical understanding it contains remain fluid and can be completely revised.' Part of the reason for this is because subsequent trials 'revisit and revise their judicial precursors' (Douglas 2006: 191). ICTR judges themselves acknowledged this possibility. Sander (2018: 557) notes that while the judges in the judgment of Théoneste Bagosora et al. (2008) concluded that the prosecution had not proven that the genocide had been planned in advance, it remained conceivable that 'newly discovered information, subsequent trials or history' (ICTR Prosecutor v. Théoneste Bagosora et al., ICTR Case No. ICTR-98-41, 18 December 2008, para 2112) would support that conclusion. While such a statement implies a desire by the judges to have been able to concur with earlier judgments, it also indicates (probably inadvertently) the vulnerability of judgments.

Using a judgment as a guide to assess the credibility of an exhibit as suggested by the ALO above would not be straightforward, as the archives contain multiple copies of the same exhibit that served different, possibly contradictory, purposes in different trials. As Tom Adami (2007: 216), former Chief Archivist and head of the Judicial Records and Archives Unit at the ICTR, notes:

> A transcript of the Rwandan [*Radio Télévision Libre des Mille Collines*] ethnic hatred radio broadcasts may be submitted as exculpatory material by one of the parties and then it may again appear as an exhibit for the opposite side. Also, the same transcripts may again appear in another case defending or refuting a different set of actions attributed to a different defendant. Records are used, re-used, interpreted, and reinterpreted according to a complex set of requirements of the prosecution and/or defense teams.

An indicator that 'future researchers' may not be as compliant as the ALO assumes is illustrated by the case of Danny Hoffman (2007), an anthropologist who published a version of the expert report he prepared for the defence in the trial of the leaders of Civil Defence Forces (CDF) Militia at the SCSL. Hoffman (2007: 640) argues that:

> I believe the Special Court transcripts and archive will be the primary historical record of the war. . . . Though there are a number of excellent books, articles, reports, and websites dedicated to analyzing or documenting the CDF, no other body collected the sheer volume of data that the Special Court did. A great deal of this material is freely available online. In my view, much of the Prosecution's interpretation of that material was inaccurate. My report and the current article are therefore meant as a dissenting voice in the CDF archive.

Hoffman values the SCSL archive, but his interpretation of it is contrary to that promoted by the prosecution and the judgments at the SCSL. Eric Ketelaar (2012: 210), a former national archivist of the Netherlands and a member of the Advisory Committee on the Archives of the UN Tribunals for the former Yugoslavia and Rwanda (2007–8) (see ICTY, 2007) argues, in the context of the ICTY, that archives never speak for themselves, rather, it is users who will determine what information they will get out of an archive. As a consequence, 'archives are never closed and never complete: every individual and every generation are allowed their own interpretation of the archive, to reinvent and reconstruct its view on and narrative of the past' (Ketelaar, 2012: 210). While Hoffman belongs to the anticipated category of 'researchers and historians' envisaged by the Prosecutor's spokesperson (Gallimore, 2008: 255), his 'dissenting voice' raises the spectre of more extreme dissent as hinted at by defence lawyers who claimed that the archives substantiated an 'untold story of the Rwanda War' (Erlinder, 2009: 20) and that 'The judgement is not made now; the judgement will be made in the future' (see Chapter 1) reversing the ALO's assumption that the judgments are a guide to interpreting the archive.

This suggests that the ICTR archives may 'face a long-term state of contestation' (Kaye, 2014: 392). Perhaps the archives will not be used as 'tools for fostering reconciliation and memory' (United Nations, 2009a: para 245) and will not be able to 'ensure that history cannot be distorted later for political ends' (United Nations, 2011b UN Doc. S/2004/616: para 28). In the context of the ICTY, Kirsten Campbell (2013: 258) employs Derrida's (1996) observation that because the creation of an archive is as much an act of forgetting as remembering, omissions from such archives will mean they come 'to symbolise dissension and disagreement'. Likewise, what is included will also fuel dissension as seen in a statement from a defence lawyer (see Chapter 1):

> The accused persons say, and keep saying, we shouldn't give up. We are putting everything on record for history. The truth will come out one way or another. Put everything on the record and then later our children will decide on the truth. People will be able to read and make their own decisions in the future. We have all the records. The judgment is not made now; the judgment will be made in the future.

And what of the assumption that it will be 'researchers and historians' (Gallimore, 2008: 255–8) who will be the principle consumers of the archive? These consumers will be multiple and unpredictable and as Michel-Rolph Trouillot (1995: 25–6) argues, not restricted to 'researchers and historians':

> theories of history ... grossly underestimate the size, the relevance, and the complexity of the overlapping sites where history is produced, notably outside of academia ... Next to professional historians we discover artisans of different kinds, unpaid or unrecognised field labourers who augment, deflect or reorganise the work of the professionals as politicians, students, fiction writers, filmmakers and participating members of the public.

Such 'artisans' will 'subject the narrative to different and unpredictable readings [and put it] to different and unpredictable' uses (Schaffer and Smith, 2004: 32).

While the 'disciplining drama of judgement' (Douglas, 2001: 175) implies permanence and univocality, the discussion above demonstrates that the archives will not, inevitably, be used in the way the prosecution's spokesperson envisaged. If such contestation is unavoidable, perhaps it should be embraced. Speaking of the ICTY archives, Ketelaar (2012: 217) welcomes the fact that it will be a 'living archive' that will 'continue to be challenged, contested, and expanded'. Like memory, 'an archive is not just an agency of storage, but a process' (Ketelaar, 2012: 217) and is, therefore, 'a space to escape from a monolithic truth, history and memory, by allowing the questioning of myth and rationality'.

CONCLUSION

Contrary to Arendt's (1994[1963]: 253) argument that 'law's main business' should be determining the guilt or innocence of the accused, many of the judges and lawyers with whom I spoke at the ICTR believed that the objective of preserving a historical record could also be pursued, a position held by many of their forebears at Nuremberg. Given law's 'relentless insistence on record keeping and remembrance' (Sarat and Kearns, 2002: 13) and 'legal testing' (Wilson, 2011: 169, 220) lawyers and judges implied that the 'historical record' should be valued, for after all 'You're going to have a version of history anyway, so better to have an accurate legal version rather than a watered down version' (prosecution lawyer). At the same time, however, lawyers and judges wanted to distinguish their endeavour from that of truth commissions and historians. I have demonstrated that such a distinction relies upon a caricature of truth commissions and obscures the similarities between the practice of law and the writing of history. I suggested that lawyers and judges sought to maintain such distinctions in order to emphasize that law is distinct because a judgement prevents 'a perpetual rewriting' (Ricouer 2004: 320). And yet, the historical record preserved in the archive is not so easily disciplined and is liable to dissenting readings and may 'face a long-term state of contestation' (Kaye, 2014: 392).

It could, however, be argued that aspirations for the ICTR archives are being over-valued. Trouillot (1995: 20) reminds us that 'Long before average citizens read [works by historians] they access history through celebrations, sites and museum visits, movies.' In the context of the ICTR, films have already established strong narratives of the 1994 Rwandan genocide: *Hotel Rwanda* (2004); *Sometimes in April*

(2005); *Shooting Dogs* (2005) (see Eltringham, 2013b), as have documentaries, memorial sites and accounts by journalists (see Keane, 1995). From that perspective, our concern may shift from the possibility that the ICTR archives may generate histories contrary to the judgments to a concern that the ICTR archives may not be consulted at all.

CONCLUSION

During a conversation with me a prosecution lawyer once mused, 'When we walk out; what was it all about?' (see Chapter 1). In 2005 I was handed a draft 'legacy' document that gave one possible answer to that question, chronicling the number of arrests, completed trials and jurisprudence bequeathed to the project of international criminal justice (ICTR, 2005b). The same emphasis is present in the 2014 video that dominates the Mechanism for International Criminal Tribunals (MICT) ICTR page (http://unictr.unmict.org/). Stating that the ICTR's 'legacy lays the foundation for a new era in international criminal justice', the emphasis is, again, placed on tangible achievements: '20,000 evidence exhibits, 27,000 hours of testimony, 93 indicted, 75 trials, 61 convictions' and a series of jurisprudential 'firsts' (the first conviction for genocide, the first conviction of a former head of government since the Nuremberg and Tokyo tribunals, the first conviction for rape as a tool of genocide, and the first convictions of members of the media for inciting genocide). While the MICT video suggests that the ICTR's work has brought 'healing' to Rwandans, no explicit reference is made to the hope expressed in the 1994 Statute that it would 'contribute to the process of national reconciliation and to the restoration and maintenance of peace' (United Nations, 1994e UN Doc. S/RES/955 (1994); see Chapter 1). Neither is a 'historical record' mentioned, despite its prominence in official statements in the latter stages of the ICTR's operation (see Chapter 5). Rather, the video describes the mission of the ICTR as having been 'to locate, apprehend and prosecute the architects of the genocide'. The emphasis, in other words, is placed squarely on the 'law's main business' of determining guilt or innocence (Arendt, 1994[1963]: 253) rather than 'grandiose statements' about 'peace' or 'reconciliation' (Mégret, 2016: para 50). The video ends by stating that the ICTR has contributed to 'a time when international law offers justice to all people, everywhere', placing the emphasis on the global project of international criminal justice rather than the specifics of post-genocide Rwanda (see Chapter 1; Eltringham, 2014).

Reflecting on such 'legacy talk', Sara Kendall and Sarah Nouwen (2016: 213) employ Zygmunt Baumen's (1992: 2) argument that institutions, just like individuals, make 'bids for immortality', by engaging in efforts to 'colonize' the future through recounting their life narratives. This echoes the argument in the Introduction that 'because the rules for constructing personal and organizational identities are very much alike' (Czarniawska, 1997: 40–50) those tasked with speaking on behalf of the ICTR portrayed it as a 'super-person' and recounted a life narrative of 'achievements'. By perpetuating the image of the ICTR as 'super-person' (Czarniawska, 1997: 40–1) with a cohesive 'life narrative' (Bauman, 1992: 2), the ICTR's 'legacy talk' continues to privilege an abstract 'super-person' over real individuals, thereby continuing to conceal the fact that law is a 'flawed human process' (Morison and Leith, 1992: vii).

As discussed in the Introduction, concealment of the fallible individual permeates the practice of law. The euphemisms of the *personae juris* ('defendant', 'Mr President', 'Madam Prosecutor') and euphemistic reference to the judges ('Chamber', 'Court' and 'Tribunal') create an image of 'transcendent justice' that is not 'confined totally to persons' (Garapon, 2001: 28), but is 'somewhere else, always out of reach' (Feldman, 2004: 193). The desire to disassociate law from the vagaries of fallible individuals was also considered in Chapter 3 where I described how the constant revision of the ICTR's RPE illustrates how arbitrary, contingent responses in the courtroom were rapidly stabilized into impersonal, universal principles by means of 'the cult of the [legal] text' (Bourdieu, 1987: 851). While revealing the particular nature of adaptation at the ICTR, this process re-affirms the observation that law is claimed to be an expression of transcendent principles but is, in reality, a continuous, textual codification of contingent practice (see Falk-Moore, 2000: 9–10).

Just as this 'cult of the [legal] text' (Bourdieu, 1987: 851) allows legal decisions to appear not as decisions by judges but as the independent 'will of the law' (Bourdieu, 1987: 828), so the promotion of the life narrative of the ICTR as 'super-person' strengthens the claim that law is stable and dispassionate (Peters, 2008: 199). 'Legacy talk', therefore, is a continuation of the autobiographical narration that occurred during the ICTR's operation in order to cultivate a 'public image of cohesion and shared belief' (Scott, 1990: 55) and suppress the 'contradictions and contingencies of practice and the plurality of perspectives' (Mosse, 2006: 938) that have been the subject of this book.

And yet, 'legacies are assessed over time, and by various parties other than the legator' (Kendall and Nouwen, 2016: 217). As a consequence, the very act of defining 'legacy' is 'somewhat daring' given that, in reality, 'it depends on external judgement and develops incrementally over time' (Stahn, 2012: 275). It is for this reason that trying to 'colonise the future' will 'remain forever disconcertingly provisional and non-definite' (Bauman, 1992: 54). As Lawrence Douglas (2006: 104) notes, international trials:

> play before multiple audiences, each of which will perceive the trial differently and will measure its success by different standards ... these perceptions will transform over the course of the years, as the dynamics of space yield to the imponderables of time.

Not only are such evaluations ongoing, attempts to claim a 'legacy' will provoke alternative versions, as seen in the *Association des Avocats de la Défense* (ADAD) dossier distributed at the 2007 Legacy Conference (see Chapter 1) and the two-day conference organized by ADAD in The Hague in 2009 entitled 'ICTR: An Independent Conference on its Legacy from the Defence Perspective'. While many of the presentations at the 2009 Conference reflected procedural issues ('ICTR Witness Protection'; 'Joint Criminal Enterprise and Command Responsibility in International Criminal Justice') others denounced the whole enterprise ('Why the ICTR has had a Zero Deterrent Effect in Africa'; 'The UN Security Council created "Victor's Impunity" at the ICTR'). The appropriation of the term 'legacy' by ADAD from the ICTR's own 2007 Conference demonstrates the irony that a term initially employed to impose a particular account provided a platform for contestation.

I also considered uncertainty regarding future assessments of the ICTR in the discussion of the archive in Chapter 5. There I quoted an ALO who assumed that a 'future researcher' would assess any item from the archive in a way that corresponded to the assessment of judges in the judgments. I suggested that this was naïve given that judgements can be revised through judicial review (if new facts are discovered) or appealed (on the basis of issues of law) and trials in other jurisdictions may also challenge ICTR judgments (see Douglas, 2001: 4). Beyond such conventional re-assessment, I quoted Eric Ketelaar (2012: 217), a former national archivist of the Netherlands and a member of the Advisory Committee on the Archives of the ICTR and ICTY, who states that given that 'an archive is not just an agency of storage, but a process' it will 'continue to be challenged, contested, and expanded'. This was demonstrated in Chapter 1 where I described how certain defence lawyers denounced the ICTR while simultaneously indicating that the archives contained material that substantiated an 'untold story of the Rwanda War' (Erlinder, 2009: 20; see Eltringham, 2017), a story different from that found in the ICTR's judgments. The example of the archives demonstrates that any attempt to colonize the future will remain 'disconcertingly provisional' (Bauman, 1992: 54). Both the co-option of 'legacy' by ADAD for the 2009 Conference and the use of the archive by defence lawyers to tell an 'untold story' suggest that the ICTR's 'legacy talk' is far from invincible.

Sarat and Kearns (2002: 12) argue that there are 'two audiences for every legal act, the audience of the present and the audience of the future'. While the discussion of legacy and the archive was concerned with audience(s) of the future, a key theme of this book has been the perspectives of a particular 'audience of the present', those who worked at the ICTR. As noted in the Introduction, judges, lawyers and others who worked at the ICTR were constantly '[re]formulating, editing, applauding, and refusing' (Czarniawska, 1997: 46) the narrative disseminated by those tasked with speaking for the ICTR. In Chapter 1, for example, I discussed the complex assessments of the ICTR by judges and lawyers. Defence lawyers held ambivalent positions, both denouncing the ICTR as 'victor's justice' but also celebrating its capacity to tell the 'untold story of the Rwanda War' (Erlinder, 2009: 20). Likewise, judges stood by the outcome of trials, but feared that the record of the ICTR would be tainted by the failure to prosecute the RPF. While official 'legacy talk' seeks to suppress this 'plurality of perspectives' (Mosse, 2006: 938), such assessments suggest that there will be a shadow 'legacy talk' carried on by those who worked at the ICTR. This shadow 'legacy talk' will, of course, be as diverse as the judges and lawyers who worked at the ICTR while official 'legacy talk' will remain resolutely monovocal.

I have argued that an important legacy (although not included in 'legacy talk') of the ad hoc, exceptional ICTR is the way it 'rendered explicit' the hidden ways in which law operates in unexceptional, domestic courtrooms. The exceptional nature of the ICTR meant that much of what lawyers and judges normally take for granted had to be 'rendered explicit' (Zoettl, 2016: 7). Chapter 3 considered seemingly unimportant details of courtroom practice (at the domestic and international levels) that are essential to 'producing and reproducing a legal system' (Zoettl, 2016: 10) and that such hidden, taken-for-granted, 'unwritten rules' are only rendered explicit when disregarded. The ICTR was a unique environment in which lawyers and judges drawn from diverse legal systems routinely transgressed one another's 'unwritten rules' in a context in which there was no consensus on the 'unwritten rules'. This required legal practitioners to articulate what would normally resist explicit description (Bourdieu, 2003[1977]: 94) thereby providing a novel insight into the role played by these 'unwritten rules'. I explored this in detail in Chapter 3 regarding lawyers sitting and standing, arguing that this is an example of 'extra-legal knowledge' (Morison and Leith, 1992: 17; see Introduction) and a component of the 'extratextual and subtextual language' of the courtroom (Martin, 2006: 10–11; see Chapter 2).

Not only does the experience of the ICTR provide scholarly insight into the role played by 'unwritten rules' in legal practice, it also allowed lawyers and judges an opportunity to become conscious of, evaluate and, in some cases, change habitual practice given that everything that 'we would normally take for granted' (prosecution lawyer) had to be discussed (see Chapter 3). In the process, some lawyers and judges displayed a lack of attachment to their habitual practice, that 'just because we have one way of doing something doesn't mean it is better' (defence lawyer) and 'Who the hell cares how things are done in the old country' (judge). As regards the encounter between practitioners from the common ('adversarial') and civil ('inquisitorial') legal systems, judges reported 'little tension' (civil law) that it had not 'created a great difference' (common law) and 'we're all playing the same game' (civil law). Judges described the encounter with alternative systems as 'enriching', 'liberating' and 'stimulating' and that 'It's the differences that create the richness.' Lawyers expressed a similar, liberating openness, that 'I've learnt to think out of the box of common law, a new way of doing things' (common law), and 'You have to decide what is best, what's efficient' (civil law). As a consequence, certain lawyers and judges left the ICTR having gone through a process in which what they had previously taken for granted had been held up for evaluative inspection. This is also a legacy of the ICTR. Just as prior experience (domestic and/or international) informed legal practitioners in their encounter with the particular needs of practising at the ICTR, so, in turn, experience of the ICTR will have become an evaluative touchstone as practitioners (re)dispersed to domestic jurisdictions and other international courts.

Staying with the theme of how the ad hoc, exceptional ICTR provided insight into the ways in which law operates in unexceptional, domestic courtrooms, in Chapter 2 I discussed how judges reiterated the importance placed in domestic courts on demeanour and the 'marginality of words' compared to the importance of the body (see Braverman, 2007: 261–3). The exceptional use of simultaneous interpretation at the ICTR brought the importance of the body into even greater relief. Interpreters' need for a 'clear view of the speaker and the room' (International Association of Conference Interpreters, 2015) in order to pick up the 'body language' made explicit what is ordinarily taken for granted by all trial participants, whether in international or domestic trials. Furthermore, the exceptional nature of the Zigiranyirazo trial (the witness and accused in two different continents) shows that the need to assess demeanour is not restricted to judges assessing the credibility of a witnesses for the final judgment, but also lawyers and judges constantly assessing one another physically as part of a 'normal visual interaction with the proceedings' (ICTR, 2006f: 16; see Chapter 3). The exceptional nature of the ICTR reiterates the general observation that 'nonverbal communication subtly effects the entire proceedings of a trial' (Levenson, 2007: 579). This further demonstrates the weakness of legal scholarship that takes transcripts as the sole unit of analysis as transcripts do not record the 'extratextual and subtextual language' of the courtroom (Martin, 2006: 10–11; see Introduction).

In Chapter 2 I also argued how the exceptional, improvised, ad hoc nature of the ICTR revealed aspects of the creation of judicial space that are otherwise naturalized and hidden in domestic court complexes. While it is rules explicitly enforced by a judge that appear to establish 'order in court', that order is, in reality, a consequence of the demarcation of a space as a 'play-ground' in which the rules of ordinary life are suspended and an 'absolute and peculiar order reigns' (Huizinga, 1949: 10). I argued, that the public, apparently marginal to the practice of law, play an important role in creating that space, that the courtroom is a privileged site because of the measured obstruction and gradual incorporation of spectators as they approach the courtroom (Garapon, 2001:

46–7). In such an environment, the visitor's body is not simply a passive receptor, but is a vehicle for the strategies of differentiating the privileged space of the courtroom. The public become embodied indicators of a privileged space when that space is supposedly privileged irrespective of their presence. While I am not the first person to note that the privileging of the courtroom as a site of authority is a product of the way that court buildings act upon members of the public (see Garapon, 2001; Hanson, 1996; Mulcahy, 2007; Taylor, 1993), the ICTR's exceptionality as an improvised court complex further affirms the role played by two seemingly unimportant elements in the practice of law: the physical space and spectators.

The exceptional nature of trials at the ICTR was also an opportunity to re-assess previous research on witness testimony. In Chapter 4, I examined the argument that Rwandan 'culture' was an impediment to Rwandans giving testimony, that, according to a prosecution lawyer, 'They're not used to narrative storytelling as a cultural thing in Rwanda.' I suggested that simultaneous interpretation, protection orders, multiple testimony and the question and answer format of witness examination were also important impediments. Regarding the question and answer format of witness examination, I argued that because a witness can only speak when answering the question that has most recently been asked of them and that only lawyers and judges are permitted to ask questions, there are 'fundamental contradictions between everyday storytelling ... and the expectations and interpretations of storytelling and retelling in court' (Eades, 2008: 210). I argued, therefore, that rather than unfamiliarity with narrative storytelling as a 'cultural thing', Rwandans may just have been unfamiliar with the question/answer format of the courtroom. On one hand, this argument was directed towards the specifics of the ICTR (the argument that Rwandan 'culture' was an impediment). On the other hand, this highlights the fact that the question and answer format of witness examination causes 'problems for any witness who is unfamiliar with the ways of thinking, believing and acting that are part of legal culture' (Eades, 2008: 223) whether in international or domestic trials.

The discussion in Chapter 4 also gave an opportunity to problematize witness statements in a context in which Rwandan witnesses gave testimony which did not correspond with previous statements. I argued that while there is an assumption that statements allow 'survivors to speak for themselves' (Hartman, 1995: 192), this is not the case given they are always dialogical, co-productions (see Langfield and Maclean,

2009), that incorporate 'foreign material' (Levi, 1986: 130) and when transformed from a question and answer interview to a narrative/summary statement certain material is rejected and the sequence of events is made to appear more coherent with features 'edited in' (McKinley, 1997: 75). While it would be rare in a domestic court for a witness to give multiple statements, at the ICTR many witnesses had provided multiple statements. My discussion of witness statements at the ICTR was, therefore, an opportunity to re-affirm that the witness statement, a central instrument in criminal trials, is far from being the witnesses 'own words'.

While the ICTR's 'legacy talk' foregrounds tangible achievements (arrests, convictions etc.) I have suggested that there is also a 'shadow legacy' carried by those who worked at the ICTR. In addition, by re-affirming the importance of 'unwritten rules'; the importance of 'seeing and being seen' in the courtroom; the role the physical space and spectators in demarcating the 'play-ground' of law; the counter-intuitive manner in which testimony is elicited; and the fabricated nature of statements, the ICTR leaves a legacy of insights into the practice of law in domestic as well as other international contexts.

This book has responded to Morison and Keith's (1992: 19) suggestion that the 'legal process, can be understood only if we move away from the academically (and popularly) construed perception of law being about abstract rules and towards a full understanding of what goes on in the real world' of lawyers and judges. This full(er) understanding, I argue, will allow a more nuanced assessment of international criminal justice, thereby requiring both detractors and advocates to be diligent in recognizing that the success/failure of such institutions according to grandiose claims is undergirded by a muddled, 'flawed human process' (Morison and Leith, 1992: vii).

BIBLIOGRAPHY

Abbink, J. and T. Salverda, eds. (2012). *The Anthropology of Elites: Power, Culture and the Complexities of Distinction*. London: Palgrave Macmillan.

Abu-Lughod, L. (1991). Writing Against Culture. In R. Fox, ed., *Recapturing Anthropology*. Santa Fe, NM: School for Advanced Research Press, pp. 137–62.

Abu-Lughod, L. (2002). Do Muslim Women Really Need Saving? Anthropological Reflections on Cultural Relativism and Its Others. *American Anthropologist*, 104(3), 783–90.

Achebe, C. (1988). *Hopes and Impediments: Selected Essays, 1965–1987*. London: Doubleday.

Adami, T. (2007). 'Who Will Be Left to Tell the Tale?' Recordkeeping and International Criminal Jurisprudence. *Archival Science*, 7(3), 213–21.

African Rights and Redress (2008). *Survivors and Post-Genocide Justice in Rwanda: Their Experiences, Perspectives and Hopes*. London: Redress.

Akhavan, P. (2005). The Crime of Genocide in the ICTR Jurisprudence. *Journal of International Criminal Justice*, 3(4), 989–1006.

Almqvist, J. (2006). The Impact of Cultural Diversity on International Criminal Proceedings. *Journal of International Criminal Justice*, 4(4), 745–64.

Ambos, K. (2003). International Criminal Procedure: 'adversarial', 'inquisitorial' or Mixed? *International Criminal Law Review*, 3(1), 1–37.

Anders, G. (2011). Testifying About 'Uncivilized Events': Problematic Representations of Africa in the Trial Against Charles Taylor. *Leiden Journal of International Law*, 24(4), 937–59.

Aptel, C. (2002). The Intent to Commit Genocide in the Case Law of the International Criminal Tribunal for Rwanda. *Criminal Law Forum*, 13(3), 273–91.

Apuuli, K. P. (2009). Procedural Due Process and the Prosecution of Genocide Suspects in Rwanda. *Journal of Genocide Research*, 11(1), 11–30.

Archambault, C. S. (2011). Ethnographic Empathy and the Social Context of Rights: 'Rescuing' Maasai Girls from Early Marriage. *American Anthropologist*, 113(4), 632–43.

Arendt, H. (1994[1963]). *Eichmann in Jerusalem: A Report on the Banality of Evil*. Harmondsworth: Penguin.

Arendt, H. (1998[1958]). *The Human Condition*, 2nd ed., Chicago: University of Chicago Press.

Asad, T. (1973). Two European Images of Non-European Rule. *Economy and Society*, 2(3), 263–77.

Askin, K. D. (1999). Sexual Violence in Decisions and Indictments of the Yugoslav and Rwandan Tribunals: Current Status. *American Journal of International Law*, 93(1), 92–123.

Atkinson, M. and P. Drew (1979). *Order in Court: The Organization of Verbal Interaction in Judicial Settings*. London: Macmillan.

Autesserre, S. (2014). *Peaceland: Conflict Resolution and the Everyday Politics of International Intervention*. New York: Cambridge University Press.

Bachmann, M. (2010). Theatre and the Drama of the Law: A 'Theatrical History' of the Eichmann Trial. *Law Text Culture*, 14(1), 94–116.

Baines, E. and B. Stewart (2011). I cannot accept what I have not done': Storytelling, Gender and Transitional Justice. *Journal of Human Rights Practice*, 3(3), 245–63.

Bajc, V. (2007). Surveillance in Public Rituals: Security Meta-Ritual and the 2005 U. S. Presidential Inauguration. *American Behavioral Scientist*, 50(12), 1648–73.

Ball, M. (1975). The Play's the Thing: An Unscientific Reflection on Courts Under the Rubric of Theater. *Stanford Law Review*, 28(1), 81–115.

Bauman, Z. (1992). *Mortality, Immortality, and Other Life Strategies*. Stanford, CL: Stanford University Press.

Baumann, G. (1992). Ritual Implicates 'others'. Rereading Durkheim in a Plural Society. In D. de Coppet, ed., *Understanding Rituals*. London and New York: Routledge, pp. 97–116.

Baylis, E. (2008). Tribunal-Hopping with the Post-Conflict Justice Junkies, *Oregon Review of International Law Symposium Issue*, 10, 361–90.

Baylis, E. (2015). What Internationals Know: Improving the Effectiveness of Post-Conflict Justice Initiatives. *Washington University Global Studies Law Review*, 14, 243–315.

Bell, C. (1992). *Ritual Theory, Ritual Practice*. New York: Oxford University Press.

Bentham, J. (1978[1827]). *Rationale of Judicial Evidence*. London: Garland.

Berk-Seligson, S. (1990). Bilingual Court Proceedings: The Role of the Court Interpreter. In J. N. Levi and A. G. Walker, eds., *Language in the Judicial Process*. New York: Plenum Press, pp. 155–201.

Betts, A. (2005). Should Approaches to Post-Conflict Justice and Reconciliation Be Determined Globally, Nationally or Locally? *European Journal of Development Research*, 17(4), 735–52.

Blommaert, J., Bock, M. and McCormick, K. (2007). Narrative Inequality in the TRC Hearings: On the Hearability of Hidden Transcripts. In C. Anthonissen and J. Blommaert, eds., *Discourse and Human Rights Violations*. Amsterdam: John Benjamins, pp. 33–64.

Boed, R. (2002). Individual Criminal Responsibility for Violations of Article 3 Common to the Geneva Conventions of 1949 and of Additional Protocol II Thereto in the Case Law of the International Criminal Tribunal for Rwanda. *Criminal Law Forum*, 13(3), 293–322.

Bohlander, M. (2006). Referring an Indictment from the ICTY and ICTR to Another Court. Rule 11BIS and the Consequences for the Law of Extradition. *The International and Comparative Law Quarterly*, 55(1), 219–26.

Bonacker, T. (2013). Global Victimhood: On the Charisma of the Victim in Transitional Justice Processes. *World Political Science Review*, 9(1), 97–129.

Bostian, I. L. (2005). Cultural Relativism in International War Crimes Prosecutions: The International Criminal Tribunal for Rwanda. *ILSA Journal of International and Comparative Law*, 12(1), 1–40.

Bourdieu, P. (1984). *Homo Academicus*. Cambridge: Polity.

Bourdieu, P. (1987). The Force of Law: Toward a Sociology of the Juridical Field. *Hastings Journal of Law*, 38(5), 814–53.

Bourdieu, P. (1990). *The Logic of Practice*. Cambridge: Polity Press.

Bourdieu, P. (1999). Site Effects. In P. Bourdieu and P. P. Ferguson, eds., *The Weight of the World: Social Suffering in Contemporary Society*. Cambridge: Polity Press, pp. 123–9.

Bourdieu, P. (2003[1977]). *Outline of a Theory of Practice*. Cambridge: Cambridge University Press.

Bourdieu, P. (1991). *Language and Symbolic Power*. Translated by John B. Thompson.Cambridge: Polity.

Bourdieu, P. and L. Wacquant (1992). *An Invitation to Reflexive Sociology*. Chicago: University of Chicago Press.

Braverman, I. (2007). The Place of Translation in Jerusalem's Criminal Trial Court. *New Criminal Law Review: An International and Interdisciplinary Journal*, 10(2), 239–77.

Brooks, P. (1996). 'The Law as Narrative and Record. In P. Brooks and P. Gewirtz, eds., *Law's Stories: Narrative and Rhetoric in the Law*. New Haven, CT: Yale University Press, pp. 14–22.

Brounéus, K. (2008). 'Truth Telling as Talking Cure? Insecurity and Retraumatization' in the Rwandan Gacaca Courts. *Security Dialogue*, 39 (1), 55–76.

Bruner, J. S. (1990). *Acts of Meaning*. London: Harvard University Press.

Buruma, I. (1995). *The Wages of Guilt: Memories of War in Germany and Japan*. London: Vintage.

Butler, J. (1988). 'Performative Acts and Gender Constitution: An Essay on Phenomenology and Feminist Theory'. *Theatre Journal*, 40(4), 519–31.

Buur, L. (2001). 'Making Findings for the Future: Representational Order and Redemption in the Work of the TRC'. *South African Journal of Philosophy*, 20 (1), 42–65.

Buur, L. (2003a). 'In the Name of the Victims': The Politics of Compensation in the Work of the South African Truth and Reconciliation Commission. In P. Gready, ed., *Political Transition: Politics and Cultures*. London: Pluto Press, pp. 148–64.

Buur, L. (2003b). Monumental History: Visibility and Invisibility in the Work of the South African Truth and Reconciliation Commission. In D. Posel and G. Simpson, eds., *Commissioning the Past: Understanding South Africa's Truth and Reconciliation Commission*. Johannesburg: Witwatersrand University Press, pp. 66–93.

Byrne, R. (2010). The New Public International Lawyer and the Hidden Art of International Criminal Trial Practice. *Connecticut Journal of International Law*, 25, 243–303.

Campbell, K. (2013). The Laws of Memory The ICTY, the Archive, and Transitional Justice. *Social and Legal Studies*, 22, 247–69.

Carlen, P. (1976). *Magistrates' Justice*. London: Martin Robertson.

Carlsson, I., H. Sung-Joo and R. Kupolati (1999). Report of the Independent Inquiry into the Actions of the United Nations During the 1994 Genocide in Rwanda. New York: United Nations.

Carr, E. H. (1987). *What Is History?* 2nd ed., London: Penguin.

Cassese, A. (2004). The ICTY: A Living and Vital Reality. *Journal of International Criminal Justice*, 61(1), 585–97.

Cerone, J. (2008). The Jurisprudential Contributions of the ICTR to the Legal Definition of Crimes Against Humanity – The Evolution of the Nexus Requirement. *New England Journal of International and Comparative Law*, 14, 191–201.

Chenault, S. (2008). 'And Since Akayesu? The Development of ICTR Jurisprudence on Gender Crimes: A Comparison of Akayesu and Muhimana. *New England Journal of International and Comparative Law*, 14, 222–37.

Christodoulidis, E. (2001). Law's Immemorial. In E. Christodoulidis and S. Veitch, eds., *Lethe's Law: Justice, Law and Ethics in Reconciliation*. Oxford: Hart, pp. 207–27.

Clark, M. M. (2005). Resisting Attrition in Stories of Trauma. *Narrative*, 13 (3), 294–8.

Clarke, K. M. (2009). *Fictions of Justice: The International Criminal Court and the Challenge of Legal Pluralism in Sub-Saharan Africa*. Cambridge: Cambridge University Press.

Clifford, J. (1988). *The Predicament of Culture: Twentieth Century Ethnography, Literature and Art*. Cambridge, MA: Harvard University Press.

Clifford, J. (1997). *Routes: Travel and Translation in the Late Twentieth Century*. Cambridge, MA: Harvard University Press.

Cohen, A. (1981). *Politics of Elite Culture: Explorations in the Dramaturgy of Power in a Modern African Society*. Berkeley: California University Press.

Cohen, F. S. (1950). Field Theory and Judicial Logic. *The Yale Law Journal*, 59 (2), 238–72.

Cole, C. M. (2007). Performance, Transitional Justice, and the Law: South Africa's Truth and Reconciliation Commission. *Theatre Journal*, 59(2), 167–87.

Collingwood, R. G. and W. J. V. D. Dussen (1993[1946]). *The Idea of History*, 2nd ed., Oxford: Clarendon.

Comaroff, J. and J. L. Comaroff (1991). *Of Revelation and Revolution: Christianity, Colonialism, and Consciousness in South Africa*. Chicago: University of Chicago Press.

Combs, N. A. (2009). Testimonial Deficiencies and Evidentiary Uncertainties in International Criminal Trial. *Journal of International Law and Foreign Affairs*, 235, 235–73.

Commonwealth Human Rights Initiative (2009). *Rwanda's Application for Membership in the Commonwealth – Report and Recommendations of CHRI*. New Delhi: Commonwealth Human Rights Initiative.

Conley, J. M. and W. M. O'Barr (1990). *Rules Versus Relationships: The Ethnography of Legal Discourse*. Chicago IL: University of Chicago Press.

Conley, J. M. and W. M. O'Barr (2005). *Just Words: Law, Language, and Power*, 2nd ed., Chicago IL: University of Chicago Press.

Cowan, J., M. Dembour and R. Wilson (2001). Introduction. In J. Cowan, M. Dembour and R. Wilson, eds., *Culture and Rights: Anthropological Perspectives*. Cambridge: Cambridge University Press, pp. 1–26.

Crosby, A. and M. B. Lykes (2011). Mayan Women Survivors Speak: The Gendered Relations of Truth Telling in Postwar Guatemala. *International Journal of Transitional Justice*, 5(3), 456–76.

Cruvellier, T. (2010). *Court of Remorse Inside the International Criminal Tribunal for Rwanda*. Translated by C. Voss. Madison: University of Wisconsin Press.

Czarniawska, B. (1997). *Narrating the Organization: Dramas of Institutional Identity*. Chicago: University of Chicago Press.

Danet, B., K. B. Hoffman, N. C. Kermish, H. J. Rafn and D. G. Stayman (1976). An Ethnography of Questioning in the Courtroom. In R. W. Shuy and A. Shnukal, eds., *Language Use and the Uses of Language*. Washington DC: Georgetown University Press, pp. 222–34.

Davidson, H. R. (2004). The International Criminal Tribunal for Rwanda's Decision in The Prosecutor v. Ferdinand Nahimana et al.: The Past, Present, and Future of International Incitement Law. *Leiden Journal of International Law*, 17(3), 505–19.

Debord, G. (1967). *The Society of the Spectacle*. Detroit, MI.: Black & Red.

Degni-Ségui, R. (1994). *Situation of Human Rights in Rwanda*. New York: United Nations.

Del Ponte, C. and C. Sudetic (2009). *Madame Prosecutor: Confrontations with Humanity's Worst Criminals and the Culture of Impunity*. New York: Other Press.

Derrida, J. (1996). *Archive Fever: A Freudian Impression*. Chicago; London: University of Chicago Press.

Dershowitz, A. M. (1996). Life is Not a Dramatic Narrative. In P. Brooks and P. Gewirtz, eds., *Law's Stories: Narrative and Rhetoric in the Law*. New Haven, CT: Yale University Press, pp. 99–105.

Des Forges, A. L. (1999). *"Leave None to Tell the Story": Genocide in Rwanda*. New York: Human Rights Watch.

Dieng, A. (2001). Africa and the Globalization of Justice: Contributions and Lessons from the International Criminal Tribunal for Rwanda. Paper presented at Justice in Africa, 30 July–2 August 2001, at Wilton Park, Sussex, England.

Dieng, A. (2003) Registrar's Note. *ICTR Newsletter*, 1(1). Arusha: ICTR.

Dixon, R. (1997). Developing International Rules of Evidence for the Yugoslav and Rwanda Tribunals. *Transnational Law and Contemporary Problems*, 7, 81–102.

Donia, R. (2012). Truths, Memories and Histories in the Archives of the International Criminal Tribunal for the Former Yugoslavia. In H. van der Wilt, J. Vervliet, G. K. Sluiter and J. H. ten Cate, eds., *The Genocide Convention: The Legacy of 60 Years*. Leiden: Brill, pp. 199–221.

Douglas, L. (2001). *The Memory of Judgment: Making Law and History in the Trials of the Holocaust*. New Haven, CT: Yale University Press.

Douglas, L. (2006). History and Memory in the Courtroom: Reflections on Perpetrator Trials. In H. R. Reginbogin and C. Safferling, eds., *The Nuremberg Trials: International Criminal Law Since 1945*. Munchen: Saur, pp. 95–105.

Douglas, L. (2006). Perpetrator Proceedings and Didactic Trials. In A. Duff, L. Farmer, S. Marshall and V. Tadros, eds., *The Trial on Trial: Volume 2: Judgment and Calling to Account*. London: Bloomsbury, pp. 191–206.

Douglas, L. (2016). Truth and Justice in Atrocity Trials. In W. A. Schabas, ed., *The Cambridge Companion to International Criminal Law*. Cambridge: Cambridge University Press, pp. 34–51.

Douglass, A. (2003). The Menchu Effect: Strategies, Lies and Approximate Truths in Texts of Witness. In A. Douglass and T. A. Vogler, eds., *Witness and Memory: The Discourse of Trauma*. New York: Routledge, pp. 55–88.

Dunstan, R. (1980). Contexts for Coercion: Analyzing Properties of Courtroom 'Questions'. *British Journal of Law and Society*, 7(1), 61–77.

Eades, D. (1996). Verbatim Courtroom Transcripts and Discourse Analysis. In H. Kniffka, ed., *Recent Developments in Forensic Linguistics*. Frankfurt: Peter Lang, pp. 241–54.

Eades, D. (2000). I Don't Think It's an Answer to the Question: Silencing Aboriginal Witnesses in Court. *Language in Society*, 29(2), 161–95.

Eades, D. (2008). Telling and Retelling Your Story in Court: Questions, Assumptions and Intercultural Implications. *Current Issues in Criminal Justice*, 20(2), 209–30.

Eastmond, M. (2007). Stories as Lived Experience: Narratives in Forced Migration Research. *Journal of Refugee Studies*, 20(2), 248–64.

Eboe-Osuji, C. (2005). Complicity in Genocide Versus Aiding and Abetting Genocide Construing the Difference in the ICTR and ICTY Statutes. *Journal of International Criminal Justice*, 3(1), 56–81.

Elias-Bursać, E. (2015). *Translating Evidence and Interpreting Testimony at a War Crimes Tribunal*. London: Palgrave.

Ellis, M. (1997). Achieving Justice Before the International War Crimes Tribunal: Challenges for the Defense Counsel. *Duke Journal Of Comparative and International Law*, 7(2), 519–36.

Eltringham, N. (2004). *Accounting for Horror: Post-Genocide Debates in Rwanda*. London: Pluto.

Eltringham, N. (2008). A War Crimes Community": The Legacy of the International Criminal Tribunal for Rwanda Beyond Jurisprudence. *New England Journal of International and Comparative Law*, 14(2), 309–18.

Eltringham, N. (2009). 'We are not a Truth Commission': Fragmented Narratives and the Historical Record at the International Criminal Tribunal for Rwanda. *Journal of Genocide Research*, 11(1), 55–79.

Eltringham, N. (2010). Judging the 'Crime of Crimes': Continuity and Improvisation at the International Criminal Tribunal for Rwanda. In A. Hinton, ed., *Transitional Justice: Global Mechanisms and Local Realities in the Aftermath of Genocide and Mass Violence*. New Brunswick, NJ: Rutgers University Press, pp. 206–26.

Eltringham, N. (2013a). 'Illuminating the Broader Context': Anthropological and Historical Knowledge at the International Criminal Tribunal for Rwanda. *Journal of the Royal Anthropological Institute*, 19(2), 338–55.

Eltringham, N. (2013b). Showing What Cannot Be Imagined: 'Shooting dogs' and 'Hotel Rwanda'. In N. Eltringham, ed., *Framing Africa: Portrayals of a Continent in Contemporary Mainstream Cinema*. Oxford: Berghahn Books, pp. 113–34.

Eltringham, N. (2014). 'When we walk out; what was it all about?': Views on 'new beginnings' from Within the International Criminal Tribunal for Rwanda. *Development and Change*, 45(3), 543–64.

Eltringham, N. (2017). 'The judgement is not made now; the judgement will be made in the future': 'politically motivated' defence lawyers and the International Criminal Tribunal for Rwanda's 'historical record'. *Humanity: An International Journal of Human Rights, Humanitarianism and*

Development. Available at http://humanityjournal.org/blog/the-judgement-is-not-made/.

Erlanger, H., B. Garth, J. Larson, E. Mertz, V. Nourse and D. Wilkins (2005). Foreword: Is It Time for a New Legal Realism? *Wisconsin Law Review*, 2, 335–63.

Erlinder, P. (2009). Preventing the Falsification of History: An Unintended Consequence of ICTR Disclosure Rules? Paper presented at International Criminal Tribunal for Rwanda: An Independent Conference on Its Legacy from the Defence Perspective, 13–15 November 2009, at Institute for Social Science, The Hague.

Errington, S. (1979). Some Comments on Style in the Meaning of the Past. *Journal of Asian Studies*, 38(2), 231–44.

Esmier, S. (2003) 1948: Law, History, Memory. *Social Text*, 21(2), 25–48.

Etienne, M. (2005) The Ethics of Cause Lawyering: An Empirical Examination of Criminal Defense Lawyers as Cause Lawyers. *The Journal of Criminal Law and Criminology*, 95(4), 1195–260.

Evans, R. J. (2002). History, Memory, and the Law: The Historian as Expert Witness. *History and Theory*, 41(3), 326–45.

Falk Moore, S. (2000). *Law as Process: An Anthropological Approach*, 2nd ed., Oxford: James Currey.

Fassin, D. and R. Rechtman (2009). *The Empire of Trauma: An Inquiry into the Condition of Victimhood*. Princeton, NJ: Princeton University Press.

Feldman, A. (1991). *Formations of Violence: The Narrative of the Body and Political Terror in Northern Ireland*. Chicago IL: University of Chicago Press.

Feldman, A. (2004). Memory Theatres, Virtual Witnessing, and the Trauma-Aesthetic. *Biography*, 27(1), 163–202.

Ferguson, J. (2006). *Global Shadows: Africa in the Neoliberal World Order*. Durham, NC: Duke University Press.

Fletcher, L. E. and H. M. Weinstein (2002). Violence and Social Repair: Rethinking the Contribution of Justice to Reconciliation. *Human Rights Quarterly*, 24(3), 573–639.

Foucault, M. (1978). *The History of Sexuality*. Harmondsworth: Penguin.

Foucault, M. (1980). 'Two Lectures', in C. Gordon, ed., *Power/Knowledge: Selected Interviews and Other writings 1972–1977*. Harlow: Harvester Wheatsheaf, pp. 78–108.

Foucault, M. (1991[1975]). *Discipline and Punish: The Birth of the Prison*. Translated by A. Sheridan. Harmondsworth: Penguin.

French, B. (2009). Technologies of Telling: Discourse, Transparency, and Erasure in Guatemalan Truth Commission Testimony. *Journal of Human Rights*, 8(1), 92–109.

GADH (2009a). 'International Criminal Tribunal for Rwanda: Model or Counter Model for International Criminal Justice?'. Geneva: Geneva

Academy of International Humanitarian Law and Human Rights. 9–11 July 2009 Geneva.

GADH (2009b). 'International Criminal Tribunal for Rwanda: Model or Counter Model for International Criminal Justice? Session 5 Debates with Prosecutors'. Geneva: Geneva Academy of International Humanitarian Law and Human Rights. 9–11 July 2009 Geneva.

Gaiba, F. (1998). *The Origins of Simultaneous Interpretation: The Nuremberg Trial*. Ottawa: University of Ottawa.

Galchinsky, M. (2010). The Problem with Human Rights Culture. *South Atlantic Review*, 75(2), 5–18.

Gallimore, T. (2008). The Legacy of the International Criminal Tribunal for Rwanda (ICTR) and Its Contributions to Reconciliation in Rwanda. *New England Journal of International and Comparative Law*, 14(2), 239–63.

Garapon, A. (2001). *Bien Juger: Essai sur le Rituel Judiciare*. Paris: Éditions Odile Jacob.

Gaskin, H. (1990). *Eyewitness at Nuremberg*. London: Arms and Armour Press.

Geertz, C. (1980). *Negara: The Theatre State in Nineteenth Century Bali*. Princeton NJ: Princeton University Press.

Geertz, C. (1983). *Local Knowledge: Fact and Law in Comparative Perspective*. New York NY: Basic Books.

Gelles, P. H. (1998). Testimonio, Ethnography and Processes of Authorship. *Anthropology Newsletter*, March 1998.

Gewirtz, P. (1996). Narrative and Rhetoric in the Law. In P. Brooks and P. Gewirtz, eds., *Law's Stories: Narrative and Rhetoric in the Law*. New Haven, CT: Yale University Press, pp. 2–13.

Gluckman, H. M. (1955). *The Judicial Process Among the Barotse of Northern Rhodesia*. Manchester University Press: Manchester.

Goffman, E. (1959). *The Presentation of Self in Everyday Life*. New York: Doubleday Anchor.

Goffman, E. (1991[1968]). *Asylums: Essays on the Social Situation of Mental Patients and Other Inmates*. Harmondsworth: Penguin.

Good, A. (2004) Expert Evidence in Asylum and Human Rights Appeals: An Expert's View. *International Journal of Refugee Law*, 16(3), 358–80.

Good, A. (2007). *Anthropology and Expertise in the Asylum Courts*. London: Routledge-Cavendish.

Gordon, G. S. (2004). War of Media, Words, Newspapers, and Radio Stations: The ICTR Media Trial Verdict and a New Chapter in the International Law of Hate Speech. *Virginia Journal of International Law*, 45, 139–97.

Gouri, H. (2004). *Facing the Glass Booth: The Jerusalem Trial of Adolf Eichmann*. Detroit, MI: Wayne State University Press.

Government of South Africa (1995). Promotion of National Unity and Reconciliation Act 34 of 1995.

Green, L. L. (2002). Gender Hate Propaganda and Sexual Violence in the Rwandan Genocide: An Argument for Intersectionality in International Law. *Columbia Human Rights Law Review*, 33(3), 733–76.

Greenfield, D. M. (2008). The Crime of Complicity in Genocide: How the International Criminal Tribunals for Rwanda and Yugoslavia Got It Wrong, and Why It Matters. *The Journal of Criminal Law and Criminology*, 98(3), 921–52.

Greenspan, H. and S. Bolkosky (2006). When Is an Interview an Interview? Notes from Listening to Holocaust Survivors. *Poetics Today*, 27(2), 431–49.

Grotowski, J., E. Barba and P. Brook (1991[1968]). *Towards a Poor Theatre*. London: Methuen.

Gunawaradana, A. D. (2000). Contributions by the International Criminal Tribunal for Rwanda to Development of the Definition of Genocide. *American Society of International Law Proceedings*, 94, 277–9.

Gupta, A. and J. Ferguson (1997). *Anthropological Locations: Boundaries and Grounds of a Field Science*. Berkeley: University of California Press.

Gusterson, H. (1997). Studying Up Revisited. *PoLAR: Political and Legal Anthropological Review*, 20(1), 114–19.

Haddad, H. N. (2011). Mobilizing the Will to Prosecute: Crimes of Rape at the Yugoslav and Rwandan Tribunals. *Human Rights Review*, 12(1), 109–32.

Haffajee, R. L. (2006). Prosecuting Crimes of Rape and Sexual Violence at the ICTR: The Application of Joint Criminal Enterprise Theory. *Harvard Journal of Law and Gender*, 29, 201–21.

Hagan, J. (2003). *Justice in the Balkans: Prosecuting War Crimes in the Hague Tribunal*. London: University of Chicago Press.

Hale, S. B. (2004). *The Discourse of Court Interpreting: Discourse Practices of the Law, the Witness and the Interpreter*. Amsterdam: John Benjamins.

Hammersley, M. and P. Atkinson (2007). *Ethnography: Principles in Practice*. London: Routledge.

Hannerz, U. (1998). Other Transnationals: Perspectives Gained from Studying Sideways. *Paideuma*, 44, 109–24.

Hanson, J. (1996). The Architecture of Justice: Iconography and Space Configuration in the English Law Court Building. *Architectural Research Quarterly*, 1(4), 50–9.

Hardt, M. and A. Negri (2000). *Empire*. London: Harvard University Press.

Harris, L. C. (2002). The Emotional Labour of Barristers: An Exploration of Emotional Labour by Status Professionals. *Journal of Management Studies*, 39(4), 553–84.

Hartman, G. H. (1995). Learning from Survivors: The Yale Testimony Project. *Holocaust and Genocide Studies*, 9(2), 192–207.

Hartmann, F. (2007). *Paix et châtiment, Les guerres secrètes de la politique et de la justice internationales* Paris: Flammarion.

Hausner, G. (1967). *Justice in Jerusalem*. London: Nelson.

Hayner, P. B. (2010). *Unspeakable Truths: Transitional Justice and the Challenge of Truth Commissions*. London: Routledge.

Hazan, P. (1998). Les crimes commis contre les Hutus ne doivent pas demeurer impunis. *Le Temps*, 18 September 1998.

Hazan, P. (2004). *Justice in a Time of War: The True Story Behind the International Criminal Tribunal for the Former Yugoslavia*. College Station, TX: Texas A&M University Press.

Henry, N. (2010). The Impossibility of Bearing Witness: Wartime Rape and the Promise of Justice. *Violence Against Women*, 16(10), 1098–119.

Heydon, J. D. and M. Ockelton (1996). *Evidence: Cases and Materials*, 4th ed., London: Butterworths.

Hibbitts, B. J. (1995). Making Motions: The Embodiment of Law in Gesture. *Journal of Contemporary Legal Issues*, 6(5), 51–81.

Hilberg, R. (1961). *The Destruction of the European Jews*. Yale CT: Yale University Press.

Hindman, H. and A.-M. Fechter (2011). Introduction. In A.-M. Fechter and H. Hindman, eds., *Inside the Everyday Lives of Development Workers: The Challenges and Futures of Aidland*. Sterling, VA: Kumarian, pp. 1–19.

Hinton, A. L. (2010). Toward an Anthropology of Transitional Justice. In A. L. Hinton, ed., *Transitional Justice: Global Mechanisms and Local Realities After Genocide and Mass Violence*. New Brunswick, NJ: Rutgers University Press, pp. 1–24.

Hinton, A. L. (2016). *Man or Monster?: The Trial of a Khmer Rouge Torturer*. Durham NC: Duke University Press.

Hinton, A. L. (2018). *The Justice Facade: Trials of Transition in Cambodia*. Oxford: Oxford University Press.

Hirondelle News (2003). ICTR/Prosecutor – Interview with Carla Del Ponte. 16 September 2003.

Hirondelle News (2009). Rwanda/UN – Kigali Reiterates Its Request to Shelter ICTR's Archives. 21 October 2009.

Hirsch, H. (1995). *Genocide and the Politics of Memory: Studying Death to Preserve Life*. Chapel Hill, NC: The University of North Carolina Press.

Hoffman, D. (2007). The Meaning of a Militia: Understanding the Civil Defence Forces of Sierra Leone. *African Affairs*, 106(425), 639–62.

Hola, B., C. Bijleveld and A. Smeulers (2011). Punishment for Genocide – Exploratory Analysis of ICTR Sentencing. *International Criminal Law Review*, 11(4), 745–73.

Huizinga, J. (1949). *Homo Ludens: A Study of the Play-Element in Culture*. London: Routledge and Kegan Paul.

Human Rights Watch (2002). *Rwanda: Deliver Justice for Victims of Both Sides*. New York: Human Rights Watch.

Human Rights Watch and FIDHR (2006). *Letter to Council Members on Eve of Meeting with Lead Prosecutor.* 12 December 2008 New York: Human Rights Watch.

Humphreys, S. (1985). Law as Discourse. *History and Anthropology*, 1(2), 241–64.

Hyde, H. M. (1964). *Norman Birkett: The Life of Lord Birkett of Ulverston.* London: H. Hamilton.

ICTR n.d. The ICTR at a Glance. Arusha: ICTR.

ICTR (1996). Directive on the Assignment of Defence Counsel. Arusha: ICTR.

ICTR (2000). Prosecutor Outlines Future Plans. Arusha: ICTR.

ICTR (2002). ICTR President Seizes Security Council. ICTR Bulletin, 6 August 2002.

ICTR (2002). Address by the Prosecutor of the International Criminal Tribunals for the former Yugoslavia and Rwanda, Mrs. Carla del Ponte to the United Nations Security Council. 29 October 2002 The Hague: ICTY.

ICTR (2004). Statement by Justice Hassan B. Jallow, Prosecutor of the International Criminal Tribunal for Rwanda to the United Nations Security Council. 29 June 2004 Arusha: ICTR.

ICTR (2005a). Testifying Before the International Criminal Tribunal for Rwanda. Arusha: ICTR.

ICTR (2005b). International Justice: The Legacy of the United Nations International Criminal Tribunal for the Former Yugoslavia and of the International Criminal Tribunal for Rwanda: Discussion Paper (Draft). Arusha: ICTR.

ICTR (2005[1995]). Rules of Procedure and Evidence. Arusha: ICTR.

ICTR (2006a). Military I – Defence Exhibit DK112 – UN Code Cable "The 'Gersoni' Report Rwanda." 16 November 2006.

ICTR (2006b). Military I – Defence Exhibit DNT257 – US Document from US Secretary of State to US Mission to UN Dated 22/09/94. 9 November 2006.

ICTR (2006c). Military I – Defence Exhibit DNT264 US Document from George E. Moose to the US Secretary of State; 12/09/94; Subject: New Human Rights Abuses in Rwanda. 17 November 2006.

ICTR (2006d). Military I – Defense Exhibit DNT 261 – Human Rights Watch, Absence of Prosecution, Continued Killings, Sept. 1994. 17 November 2006.

ICTR (2006e). *Prosecutor v. Protais Zigiranyirazo* Case No. ICTR-2001–73-AR 73, Decision on Defence and Prosecution Motions Related to Witness ADE. 31 January 2006 Arusha: ICTR.

ICTR (2006f). *Prosecutor v. Protais Zigiranyirazo* Case No. ICTR-2001–73-AR 73, Decision on Interlocutory Appeal Regarding Michel Bagaragaza Testimony. 30 October 2006 Arusha: ICTR.

ICTR (2006g). *Prosecutor v. Protais Zigiranyirazo* Case No. ICTR-2001-73-AR 73, Protais Zigiranyirazo. Reply Brief: Appeal from the Extremely Confidential Decision on Defense Motion Concerning the Hearing of Witness ADE. 6 July 2006 Arusha: ICTR.

ICTR (2007). Tribunals Launch Archiving Study. The Hague: ICTY.

ICTY (1999). The Code of Ethics of Interpreters and Translators Employed by the International Criminal Tribunal for the Former Yugoslavia. The Hague: ICTY.

Ingold, T. (1993). The Art of Translation in a Continuous World. In G. Pálsson, ed., *Beyond Boundaries: Understanding, Translation And Anthropological Discourse*. Oxford: Berg, pp. 210–30.

International Association of Conference Interpreters (2015). *Code of Professional Ethics*. Geneva: AICC. Available at https://aiic.net/page/6724.

International Crisis Group (2003). *Tribunal Penal International Pour le Rwanda: Pragmatisme de Rigueur*. Brussels: International Crisis Group.

International Military Tribunal (1945). *Charter of the International Military Tribunal – Annex to the Agreement for the Prosecution and Punishment of the Major War Criminals of the European Axis*. Nuremberg: International Military Tribunal.

International Military Tribunal (1947). *Trial of the Major War Criminals Before the International Military Tribunal*. Vol. I. Nuremberg: International Military Tribunal.

International Military Tribunal for the Far East (1945). *Charter of the International Military Tribunal for the Far East*. Tokyo: International Military Tribunal.

IRIN (2001). Government Puts Genocide Victims at 1.07 Million. Integrated Regional Information Network for Central and Eastern Africa.

Jackson, B. (1990). Narrative Theories and Legal Discourse. In C. Nash, ed., *Narrative in Culture: The Uses of Storytelling in the Sciences, Philosophy, and Literature*. London: Routledge, pp. 23–50.

Jackson, M. (2002). *The Politics of Storytelling: Violence, Transgression, and Intersubjectivity*. Copenhagen: Museum Tusculanum Press.

Jackson, M. (2005). Storytelling Events, Violence, and the Appearance of the Past. *Anthropological Quarterly*, 78(2), 355–76.

Jacob, R. (1994). *Images de la Justice: Essai sur l'iconographie judiciaire du Moyen Âge à l'Âge classique*. Paris: Le Léopard d'Or.

Jalloh, C. C., A. Marong and D. M. Kinnecome (2007). Concurrent Jurisdiction at the ICTR: Should the Tribunal Refer Cases to Rwanda? In E. Decaux, ed., *Human Rights to International Criminal Law: Studies in Honour of an African Jurist: Judge Laity Kama*. Leiden: Martinus Nijhoff Brill, pp. 159–201.

Jay, M. (1992). Of Plots, Witnesses, and Judgements. In S. Friedländer, ed., *Probing the Limits of Representation: Nazism and the "final solution."* Cambridge, MA: Harvard University Press, pp. 97–107.

Johnson, T. A. M. (2011). On Silence, Sexuality and Skeletons: Reconceptualizing Narrative in Asylum Hearings. *Social and Legal Studies,* 20(1), 57–78.

Jönsson, L. and P. Linell (1991). Story Generations: From Dialogical Interviews to Written Reports in Police Interrogations. *Text and Talk,* 2 (3), 419–40.

Jordash, W. (2009). The Practice of 'Witness Proofing' in International Criminal Tribunals: Why the International Criminal Court Should Prohibit the Practice. *Leiden Journal of International Law,* 22(3), 501–23.

Kahane, D. (2003). Dispute Resolution and the Politics of Cultural Generalization. *Negotiation Journal,* 19(1), 5–27.

Kapferer, B. (1986). Performance and the Structuring of Meaning and Experience. In V. Turner and E. M. Bruner, eds., *The Anthropology of Experience.* Champaign IL: University of Illinois Press pp. 188–203.

Kapferer, B. (1997). *The Feast of the Sorcerer: Practices of Consciousness and Power.* Chicago IL: University of Chicago Press.

Karton, J. D. H. (2008). Lost in Translation: International Criminal Courts and the Legal Implications of Interpreted Testimony. *Vanderbilt Journal of Transnational Law,* 41(1), 1–54.

Kaye, D. (2014). Archiving Justice: Conceptualizing the Archives of the United Nations International Criminal Tribunal for the Former Yugoslavia. *Archival Science,* 14(3), 381–96.

Keane, F. (1995). *Season of Blood: A Rwandan Journey.* London: Viking.

Keller, A. N. (2001). Punishment for Violations of International Criminal Law: An Analysis of Sentencing at the ICTY and ICTR. *Indiana International and Comparative Law Review,* 12(1), 53–74.

Kelsall, T. (2009). *Culture Under Cross-Examination: International Justice and the Special Court for Sierra Leone.* Cambridge: Cambridge University Press.

Kendall, S. and S. M. H. Nouwen (2014). Representational Practices at the International Criminal Court: The Gap Between Juridified and Abstract Victimhood. *Law and Contemporary Problems,* 76(3&4), 235–62.

Kendall, S. and S. M. H. Nouwen (2016). Speaking of Legacy: Toward an Ethos of Modesty at the International Criminal Tribunal for Rwanda. *The American Journal of International Law,* 110(2), 212–32.

Kennedy, D. W. (2002). The International Human Rights Movement: Part of the Problem? *Harvard Human Rights Journal,* 15, 100–25.

Kent, L. (2011). Local Memory Practices in East Timor: Disrupting Transitional Justice Narratives. *International Journal of Transitional Justice,* 5(3), 434–55.

Kessler-Harris, A. (1986). Equal Employment Opportunity Commission v. Sears, Roebuck and Company: A Personal Account. *Radical History Review*, 1986(35), 57–79.

Ketelaar, E. (2012). Truths, Memories and Histories in the Archives of the International Criminal Tribunal for the Former Yugoslavia. In H. van der Wilt, J. Vervliet, G. K. Sluiter and J. H. ten Cate, eds., *The Genocide Convention: The Legacy of 60 Years*. Leiden: Brill, pp. 201–22.

Khan, S. M. (2000). *The Shallow Graves of Rwanda*. London: I.B. Tauris.

Komter, M. (2006) From Talk to Text: The Interactional Construction of a Police Record. *Research on Language in Social Interaction*, 39(3), 201–28.

Koomen, J. (2013).'Without These Women, the Tribunal Cannot Do Anything': The Politics of Witness Testimony on Sexual Violence at the International Criminal Tribunal for Rwanda. *Signs*, 38(2), 253–77.

Koomen, J. (2014a). Language Work at International Criminal Courts. *International Feminist Journal of Politics*, 16(4), 581–600.

Koomen, J. (2014b). Global Governance and the Politics of Culture: Campaigns Against Female Circumcision in East Africa. *Gender, Place & Culture*, 21(2), 244–61.

Koskenniemi, M. (2002). Between Impunity and Show Trials. *Max Planck Yearbook of United Nations Law Online*, 6(1), 1–35.

Langfield, M. and P. Maclean (2009). Multiple Framings: Survivor and Non-Survivor Interviewers in Holocaust Video Testimony. In N. Adler, S. Leydesdorff, M. Chamberlain and L. Neyzi, eds., *Memories of Mass Repression: Narrating Life Stories in the Aftermath of Atrocity*. Somerset, NJ: Transaction, pp. 199–218.

Latour, B. (2004). Scientific Objects and Legal Objectivity. In A. Pottage and M. Mundy, eds., *Law, Anthropology and the Constitution of the Social: Making Persons and Things*. Cambridge: Cambridge University Press, pp. 73–114.

Laub, D. (1992). An Event Without a Witness: Truth, Testimony and Survival. In S. Felman and D. Laub, eds., *Testimony: Crises of Witnessing in Literature, Psychoanalysis, and History*. New York; London: Routledge, pp. 75–92.

Lawrence, S. N. (2001). Cultural (In)sensitivity: The Dangers of a Simplistic Approach to Culture in the Courtroom. *Canadian Journal of Women and the Law*, 13(1), 107–36.

Lefebvre, H. (1991). *The Production of Space*. Oxford: Basil Blackwell.

Levenson, L. L. (2007). Courtroom Demeanor: The Theater of the Courtroom. *Minnesota Law Review*, 92, 573–633.

Levi, P. (1986). The Memory of Offense. In G. Hartman, ed., *Bitburg in Moral and Political Perspective*. Bloomington IN: Indiana University Press, pp. 131–7.

Llewellyn, K. N. (1930). A Realistic Jurisprudence – The Next Step. *Columbia Law Review*, 30(4), 431–65.

Lowenthal, D. (1985). *The Past Is a Foreign Country.* Cambridge: Cambridge University Press.

Luchjenbroers, J. (1997). 'In your own words . . . ' Questions and Answers in a Supreme Court Trial. *Journal of Pragmatics,* 27(4), 477–503.

Lundy, P. and M. McGovern (2008). Whose Justice? Rethinking Transitional Justice from the Bottom Up. *Journal of Law and Society,* 35(2), 265–92.

MacKinnon, C. A. (2006). Defining Rape Internationally: A Comment on Akayesu. *Columbia Journal of Transnational Law,* 44, 940–58.

Madlingozi, T. (2010). On Transitional Justice Entrepreneurs and the Production of Victims. *Journal of Human Rights Practice,* 2(2), 208–28.

Maier, C. S. (2000). Doing History, Doing Justice: The Narrative of the Historian and the Truth Commission. In R. Rotberg and D. Thompson, eds., *Truth v. Justice: The Morality of Truth Commission.* Princeton, NJ: Princeton University Press, pp. 261–78.

Mamdani, M. (2000). The Truth According to the TRC. In I. Amadiume and A. An-Na'im, eds., *The Politics of Memory: Truth, Healing and Social Justice.* London: Zed Books, pp. 176–83.

Mamiya, R. (2007). Taking Judicial Notice of Genocide? The Problematic Law and Policy of the Karemera Decision. *Wisconsin International Law Journal,* 25, 1–22.

Marcus, G. E. (1983). *Elites: Ethnographic Issues.* Albuquerque: University of New Mexico Press.

Markowitz, L. (2001). Finding the Field: Notes on the Ethnography of NGOs. *Human Organization,* 60(1), 40–46.

Martin, C. (2006). Bodies of Evidence. *The Drama Review,* 50(3), 8–15.

Matoesian, G. M. (1993). *Reproducing Rape: Domination Through Talk in the Courtroom.* Cambridge: Polity Press.

Mbembe, J. A. (2001). *On the Postcolony.* Berkeley, CA: University of California Press.

McDougall, C. (2006). The Sexual Violence Jurisprudence of the International Criminal Tribunal for the Former Yugoslavia and the International Criminal Tribunal for Rwanda: The Silence Has Been Broken but There's Still a Lot to Shout About. In U. Dolgopol and J. Gardam, eds., *The Challenge of Conflict: International Law Responds.* Leiden, Boston MA: Martinus Nijhoff, pp. 331–46.

McEvoy, K. (2007). Beyond Legalism: Towards a Thicker Understanding of Transitional Justice. *Journal of Law and Society,* 34(4), 411–40.

McEvoy, K. (2008). Letting Go of Legalism: Developing a 'Thicker' Version of Transitional Justice. In K. McEvoy and L. McGregor, eds., *Transitional Justice from Below: Grassroots Activism and the Struggle for Change.* London: Hart Publishing, pp. 15–46.

McEvoy, K. (2011). What Did the Lawyers Do During the 'War'? Neutrality, Conflict and the Culture of Quietism. *The Modern Law Review,* 74(3), 350–84.

McEvoy, K. and K. McConnachie (2013). Victims and Transitional Justice: Voice, Agency and Blame. *Social and Legal Studies*, 22(4), 489–513.

McEvoy, K. and L. McGregor eds. (2008). *Transitional Justice from Below: Grassroots Activism and the Struggle for Change*. Oxford: Hart.

McKinley, M. (1997). Life Stories, Disclosure and the Law. *PoLAR: Political and Legal Anthropology Review*, 20(2), 70–82.

Meierhenrich, J. (2013). The Practice of International Law: A Theoretical Analysis. *Law and Contemporary Problems*, 76(3–4), 1–83.

Mégret, F. (2011). The Legacy of the ICTY as Seen Through Some of Its Actors and Observers. *Goettingen Journal of International Law*, 3(3), 1011–52.

Mégret, F. (2016). International Criminal Justice as a Juridical Field. *Champ Pénal/Penal Field*, 13.

Melman, J. (2011). Possibility of Transfer: A Comprehensive Approach to the International Criminal Tribunal for Rwanda's Rule 11Bis to Permit Transfer to Rwandan Domestic Courts. *Fordham Law Review*, 79(3), 1271–332.

Melvern, L. (2000). *A People Betrayed: The Role of the West in Rwanda's Genocide*. London: Zed.

Merry, S. E. (1986). Everyday Understandings of the Law in Working-Class America. *American Ethnologist*, 13(2), 253–70.

Merry, S. E. (2003). Human Rights Law and the Demonization of Culture (And Anthropology Along the Way). *PoLAR: Political and Legal Anthropology Review*, 26(1), 55–76.

Merry, S. E. (2006a). New Legal Realism and the Ethnography of Transnational Law. *Law and Social Inquiry*, 31(4), 975–95.

Merry, S. E. (2006b). Transnational Human Rights and Local Activism: Mapping the Middle. *American Anthropologist*, 108(1), 38–51.

Merry, S. E. (2011). Measuring the World: Indicators, Human Rights, and Global Governance. *Current Anthropology*, 52(3), S83–S95.

Mettraux, G. (2002). Crimes Against Humanity in the Jurisprudence of the International Criminal Tribunals for the Former Yugoslavia and for Rwanda. *Harvard International Law Journal*, 43(1), 237–316.

Miller, D. (1987). *Material Culture and Mass Consumption*. Oxford: Basil Blackwell.

Moghalu, K. C. (2002). Image and Reality of War Crimes Justice: External Perceptions of the International Criminal Tribunal for Rwanda. *The Fletcher Forum of World Affairs*, 26(2), 21–46.

Moghalu, K. C. (2005). *Rwanda's Genocide: The Politics of Global Justice*. New York: Palgrave Macmillan.

Montgomery, H. (2001). Imposing Rights? A Case Study of Child Prostitution in Thailand. In J. Cowan, M. Dembour and R. Wilson, eds., *Culture and Rights: Anthropological Perspectives*. Cambridge: Cambridge University Press, pp. 80–101.

Morison, J. and P. Leith (1992). *The Barrister's World and the Nature of Law*. Milton Keynes: Open University Press.

Morris, M. H. (1997). The Trials of Concurrent Jurisdiction: The Case of Rwanda. *Duke Journal of Comparative and International Law*, 7, 349–74.

Møse, E. (2005). Main Achievements of the ICTR. *Journal of International Criminal Justice*, 3(4), 920–43.

Mosse, D. (2006). Anti-Social Anthropology? Objectivity, Objection, and the Ethnography of Public Policy and Professional Communities. *Journal of the Royal Anthropological Institute*, 12(4), 935–56.

Mosse, D. (2011). Introduction: The Anthropology of Expertise and Professionals in International Development. In D. Mosse, ed., *Adventures in Aidland: The Anthropology of Professionals in International Development*. Oxford: Berghahn, pp. 1–32.

Mudimbe, V. Y. (1994). *The Idea of Africa*. London: Indiana University Press.

Mujuzi, J. D. (2010). Steps Taken in Rwanda's Efforts to Qualify for the Transfer of Accused from the ICTR. *Journal of International Criminal Justice*, 8(1), 237–48.

Mulcahy, L. (2007). Architects of Justice: the Politics of Courtroom Design. *Social Legal Studies*, 16(3), 383–403.

Mulcahy, L. (2011). *Legal Architecture: Justice, Due Process and the Place of the Law*. New York: Routledge.

Mutua, M. (2001). Savages, Victims and Saviours: The Metaphor of Human Rights. *Harvard International Law Journal*, 42(1), 201–45.

Nader, L. (1969). Up the Anthropologist – Perspectives Gained from Studying Up. In D. Hymes, ed., *Reinventing Anthropology*. Ann Arbor, MI: University of Michigan Press, pp. 284–311.

Nahamya, E. and R. Diarra (2002). Disclosure of Evidence Before the International Criminal Tribunal for Rwanda. *Criminal Law Forum*, 13(3), 339–63.

Neave, A. (1978). *Nuremberg: A Personal Record of the Trial of the Major Nazi War Criminals*. London: Hodder and Stoughton.

Nelaeva, G. (2010). The Impact of Transnational Advocacy Networks on the Prosecution of Wartime Rape and Sexual Violence: The Case of the ICTR. *International Social Science Review*, 85(1/2), 3–27.

Niang, M. M. (2002). The Right to Counsel Before the International Criminal Tribunal for Rwanda. *Criminal Law Forum*, 13(3), 323–38.

Nice, G. (2001). Trials of Imperfection. *Leiden Journal of International Law*, 14 (2), 383–97.

Nicolini, D. (2013). *Practice Theory, Work, and Organization: An Introduction*. Oxford: Oxford University Press.

Nourse, V. and G. Shaffer (2010). Varieties of New Legal Realism: Can a World Order Prompt a New Legal Theory? *Cornell Law Review*, 95, 61–137.

Nsanzuwera, F.-X. (2005). The ICTR Contribution to National Reconciliation. *Journal of International Criminal Justice*, 3(4), 944–49.

O'Connell, J. (2005). Gambling with the Psyche: Does Prosecuting Human Rights Violators Console Their Victims? *Harvard International Law Journal*, 46(2), 295–345.

Obote-Odora, A. (2001). Drafting of Indictments for the International Criminal Tribunal for Rwanda. *Criminal Law Forum*, 12(3), 335–58.

Obote-Odora, A. (2002). Complicity in Genocide as Understood Through the ICTR Experience. *International Criminal Law Review*, 2(4), 375–408.

Obote-Odora, A. (2004). Criminal Responsibility of Journalists Under International Criminal Law. *Nordic Journal of International Law*, 73(3), 307–23.

Obote-Odora, A. (2005). Rape and Sexual Violence in International Law: ICTR Contribution. *New England Journal of International and Comparative Law*, 12(1), 135–59.

Oosterlinck, C., D. Van Schendel, J. Huon, J. Sompayrac and O. Chavanis (2012). 'Rapport D'expertise: Destruction En Vol Du Falcon 50 Kigali (Rwanda)' ['Expert Report: Destruction in Flight of the Falcon 50 Kigali (Rwanda)']. Paris: Cour d'appel de Paris Tribunal de Grande Instance de Paris.

Oosterveld, V. (2005). Gender-Sensitive Justice and the International Criminal Tribunal for Rwanda: Lessons Learned for the International Criminal Court. *New England Journal of International and Comparative Law* 12(1), 119–33.

Orentlicher, D. F. (1991). Settling Accounts: The Duty to Prosecute Human Rights Violations of a Prior Regime. *The Yale Law Journal*, 100(8), 2537–615.

Overdulve, C. M. (1997). Fonction de la langue et de la communication au Rwanda. *Nouvelle Revue de Science Missionnaire*, 53(4), 271–83.

Parker, J. (2011). The Soundscape of Justice. *Griffith Law Review*, 20(4), 962–93.

Parkin, D. (1992). Ritual as Spatial Direction and Bodily Division. In D. de Coppet, ed., *Understanding Rituals*. London and New York: Routledge, pp. 11–25.

Passmore, J. (1974). The Objectivity of History. In P. Gardiner, ed., *The Philosophy of History*. Oxford: Oxford University Press, pp. 145–60.

Peskin, V. (2008). *International Justice in Rwanda and the Balkans: Virtual Trials and the Struggle for State Cooperation*. Cambridge: Cambridge University Press.

Peters, J. S. (2008). Legal Performance Good and Bad. *Law, Culture and the Humanities*, 4(2), 179–200.

Philips, S. U. (1998). *Ideology in the Language of Judges: How Judges Practice Law, Politics and Courtroom Control*. Oxford: Oxford University Press.

Pirie, F. and J. Rogers (2012). Pupillage: The Shaping of a Professional Elite. In J. Abbink and T. Salverda, eds., *The Anthropology of Elites: Power, Culture and the Complexities of Distinction*. London: Palgrave Macmillan, pp. 139–61.

Pitt-Rivers, J. (1986). Un Rite de Passage de la Société Moderne: Le Voyage Aérien. In P. Centlivres and J. Hainard, eds., *Les rites de passage aujourd'hui. Actes du colloque de Neuchâtel 1981*. Lausanne: Editions L'Age d'Homme, pp. 115–30.

Portelli, A. (1981). The Peculiarities of Oral History. *History Workshop*, 12(1), 96–107.

Portelli, A. (1985). Oral Testimony, the Law and the Making of History: The 'April 7' Murder Trial. *History Workshop Journal*, 20(1), 5–35.

Pottier, J. (2002). *Re-Imagining Rwanda: Conflict, Survival and Disinformation in the Late Twentieth Century*. Cambridge: Cambridge University Press.

Pound, R. (1910). Law in Books and Law in Action. *American Law Review*, 44, 12–36.

Pozen, J. (2005). Justice Obscured: The Non-Disclosure of Witnesses' Identities in ICTR Trials. *New York University Journal of International Law and Politics*, 38(1–2), 281–322.

Radcliffe-Brown, A. R. (1955[1940]). Preface. In M. Fortes and E. Evans-Prichard, eds., *African Political Systems*. Oxford: Oxford University Press and International African Institute, pp. xi–xxiii.

Rearick, D. J. (2003). Innocent Until Alleged Guilty: Provisional Release at the ICTR. *Harvard International Law Journal*, 44(2), 577–95.

Redfield, P. (2012). The Unbearable Lightness of Expats: Double Binds of Humanitarian Mobility. *Cultural Anthropology*, 27(2), 358–82.

Redwood, H. (2017) Archives of Knowledge, Ownership and Contestation at the ICTR's Archive. *Humanity: An International Journal of Human Rights, Humanitarianism and Development*. Available at http://humanityjournal.org/blog/archives-of-knowledge/.

Reydams, L. (2005). The ICTR Ten Years On: Back to the Nuremberg Paradigm? *Journal of International Criminal Justice*, 3(4), 977–88.

Ricoeur, P. (2004). *Memory, History, Forgetting*. Chicago IL: University of Chicago Press.

Ricoeur, P. and J. B. Thompson (1981). *Hermeneutics and the Human Sciences: Essays on Language, Action and Interpretation*. Cambridge: Cambridge University Press.

Riles, A. (2006). Anthropology, Human Rights, and Legal Knowledge: Culture in the Iron Cage. *American Anthropologist*, 108(1), 52–65.

Robben, A. C. G. M. (2010). Testimonies, Truths, and Transitions of Justice in Argentina and Chile. In A. L. Hinton, ed., *Transitional Justice: Global Mechanisms and Local Realities in the Aftermath of Genocide and Mass Violence*. New Brunswick, NJ: Rutgers University Press, pp. 179–205.

Rock, F. (2001). The Genesis of a Witness Statement. *Forensic Linguistics*, 8 (2), 1350–771.

Rock, P. (1993). *The Social World of an English Crown Court: Witness and Professionals in the Crown Court Centre at Wood Green*. Oxford: Oxford University Press.

Rogers, J. (2012). Shadowing the Bar: Studying an English Professional Elite. *Historical Reflections*, 36(3), 39–57.

Röling, B. V. A. and A. E. Cassese (1993). *The Tokyo Trial and Beyond: Reflections of a Peacemonger*. Cambridge: Polity Press.

Ross, F. C. (2003). *Bearing Witness: Women and the Truth and Reconciliation Commission in South Africa*. London: Pluto Press.

Rousso, H. (2001). *The Haunting Past: History, Memory, and Justice in Contemporary France*. Philadelphia, PA: University of Pennsylvania Press.

Rukebesha, A. (1985). *Esoterisme et communication sociale*. Kigali: Éditions Printer Set.

Ruzibiza, A. J. (2005). *Rwanda, l'histoire secrète*. Paris: Panama.

Said, E. 2003[1978]. *Orientalism*. London: Penguin.

Sander, B. (2018). History on Trial: Historical Narrative Pluralism Within and Beyond International Criminal Courts. *International and Comparative Law Quarterly*, 67(3), 547–76.

Sarat, A. and T. R. Kearns (2002). Writing History and Registering Memory. In A. Sarat and T. R. Kearns, eds., *History, Memory and the Law*. Ann Arbor, MI: University of Michigan Press, pp. 1–24.

Sarat, A. and S. A. Scheingold (1998). *Cause Lawyering: Political Commitments and Professional Responsibilities*. Oxford: Oxford University Press.

Sarfaty, G. A. (2009). Why Culture Matters in International Institutions: The Marginality of Human Rights at the World Bank. *American Journal of International Law*, 103, 647–83.

Sartre, J.-P. (1984[1965]). *Nausea*. Harmondsworth: Penguin.

Schabas, W. (2000). Groups Protected by the Genocide Convention: Conflicting Interpretations from the International Criminal Tribunal for Rwanda. *Ilsa Journal of International and Comparative Law*, 6(2), 375–87.

Schaffer, K. and S. Smith (2004). *Human Rights and Narrated Lives: The Ethics of Recognition*. Basingstoke: Palgrave Macmillan.

Scharf, M. P. (1999). The Amnesty Exception to the Jurisdiction of the International Criminal Court. *Cornell International Law Journal*, 32(2), 507–27.

Schauer, F. (2013). Legal Realism Untamed. *Texas Law Review*, 91(4), 749–80.

Schechner, R. (1985). *Between Theater and Anthropology*. Philadelphia PA: University of Pennsylvania Press.

Schutz, A. (1962). Common-Sense and Scientific Interpretation of Human Action'. In M. A. Natanson, ed., *Collected Papers I: The Problem of Social Reality*. The Hague: Nijhoff, pp. 3–47.

Schwöbel-Patel, C. (2016). Spectacle in International Criminal Law: The Fundraising Image of Victimhood. *London Review of International Law*, 4(2), 247–74.

Scott, J. C. (1990). *Domination and the Arts of Resistance: Hidden Transcripts*. New Haven, CT: Yale University Press.

Selimovic, J. M. (2010). Perpetrators and Victims: Local Responses to the International Criminal Tribunal for the Former Yugoslavia. *Focaal*, 57 (2010), 50–61.

Shannon, K. G. (2006). Passing the Poisoned Chalice: Judicial Notice of Genocide by the ICTR. *Revue québécoise de droit international*, 19(2), 95–122.

Sharratt, S. (2011). *Gender, Shame and Sexual Violence: The Voices of Witnesses and Court Members at War Crimes Tribunals*. Farnham: Ashgate.

Shaw, R. (2007). Memory Frictions: Localizing the Truth and Reconciliation Commission in Sierra Leone. *The International Journal of Transitional Justice*, 1(2), 183–207.

Shaw, R. and L. Waldorf (2010). Introduction: Localizing Transitional Justice: Interventions and Priorities After Mass Violence. In R. Shaw, L. Waldorf and P. Hazan, eds., *Localizing Transitional Justice: Interventions and Priorities After Mass Violence*. Stanford, CA: Stanford University Press, pp. 3–26.

Sibomana, A., L. Guilbert, H. Deguine and C. Tertsakian (1999). *Hope for Rwanda: Conversations with Laure Guilbert and Herve Deguine*. London: Pluto Press.

Sloane, R. D. (2007). Sentencing for the 'Crime of Crimes': The Evolving 'Common Law' of Sentencing of the International Criminal Tribunal for Rwanda. *Journal of International Criminal Justice*, 5(3), 713–34.

Sluiter, G. (2005). The ICTR and the Protection of Witnesses. *Journal of International Criminal Justice*, 3(4), 962–76.

Sommerlad, H. (2007). Researching and Theorizing the Processes of Professional Identity Formation. *Journal of Law and Society*, 34(2), 190–217.

Sontag, S. (1966). *Against Interpretation, and Other Essays*. New York: Farrar.

Spivak, G. C. (1988). Can the Subaltern Speak? In C. Nelson and L. Grossberg, eds., *Marxism and the Interpretation of Culture*. Urbana, IL: University of Illinois Press, pp. 271–313.

Stahn, C. (2012). Between 'Faith' and 'Facts': By What Standards Should We Assess International Criminal Justice? *Leiden Journal of International Law*, 25 (2), 251–83.

Stave, B. M., M. Palmer and L. Frank (1998). *Witnesses to Nuremberg: An Oral History of American Participants at the War Crimes Trials*. New York: Twayne Publishers.

Steinitz, M. (2007). The International Criminal Tribunal for Rwanda as the Theater: The Social Negotiation of the Moral Authority of International Law. *Journal International Law and Policy*, 5(1), 1–31.

Stern, L. (2001). At the Junction of Cultures: Interpreting at the International Criminal Tribunal for the Former Yugoslavia in Light of Other International Interpreting Practices. *Judicial Review*, 5(3), 255–74.

Stier, O. B. (2003). *Committed to Memory: Cultural Mediations of the Holocaust*. Amherst MA: University of Massachusetts Press.

Stover, E. (2005). *The Witnesses: War Crimes and the Promise of Justice in the Hague*. Philadelphia, PA: University of Pennsylvania Press.

Sunga, L. S. (1995). The Commission of Experts on Rwanda and the Creation of the International Tribunal for Rwanda. *Human Rights Law Journal*, 16 (1–3), 121–4.

Szoke-Burke, S. (2012). Avoiding Belittlement of Human Suffering: A Retributivist Critique of ICTR Sentencing Practices. *Journal of International Criminal Justice*, 10(3), 561–80.

Tanner, H. H. (1999). History vs. The Law: Processing Indians in the American Legal System. *University of Detroit Mercy Law Review*, 76, 693–708.

Taussig, M. T. (1992). *The Nervous System*. London: Routledge.

Taylor, K. F. (1993). *In the Theatre of Criminal Justice: The Palais de Justice in Second Empire Paris*. Princeton NJ: Princeton University Press.

Taylor, T. (1992). *The Anatomy of the Nuremberg Trials: A Personal Memoir*. London: Bloomsbury.

Thalmann, V. (2008). French Justice's Endeavours to Substitute for the ICTR. *Journal of International Criminal Justice*, 6(5), 995–1002.

Theidon, K. (2007). Gender in Transition: Common Sense, Women and War. *Journal of Human Rights*, 6(3), 453–78.

Thomas, R. J. (1995). Interviewing Important People in Big Companies. In R. Herz and J. Imber, eds., *Studying Elites Using Qualitative Methods*. London: Sage Books, pp. 3–17.

Ticktin, M. (1999). Selling Suffering in the Courtroom and Marketplace: An Analysis of the Autobiography of Kiranjit Ahluwalia. *PoLAR: Political and Legal Anthropology Review*, 22(1), 24–41.

Tochilovsky, V. (2004). International Criminal Justice: 'Strangers in the Foreign System', *Criminal Law Forum*, 15(3), 319–44.

Trouillot, M.-R. (1995). *Silencing the Past: Power and the Production of History*. Boston, MA: Beacon.

Trouillot, M.-R. (2003). *Global Transformations: Anthropology and the Modern World*. London: Palgrave Macmillan.

Tsing, A. L. (2005). *Friction: An Ethnography of Global Connection*. Princeton, NJ: Princeton University Press.

Turner, J. I. (2008). Defense Perspectives on Law and Politics in International Criminal Trials. *Virginia Journal of International Law*, 48(3), 529–94.

United, Nations (1946). Report of the Secretary-General: Official Seal and Emblem of the United Nations. 15 October 1946. New York: United Nations. UN Doc. A/107 (1946).

United Nations (1948). Convention on the Privileges and Immunities of the United Nations. 13 February 1946. New York: United Nations

United Nations (1961). Vienna Convention on Diplomatic Relations. 18 April 1961. New York: United Nations.

United Nations (1993). Resolution 827 (1993) Adopted by the Security Council at Its 3217th Meeting. 25 May 1993. New York: United Nations. UN Doc. S/RES/827 (1993).

United Nations (1994a). General Assembly Official Records Forty-Ninth Session 21st Meeting. 6 October 1994. New York: United Nations General Assembly. UN Doc. A/49/PV.2.

United Nations (1994b). Letter dated 1 October 1994 from the Secretary General to the President of the Security Council transmitting the interim report of Commission of Experts on the evidence of grave violations of international humanitarian law in Rwanda, including possible acts of genocide (Annex: Preliminary Report of the Independent Commission of Experts established in accordance with Security Council Resolution 935 (1994)). 4 October 1994. New York: United Nations. UN Doc. S/1994/1125.

United Nations (1994c). Letter dated 28 September 1994 from the Permanent Representative of Rwanda to the United Nations. 29 September 1994. New York: United Nations. UN Doc. S/1994/1115.

United Nations (1994d). Letter from the Secretary-General to the President of the Security Council transmitting the final report of the Commission of Experts (Annex: Final Report of the Commission of Experts established pursuant to Security Council Resolution 935 (1994)). 9 December 1994. New York: United Nations. UN Doc. S/1994/1405.

United Nations (1994e). Resolution 955 (1994) Adopted by the Security Council at Its 3453rd Meeting. 8 November 1994. New York: United Nations. UN Doc. S/RES/955 (1994).

United Nations (1994f) Transcript of the 3453rd Meeting of the United Nations Security Council. 8 November 1994. New York: United Nations. UN Doc. S/PV.3453.

United Nations (1995). Report of the Secretary-General Pursuant to Paragraph 5 of Security Council Resolution 955 (1994). 13 February 1995. New York: United Nations. UN Doc. S/1995/13.

United Nations (1996a). Report of the ICTR. New York: United Nations. UN Doc. A/51/399.

United Nations (1996b). *The United Nations and Rwanda, 1993–1996.* New York: United Nations.

United Nations (1999a) Report of the Expert Group to Conduct a Review of the Effective Operation and Functioning of the ICTY and the ICTR. 22 November 1999. New York: United Nations. UN Doc. A/54/634.

United Nations (1999b). Report to the United Nations General Assembly by the President of the ICTR Annual Report of the ICTR. 7 September 1999. New York: United Nations. UN Doc. A/54/315.

United Nations (2003a). Report to the United Nations General Assembly by the President of the ICTR 8th Annual Report of the ICTR. 11 July 2003. New York: United Nations. UN Doc. A/58/140.

United Nations (2003b). Security Council Resolution 1503 (2003) Adopted by the Security Council at Its 4817th Meeting. 28 August 2003. New York: United Nations. UN Doc. S/RES/1503 (2003).

United Nations (2003c). Security Council Resolution 1504 (2003) Adopted by the Security Council at Its 4819th Meeting. 4 September 2003. New York: United Nations. UN Doc. S/RES/1504 (2003).

United Nations (2008). Address to the United Nations General Assembly by the President of the ICTR 13th Annual Report of the ICTR. 13 October 2008. New York: United Nations. UN Doc. A/63/209.

United Nations (2009a). Report of the Secretary-General on the Administrative and Budgetary Aspects of the Options for Possible Locations for the Archives of the International Tribunal for the Former Yugoslavia and the International Criminal Tribunal for Rwanda and the Seat of the Residual Mechanisms for the Tribunals. 21 May 2009. New York: United Nations. UN Doc. S/2009/258.

United Nations (2009b). Security Council Resolution 1901 (2009) Adopted by the Security Council at Its 6243rd Meeting. 16 December 2009. New York: United Nations. UN Doc. S/RES/1901 (2009).

United Nations (2010). Security Council Resolution 1966 (2010) Adopted by the Security Council at Its 6463rd Meeting. 22 December 2010. New York: United Nations. UN Doc. S/RES/1966 (2010).

United Nations (2011a). 6678th Meeting of the Security Council Monday, Wednesday, 7 December 2011, 3 pm. New York: United Nations. UN Doc. S/PV.6678.

United Nations (2011b). The Rule of Law and Transitional Justice in Conflict and Post-Conflict Societies. New York: United Nations. UN Doc. S/2011/634.

United Nations (2015). Address to the United Nations General Assembly by the President of the ICTR 20th Annual Report of the ICTR. 13 October 2015. New York: United Nations. UN Doc. A/70/218.

United Nations Wire (2002). Del Ponte Protests to Security Council That Rwanda Is Not Co-Operating. UN Wire/United Nations Foundation. 25 July 2002.

van den Herik, L. J. (2005). ICTR at Sunset: An Evaluation of the Prosecution's Strategy (1994–2004). *International Studies Journal*, 2(2), 37–68.

van Gennep, A. (1960). *The Rites of Passage*. London: Routledge.

Van Schaak, B. (2009). Obstacles on the Road to Gender Justice: The International Criminal Tribunal for Rwanda as Object Lesson. *American University Journal of Gender, Social Policy and the Law*, 17(2), 355–400.

Vansina, J. (1965). The Documentary Interview. *African Studies Review*, 8(2), 9–14.

Vansina, J. (2006[1961]). *Oral Tradition: A Study in Historical Methodology*. New Brunswick NJ: Transaction Publishers.

Verdoolaege, A. (2002). 'The Human Rights Violations Hearings of the South African TRC: A Bridge Between Individual Narratives of Suffering and a Contextualizing Master-Story of Reconciliation'. Available at http://cas1 .elis.ugent.be/avrug/trc/02_08.htm.

Verdoolaege, A. (2006). Managing Reconciliation at the Human Rights Violations Hearings of the South African TRC. *The Journal of Human Rights*, 5(1), 61–80.

Vinjamuri, L. and J. Snyder (2004). Advocacy and Scholarship in the Study of International War Crime Tribunals and Transitional Justice. *Annual Review of Political Science*, 7(1), 345–62.

Wald, P. M. (2000). Judging War Crimes. *Chicago Journal of International Law*, 1(1), 189–96.

Wald, P. M. (2001a). The International Criminal Tribunal for the Former Yugoslavia Comes of Age: Some Observations on Day-to-Day Dilemmas of the International Court. *Washington University Journal of Law and Policy*, 5, 87–118.

Wald, P. M. (2001b). To Establish Incredible Events by Credible Evidence: The Use of Affidavit Testimony in Yugoslavia War Crimes Tribunal Proceedings. *Harvard International Law Journal*, 42(2), 535–53.

Wald, P. M. (2002). Dealing with Witnesses in War Crime Trials: Lessons from the Yugoslav Tribunal. *Yale Human Rights and Development Law Journal*, 5(1), 217–39.

Wald, P. M. (2004a). ICTY Judicial Proceedings: An Appraisal from Within. *Journal of International Criminal Justice*, 2(2), 466–73.

Wald, P. M. (2004b). Reflections on Judging: At Home and Abroad. *University of Pennsylvania Journal of Constitutional Law*, 7(1), 219–48.

Wald, P. M. (2006). International Criminal Courts – A Stormy Adolescence. *Virginia Journal of International Law*, 46, 319–46.

Walker, A. G. (1986). The Verbatim Record: The Myth and Reality. In S. Fisher and A. D. Todd, eds., *Discourse and Institutional Authority:*

Medicine, Education, and Law. Norwood, NJ: Ablex Publishing Corporation, pp. 205–22.

Weinstock, N. N. (1986). Expert Opinion and Reform in Anglo-American, Continental, and Israeli Adjudication. *Hastings International and Comparative Law Review,* 10, 9–55.

West, R. (1984[1955]). *A Train of Powder.* London: Virago.

Williamson, J. A. (2002). Command Responsibility in the Case Law of the International Criminal Tribunal for Rwanda. *Criminal Law Forum,* 13(3), 365–84.

Wilson, R. A. (2001). *The Politics of Truth and Reconciliation in South Africa: Legitimizing the Post-Apartheid State.* Cambridge: Cambridge University Press.

Wilson, R. A. (2007). Tyrannosaurus Lex: The Anthropology of Human Rights and Transnational Law. In M. Goodale and S. E. Merry, eds., *The Practice of Human Rights: Tracking Law Between the Global and the Local.* Cambridge: Cambridge University Press, pp. 342–69.

Wilson, R. A. (2011). *Writing History in International Criminal Trials.* Cambridge: Cambridge University Press.

Wilson, R. A. (2003). Anthropological Studies of National Reconciliation Processes. *Anthropological Theory,* 3(3), 367–87.

Wladimiroff, M. (1999). The Assignment of Defence Counsel before the International Criminal Tribunal for Rwanda. *Leiden Journal of International Law,* 12(4), 957–68.

Wood, S. K. (2004). Woman Scorned for the Least Condemned War Crime: Precedent and Problems with Prosecuting Rape as a Serious War Crime in the International Criminal Tribunal for Rwanda. *Columbia Journal of Gender and Law,* 13, 274–327.

Woolford, A. (2010). Genocide, Affirmative Repair, and the British Colombia Treaty Process. in A. L. Hinton, ed., *Transitional Justice: Global Mechanisms and Local Realities in the Aftermath of Genocide and Mass Violence.* New Brunswick, NJ: Rutgers University Press, pp. 137–56.

Zoettl, P. A. (2016). Let Justice Be Done: A Performative View on Portuguese Criminal Trial Procedures. *Communication and Critical/Cultural Studies,* 13(4), 400–15.

Zorzi Giustiniani, F. (2008). Stretching the Boundaries of Commission Liability: The ICTR Appeal Judgment in Seromba. *Journal of International Criminal Justice,* 6(4), 783–99.

INDEX

Africa
    African 'culture' as impediment, 120–1,
        128–9
    as 'paradigm of difference', 123–4
Akayesu, Jean Paul, 129, 162, 176
Anders, Gerhard, 124
Annan, Kofi, 31, 40, 50
Arendt, Hannah, 60, 147, 154–5, 157–8, 161,
    168, 179
Arusha International Conference Centre
    (AICC), 66–8
Association des Avocats de la Défense (ADAD),
    43, 47, 183–4

Bagaragaza, Michael, 80, 83
Ball, Milner, 15, 61, 64, 168
Baylis, Elena, 9, 12, 14, 105
Bell, Catherine, 65, 72
Berk-Seligson, Susan, 96, 98
Birkett, Norman, 4, 54, 100, 154
Bourdieu, Pierre, 7, 17, 105–8, 115
Buur, Lars, 5, 163
Byrne, Rosemary, 5, 86, 93

Campbell, Kirsten, 155, 178
Carlen, Pat, 61, 71
Clarke, Kamari, 12, 125
Clifford, James, 58, 153
Collingwood, R.G., 171
Combs, Nancy, 119, 120–1, 127, 128, 141
Conley, John, 4, 32, 93–4, 133
culture
    as barrier, 120–1
    essentialization of, 121–3
    legal culture, 124, 135–6, 137, 187

Del Ponte, Carla, 40–1, 46
Douglas, Lawrence, 62, 176, 183
Duch, trial of. *See* Extraordinary Chambers in
    the Courts of Cambodia (ECCC)

Eades, Diana, 133, 148
East African Community (EAC), 66, 67–8
Eichmann, Adolf, 60, 154
Erlinder, Peter, 49–50

ethnographic research, 22
Etienne, Margareth, 47–8
Extraordinary Chambers in the Courts of
    Cambodia (ECCC), 9, 60, 122, 149

Foucault, Michel, 64–5

Garapon, Antoine, 19, 65, 68, 70, 73, 75,
    76
genocide,
    Rwandan genocide, 1–2, 38–9, 52, 156,
        176
Gersony, Robert, 39
Goffman, Erving, 70–1, 77, 106, 107

Hanson, Julienne, 59, 69, 76–7
Hibbitts, Bernard, 10, 83
Hinton, Alexander, 9, 24, 60, 122, 149, 166
Hoffman, Danny, 177–8
Huizinga, Johan, 61

international criminal justice, 6, 13, 23–5,
    27–37, 50–1, 55, 151, 153, 181,
    182
    literature, 57
International Criminal Tribunal for Rwanda
    (ICTR),
    'super-person', 17–19, 55, 182–3
    'the Tribunal', 15, 17–18, 51, 53, 115
    transcendent justice, 16, 18, 112, 182
    1994 Resolution, 36
    1994 Statute, 17, 27, 31–2, 34, 36–7, 45, 51,
        80, 85, 99–100, 113, 126, 181
    2007 Symposium, 183
    Appeals Chamber, 80, 81, 142
    as challenging the culture of impunity, 26,
        27, 29, 31, 36
    Assistant Legal Officer (ALO), 8, 34, 53, 72,
        73, 79, 86, 114, 135, 175
    completion strategy, 38, 41, 42, 162
    courtroom as 'play-ground', 59, 65, 69, 70,
        82, 108, 186, 188
    courtroom etiquette, 107–10, 166
    interpreters, 77–8, 89–90, 93, 94–5, 96–8,
        129, 132, 186

Code of Professional Ethics of the
    International Association of
    Conference Interpreters, 59
judges, 15–16, 27, 51–4
    courtroom as privileged space, 70–2
    criteria, 34
    motivations, 35
judgments, 129–31, 176
lawyers
    common and civil lawyers, 100–5, 109–10
    defence lawyer requirements, 34
    evaluation of the ICTR, 48–50
    habitual practice, 76, 77, 91–5, 99, 107–9,
        185
    motivations, 34–5, 47–8
Office of the Prosecutor, 2, 3, 41
reconciliation, 23, 26–8, 29, 31–3, 36, 52,
    181
researchers and historians, 155–6, 167–8,
    173, 174–5, 178
Rules of Procedure and Evidence (RPE or
    RPEs), 16, 62, 87–8, 99–100, 112–16,
    117, 131, 137, 176, 182
testimony, 118–20, 148, 149, 174
    assessments of, 91
the archives, 3–4, 21, 153, 155–7, 162,
    173–5, 177, 178–9, 183–4
the 'historical record', 26, 49–50, 152–3,
    156–62, 173, 179
transcripts, 3, 8, 58, 62, 79, 81–2, 89–90, 94,
    96, 119, 139, 162, 177
trials, 20, 22, 38, 48–50, 58, 78, 99, 129, 141,
    156, 158, 159, 162, 174–6
UN security check, 66, 67–8
victor's justice, 26, 38, 41, 43–5, 47, 49, 51,
    52, 184
witnesses, 15, 46, 58, 77–82, 94, 99, 118–19,
    124, 131, 134, 135–7, 151, 162
    cultural differences, 127–8, 130
    demeanour, 78–80, 81, 82, 91
    pre-trial preparation, 132–3
    protected witnesses, 63, 64, 97, 119,
        138–9, 159
    statements, 141–8, 150–1,
        170
    victim-witness, 126–7, 135
International Criminal Tribunal for the
    Former Yugoslavia (ICTY), 3, 29, 97,
    100, 155
international criminal tribunals, 11–12, 24, 28,
    125, 156
as sites of local 'vernacularisation', 13, 85–6
literature, 4

Kearns, Thomas, 156, 161, 184
Kelsall, Tim, 6, 120–1, 127, 128
Kendall, Sara, 125, 126, 182

Ketelaar, Eric, 177, 179, 184
Koomen, Jonneke, 6, 132

Lawrence, Sonia, 123
legal formalism, 7
legal realism, 7
Levenson, Laurie, 60
LiveNote, 8, 81–2, 96
Llewellyn, Karl, 7

Mamdani, Mahmood, 164
Martin, Carol, 58
McConnachie, Kirsten, 125
McEvoy, Kieran, 5, 11, 33, 125
McKinley, Michelle, 123, 146
Mechanism for International Criminal
    Tribunals (MICT), 3, 181
Mégret, Frédéric, 28, 31, 86, 153
Meierhenrich, Jens, 6–7, 14, 19,
    105
Merry, Sally, 33, 85, 122

Neave, Airey, 100, 153
New Legal Realism (NLR), 7, 12
Nouwen, Sarah, 125, 126, 182
Nuremberg Trials, 4, 19, 30, 57, 88, 99, 153–4,
    161

O'Barr, William, 4, 32, 93–4
Overdulve, Cornelis-Marinus, 121–2, 126,
    127, 130

Parkin, David, 113
practice theory, 6–7

Rock, Paul, 69, 70
Rousso, Henry, 154–5
Ruzibiza, Joshua, 50, 52
Rwanda,
    'culture', 121, 129–30
        as impediment, 126, 127–8, 151
        capacity for narrative storytelling, 133–7
    government obstruction, 40, 41, 45
    'local' objectives, 29, 33, 36
    post-genocide Rwandan Government, 1, 3
    untold story of the Rwanda War, 49, 50, 55,
        178, 184
Rwandan Patriotic Front/Army (RPF/A), 1,
    28, 37, 38–42, 44–7, 49, 51–4

Sander, Barrie, 176
Sarat, Austin, 156, 161, 184
Schwöbel-Patel, Christine, 123, 125
simultaneous interpretation, 89–95, 98–9,
    131–3, 186
South African Truth and Reconciliation
    Commission (SATRC), 5, 163–5

Special Court for Sierra Leone (SCSL), 6, 36, 120, 121, 124, 177
Stone Peters, Julie, 16, 60, 148

Taylor, Telford, 57
transcripts, 9, 57–8, 77, 120, 141
transitional justice, 4, 11–14, 87, 125
Trouillot, Michel-Rolph, 178, 179
truth commission, 158, 161–5, 179
Turner, Jenia Iontcheva, 5, 35, 155

United Nations
   Commission of Experts, 1, 38–40

High Commissioner for Refugees (UNHCR), 38–9
Secretary General, 1, 39
Security Council, 1–2, 3, 28–9, 40, 52

Verdoolaege, Annelies, 163–4

Wilson, Richard, 6, 8, 155, 173

Zigiranyirazo, Protais, 80–1, 83
Zoettl, Peter, 7, 60–1, 71, 87–8, 107, 108, 116

CAMBRIDGE STUDIES IN LAW AND SOCIETY

Books in the Series

Diseases of the Will: Alcohol and the Dilemmas of Freedom
Mariana Valverde

The Politics of Truth and Reconciliation in South Africa: Legitimizing the Post-Apartheid State
Richard A. Wilson

Modernism and the Grounds of Law
Peter Fitzpatrick

Unemployment and Government: Genealogies of the Social
William Walters

Autonomy and Ethnicity: Negotiating Competing Claims in Multi-Ethnic States
Yash Ghai

Constituting Democracy: Law, Globalism and South Africa's Political Reconstruction
Heinz Klug

The Ritual of Rights in Japan: Law, Society, and Health Policy
Eric A. Feldman

Governing Morals: A Social History of Moral Regulation
Alan Hunt

The Colonies of Law: Colonialism, Zionism and Law in Early Mandate Palestine
Ronen Shamir

Law and Nature
David Delaney

Social Citizenship and Workfare in the United States and Western Europe: The Paradox of Inclusion
Joel F. Handler

Law, Anthropology, and the Constitution of the Social: Making Persons and Things
Edited by Alain Pottage and Martha Mundy

Judicial Review and Bureaucratic Impact: International and Interdisciplinary Perspectives
Edited by Marc Hertogh and Simon Halliday

Immigrants at the Margins: Law, Race, and Exclusion in Southern Europe
Kitty Calavita

Lawyers and Regulation: The Politics of the Administrative Process
Patrick Schmidt

Law and Globalization from Below: Toward a Cosmopolitan Legality
Edited by Boaventura de Sousa Santos and Cesar A. Rodriguez-Garavito

Public Accountability: Designs, Dilemmas and Experiences
Edited by Michael W. Dowdle

Law, Violence and Sovereignty among West Bank Palestinians
Tobias Kelly

Legal Reform and Administrative Detention Powers in China
Sarah Biddulph

The Practice of Human Rights: Tracking Law between the Global and the Local
Edited by Mark Goodale and Sally Engle Merry

Judges beyond Politics in Democracy and Dictatorship: Lessons from Chile
Lisa Hilbink

Paths to International Justice: Social and Legal Perspectives
Edited by Marie-Bénédicte Dembour and Tobias Kelly

Law and Society in Vietnam: The Transition from Socialism in Comparative Perspective
Mark Sidel

Constitutionalizing Economic Globalization: Investment Rules and Democracy's Promise
David Schneiderman

The New World Trade Organization Knowledge Agreements: 2nd Edition
Christopher Arup

Justice and Reconciliation in Post-Apartheid South Africa
Edited by François du Bois and Antje du Bois-Pedain

Militarization and Violence against Women in Conflict Zones in the Middle East: A Palestinian Case-Study
Nadera Shalhoub-Kevorkian

Child Pornography and Sexual Grooming: Legal and Societal Responses
Suzanne Ost

Darfur and the Crime of Genocide
John Hagan and Wenona Rymond-Richmond

Fictions of Justice: The International Criminal Court and the Challenge of Legal Pluralism in Sub-Saharan Africa
Kamari Maxine Clarke

Conducting Law and Society Research: Reflections on Methods and Practices
Simon Halliday and Patrick Schmidt

Planted Flags: Trees, Land, and Law in Israel/Palestine
Irus Braverman

Culture under Cross-Examination: International Justice and the Special Court for Sierra Leone
Tim Kelsall

Cultures of Legality: Judicialization and Political Activism in Latin America
Javier Couso, Alexandra Huneeus, and Rachel Sieder

Courting Democracy in Bosnia and Herzegovina: The Hague Tribunal's Impact in a Postwar State
Lara J. Nettelfield

The Gacaca Courts, Post-Genocide Justice and Reconciliation in Rwanda: Justice without Lawyers
Phil Clark

Law, Society, and History: Themes in the Legal Sociology and Legal History of Lawrence M. Friedman
Edited by Robert W. Gordon and Morton J. Horwitz

After Abu Ghraib: Exploring Human Rights in America and the Middle East
Shadi Mokhtari

Adjudication in Religious Family Laws: Cultural Accommodation, Legal Pluralism, and Gender Equality in India
Gopika Solanki

Water on Tap: Rights and Regulation in the Transnational Governance of Urban Water Services
Bronwen Morgan

Elements of Moral Cognition: Rawls' Linguistic Analogy and the Cognitive Science of Moral and Legal Judgment
John Mikhail

Mitigation and Aggravation at Sentencing
Edited by Julian V. Roberts

Institutional Inequality and the Mobilization of the Family and Medical Leave Act: Rights on Leave
Catherine R. Albiston

Authoritarian Rule of Law: Legislation, Discourse and Legitimacy in Singapore
Jothie Rajah

Law and Development and the Global Discourses of Legal Transfers
Edited by John Gillespie and Pip Nicholson

Law against the State: Ethnographic Forays into Law's Transformations
Edited by Julia Eckert, Brian Donahoe, Christian Strümpell and Zerrin Özlem Biner

Transnational Legal Ordering and State Change
Edited by Gregory C. Shaffer

Legal Mobilization under Authoritarianism: The Case of Post-Colonial Hong Kong
Waikeung Tam

Complementarity in the Line of Fire: The Catalysing Effect of the International Criminal Court in Uganda and Sudan
Sarah M. H. Nouwen

Political and Legal Transformations of an Indonesian Polity: The Nagari from Colonisation to Decentralisation
Franz von Benda-Beckmann and Keebet von Benda-Beckmann

Pakistan's Experience with Formal Law: An Alien Justice
Osama Siddique

Human Rights under State-Enforced Religious Family Laws in Israel, Egypt, and India
Yüksel Sezgin

Why Prison?
Edited by David Scott

Law's Fragile State: Colonial, Authoritarian, and Humanitarian Legacies in Sudan
Mark Fathi Massoud

Rights for Others: The Slow Home-Coming of Human Rights in the Netherlands
Barbara Oomen

European States and Their Muslim Citizens: The Impact of Institutions on Perceptions and Boundaries
Edited by John R. Bowen, Christophe Bertossi, Jan Willem Duyvendak, and Mona Lena Krook

Environmental Litigation in China: A Study in Political Ambivalence
Rachel E. Stern

Indigeneity and Legal Pluralism in India: Claims, Histories, Meanings
Pooja Parmar

Paper Tiger: Law, Bureaucracy and the Developmental State in Himalayan India
Nayanika Mathur

Religion, Law and Society
Russell Sandberg

The Experiences of Face Veil Wearers in Europe and the Law
Edited by Eva Brems

The Contentious History of the International Bill of Human Rights
Christopher N. J. Roberts

Transnational Legal Orders
Edited by Terence C. Halliday and Gregory Shaffer

Lost in China? Law, Culture and Society in Post-1997 Hong Kong
Carol A. G. Jones

Security Theology, Surveillance and the Politics of Fear
Nadera Shalhoub-Kevorkian

Opposing the Rule of Law: How Myanmar's Courts Make Law and Order
Nick Cheesman

The Ironies of Colonial Governance: Law, Custom and Justice in Colonial India
James Jaffe

The Clinic and the Court: Law, Medicine and Anthropology
Edited by Ian Harper, Tobias Kelly, and Akshay Khanna

A World of Indicators: The Making of Government Knowledge through Quantification
Edited by Richard Rottenburg, Sally Engle Merry, Sung-Joon Park, and Johanna Mugler

Contesting Immigration Policy in Court: Legal Activism and Its Radiating Effects in the United States and France
Leila Kawar

The Quiet Power of Indicators: Measuring Governance, Corruption, and Rule of Law
Edited by Sally Engle Merry, Kevin Davis, and Benedict Kingsbury

Investing in Authoritarian Rule: Punishment and Patronage in Rwanda's Gacaca Courts for Genocide Crimes
Anuradha Chakravarty

Contractual Knowledge: One Hundred Years of Legal Experimentation in Global Markets
Edited by Grégoire Mallard and Jérôme Sgard

Iraq and the Crimes of Aggressive War: The Legal Cynicism of Criminal Militarism
John Hagan, Joshua Kaiser, and Anna Hanson

Culture in the Domains of Law
Edited by René Provost

China and Islam: The Prophet, the Party, and Law
Matthew S. Erie

Diversity in Practice: Race, Gender, and Class in Legal and Professional Careers
Edited by Spencer Headworth and Robert Nelson

A Sociology of Constitutions: Constitutions and State Legitimacy in Historical-Sociological Perspective
Chris Thornhill

A Sociology of Transnational Constitutions: Social Foundations of the Post-National Legal Structure
Chris Thornhill

Shifting Legal Visions: Judicial Change and Human Rights Trials in Latin America
Ezequiel A. González Ocantos

The Demographic Transformations of Citizenship
Heli Askola

Criminal Defense in China: The Politics of Lawyers at Work
Sida Liu and Terence C. Halliday

Contesting Economic and Social Rights in Ireland: Constitution, State and Society, 1848–2016
Thomas Murray

Buried in the Heart: Women, Complex Victimhood and the War in Northern Uganda
Erin Baines

Palaces of Hope: The Anthropology of Global Organizations
Edited by Ronald Niezen and Maria Sapignoli

The Politics of Bureaucratic Corruption in Post-Transitional Eastern Europe
Marina Zaloznaya

Revisiting the Law and Governance of Trafficking, Forced Labor and Modern Slavery
Edited by Prabha Kotiswaran

Incitement on Trial: Prosecuting International Speech Crimes
Richard Ashby Wilson

Criminalizing Children: Welfare and the State in Australia
David McCallum

Global Lawmakers: International Organizations in the Crafting of World Markets
Susan Block-Lieb and Terence C. Halliday

Duties to Care: Dementia, Relationality and Law
Rosie Harding

Insiders, Outsiders, Injuries, and Law: Revisiting "The Oven Bird's Song"
Edited by Mary Nell Trautner

Hunting Justice: Displacement, Law, and Activism in the Kalahari
Maria Sapignoli

Injury and Injustice: The Cultural Politics of Harm and Redress
Edited by Anne Bloom, David M. Engel, and Michael McCann

Ruling before the Law: The Politics of Legal Regimes in China and Indonesia
William Hurst

The Powers of Law: A Comparative Analysis of Sociopolitical Legal Studies
Mauricio García-Villegas

A Sociology of Justice in Russia
Edited by Marina Kurkchiyan and Agnieszka Kubal

Constituting Religion: Islam, Liberal Rights, and the Malaysian State
Tamir Moustafa

The Invention of the Passport: Surveillance, Citizenship and the State, Second Edition
John C. Torpey

Law's Trials: The Performance of Legal Institutions in the US "War on Terror"
Richard L. Abel

Law's Wars: The Fate of the Rule of Law in the US "War on Terror"
Richard L. Abel

Transforming Gender Citizenship: The Irresistible Rise of Gender Quotas in Europe
Edited by Eléonore Lépinard and Ruth Rubio-Marín

Muslim Women's Quest for Justice: Gender, Law and Activism in India
Mengia Hong Tschalaer

Children as 'Risk': Sexual Exploitation and Abuse by Children and Young People
Anne-Marie McAlinden

The Legal Process and the Promise of Justice: Studies Inspired by the Work of Malcolm Feeley
Jonathan Simon, Rosann Greenspan, Hadar Aviram

Sovereign Exchanges: Gifts, Trusts, Reparations, and Other Fetishes of International Solidarity
Grégoire Mallard

Measuring Justice: Quantitative Accountability and the National Prosecuting Authority in South Africa
Johanna Mugler

Negotiating the Power of NGOs: Women's Legal Rights in South Africa
Reem Wael

Indigenous Water Rights in Law and Regulation: Lessons from Comparative Experience
Elizabeth Jane Macpherson

The Edge of Law: Legal Geographies of a War Crimes Court
Alex Jeffrey

Everyday Justice: Law, Ethnography and Injustice
Sandra Brunnegger